INTRODUCING THE NEW *SAT*

THE COLLEGE BOARD'S OFFICIAL GUIDE

EDUCATORS PUBLISHING SERVICE, INC.
31 Smith Place
Cambridge, MA 02138-1000

INTRODUCING
THE NEW *SAT*
THE COLLEGE BOARD'S
OFFICIAL GUIDE

College Entrance Examination Board, New York

The College Board is a national nonprofit association that champions educational excellence for all students through the ongoing collaboration of more than 2,900 member schools, colleges, universities, education systems, and associations. The Board promotes—by means of responsive forums, research, programs, and policy development—universal access to high standards of learning, equity of opportunity, and sufficient financial support so that every student is prepared for success in college and work.

Copies of this book are available from your bookseller or may be ordered from College Board Publications, Box 886, New York, New York, 10101-0886. The price is $12.

Editorial inquiries concerning this book should be addressed to the College Board, 45 Columbus Avenue, New York, New York 10023-6992.

Cover design by Terrence M. Fehr. Interior design by Florence Dara Silverman. Photographs by Hugh Rogers.

International Standard Book Number: 0-87447-456-6

Library of Congress Card Catalog Number: 92-972101

Contents

Preface

The introduction of a new SAT in March of 1994 has elicited a variety of concerns and questions from parents, teachers, school counselors, and most notably, the students who will be taking the new test. This book is intended first and foremost to clearly explain what has been changed and to give those students an opportunity to become familiar with the different types of questions they will encounter. It also offers a variety of strategies for test takers both for approaching the SAT as a whole and for tackling specific types of questions. Our intention was not to present a hard and fast method for taking the test, but to give students the tools with which to approach the SAT in a positive frame of mind. Not all students will be comfortable with every bit of advice given. So the practice questions can be used to try out different strategies as well as for test familiarity. While every effort has been made to ensure that the contents of this book are as up-to-date as possible, students are urged to consult the free publication, *Taking the SAT I*, for the most current information on the test.

How This Book is Organized

This book is divided into five parts. The first is a general introduction to the new SAT I: Reasoning Test and SAT II: Subject Tests. It is meant to indicate what the specific changes are. This section should be helpful to teachers and guidance counselors in assisting students to prepare for the new tests and will also serve as a brief review for students.

The second section contains test-taking strategies. It is not intended to help students "psych out" the test. Instead, the section is meant to help students develop sound techniques that will enable them to do their best in what, for some, can be an offputting situation. The section should also enable students to approach the SAT with realistic expectations. We recommend that students try out the different techniques using either the practice verbal and mathematical questions given in Parts Three and Four or other SAT test-preparation materials.

Parts Three and Four deal specifically with the Verbal and Mathematical sections of the new SAT. They contain an in-depth discussion of each type of question a student will encounter on the test, as well as hints and strategies for answering them. Students should use these sections to become familiar with the questions, the test instructions, and the kind of answer required. Particular attention should be paid to the Student-Produced Response (Grid-in) questions in the mathematical section. This type of question is new and requires that the answers be given in specific formats. Students should also become familiar with the paired Reading Passage format, which requires them to answer questions comparing and contrasting two related passages.

Of necessity, the sections dealing with the Verbal and Mathematical questions are arranged somewhat differently. Part Three, which deals with the verbal questions, contains two sets of practice questions in Chapters 7 and 8. Those in Chapter 7 are accompanied not only by answers, but by explanations and hints, as well. Students can use the explanations and hints to hone their skills and develop their test-taking strategies. The questions in Chapter 8 are intended for students to use independently to check their progress and identify areas where further review is needed. After completing the practice questions, students may want to review specific material in Chapters 6 and 7 before taking the practice test.

Part Four contains two chapters. The first, Mathematics Review, describes the concepts and operations that will appear on the SAT. It is not intended to replace a solid high school mathematics program, but should help the reader identify strengths and areas where further review is needed. Chapter 10 contains practice questions arranged by type of question—Multiple Choice, Quantitative Comparison, and Grid-in— followed by complete solutions to each one. While the solutions given reflect current classroom practice, we fully realize that many roads lead to Rome. Students should use the techniques they are most comfortable with to solve the problems and shouldn't be concerned if their methods are different from the ones given. On the other hand, if a student has difficulty with particular types of problems, studying the sample solutions should help him or her develop the skills needed to solve similar problems in the future.

The final section contains a practice test. We recommend taking it under timed conditions and using the results along with Part Two of this book to set realistic goals for the actual test-taking experience.

How to Use This Book

Introducing the New SAT provides readers with ample opportunity for practicing with the different types of questions that will appear on the new SAT. While the best preparation for the test is still a solid course of study in high school, the practice questions should help students— and their teachers, parents, and counselors—identify strengths and areas that will require additional work. In this sense, it should help readers with long-term preparation for the SAT and beyond. On the other hand, the hint boxes and marginal notes will allow readers to quickly find and review important information shortly before taking the test. Each chapter also includes a table of contents, so that needed material is easily accessible. We hope that you will find this book both easy-to-use and helpful.

PART ONE

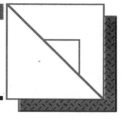

Introducing the New SAT

- ■ Chapter 1   What's New in the Test?
- ■ Chapter 2   SAT II: Subject Tests

CHAPTER 1

What's New in the Test?

Why Make Changes?

The SAT has been changed because education has changed. In general, the changes were made so that the test better reflects the type of work you will do when you get to college. Remember, the purpose of the test is to predict how well you will do, academically, in your freshman year. The more the tasks in the test are like the tasks you will face in college, the better the job the test will do.

High school and college teachers from all around the country suggested that the new SAT should continue to emphasize *thinking* more than memorizing; that is, emphasize the ability to *use* information, knowledge, and skills, more than testing whether you have information, knowledge, and skills. The changes in the SAT reflect this advice.

What's the Same?

Purpose

The purpose of the SAT I: Reasoning Test is the same as it has been for years, namely, to help predict how you will do in college. More specifically, the SAT I was and is designed to help predict your freshman grades, so that admission officers can make better decisions about your chances of succeeding in the courses you will take at their colleges.

This purpose has not changed. In fact, it is because the purpose has remained the same that the test has been changed. High school curriculums have changed. So the test had to change in order to continue to do its traditional job.

Content

The basic content of the new SAT I is very similar to that of the old. There are still two sections—verbal and math. However, there are some changes in the types of questions and in the abilities tapped by the questions.

Question Types

The old SAT had six types of questions. Five of these types of questions have been kept on the new test. Only the Antonym questions have been dropped. An additional type of question was added to the math test that requires you to grid-in your answers. This will be discussed a bit later in this chapter.

The SAT I will still be three hours long, and it will still be divided into six sections. (One of these sections will be divided into two 15-minute sections.) There will be some changes in the total number of math and verbal questions, however. And the TSWE (Test of Standard Written English) has been dropped.

Verbal	Old SAT	New SAT I
Reading Passages and Questions	yes	yes
Analogies	yes	yes
Antonyms	yes	no
Sentence Completions	yes	yes

Math	Old SAT	New SAT I
Regular Multiple-Choice Math	yes	yes
Quantitative Comparisons	yes	yes
Grid-in Answers	no	yes

Scoring

Raw scores will still be computed using a formula. That means you get one point for each right answer and a fraction of a point is taken off for each wrong answer to a multiple-choice question. (There's no penalty for a wrong answer on the math grid-in questions.)

Scores will still be converted to the familiar 200 to 800 scale, and scores on the new SAT I can be compared to scores on the old test.

What's Different?

What's New in Math?

- Grid-in questions will require you to produce your own answers;
- Problem solving and math reasoning will be emphasized;
- Calculators will be permitted—in fact, they are recommended.

There is one new type of question—the "grid-in." (On the test it's called "student-produced response.") This isn't the typical SAT multiple-choice question. In fact, it's not a multiple-choice question at all! You won't be given answers. Instead, you have to figure out the answer and grid it in. Without getting into the details (see the chapter "Preparing for the Math Test" in Part IV for more), the answer grid will look like the one at the top of page 6.

If your answer to the question is "20.3," you will write in your answer at the top of the grid *and* fill in the ovals—column by column—that correspond to your answer.

The grid-in questions will be similar to the other types of math questions. But the grid lets you express your answers as either decimals

or fractions. (You use the slashes on the second row of the grid to indicate fraction bars.) There are strict rules for how you translate between fractions and decimals. These rules are reviewed in Part IV.

Questions on the new test will still require that you reason out what to do to answer them. In general, you will find that it is as important to figure out what you should do to answer the question as it is to do the figuring. There will be plenty of examples of the types of questions you'll be seeing on the test in Part IV.

Calculators Recommended

The use of calculators on the math sections of the new SAT is permitted and it is recommended that students bring one to the exam. While no question will require a calculator to determine the answer, field trials of the new SAT have indicated that students who used calculators did slightly better on the test than those who did not.

Although many different factors contribute to students' performance on the math sections of the SAT, on average, students with solid mathematics preparation who use calculators on a regular basis are likely to do better on the test than students without this preparation.

While no question will require the use of a calculator, the College Board recommends that students bring a calculator with them when they take the new SAT. The use of calculators is discussed more fully in Part IV of this book, Mathematical Reasoning.

What's New in the Verbal Section?

- **Longer reading passages;**
- **Double reading passages;**
- **Vocabulary-in-context questions.**

There are no new types of verbal questions, but there are some changes in what some of the old standbys ask. You'll find the changes in the Sentence Completion and Critical Reading sections.

Critical Reading

The basic format of the Reading questions won't change. There will still be reading passages followed by questions that refer to the passages. You will find some differences in those passages, however.

- Passages will be longer. In fact, there will be some double passages, where you will be asked to make comparisons between what is said in two related passages.
- The new passages are intended to arouse the interest of the test takers. But since "interesting" is a matter of personal taste, not every passage will be exciting to everyone who takes the test. Even if you're not especially interested in the topics, however, the new passages are designed to be readable and accessible.
- The old SAT limited the number of questions following any one passage to 5 or sometimes 6. You may find as many as 12 or 13 questions on some of the longer reading passages in the new SAT.

Reading Questions

There are two very broad categories of reading questions. Some ask what the author says, and others ask what the author means.

- There will be more emphasis on what the author means or suggests in the new SAT I, with fewer questions that ask only about the facts of the passage.
- There will be some vocabulary questions in the reading sections. These questions will focus on what the words mean *as they are used in the passage.*
- There will be some questions that ask you to compare two related reading passages.

Sentence Completions

Sentence Completions will include some questions that are straightforward vocabulary-in-context questions. There will also be Sentence Completions that combine vocabulary and reasoning. In the second type, understanding the sentence is as important as knowing the vocabulary.

What Not to Expect

The old SAT verbal sections had four types of questions. The new SAT I verbal sections have only three types. Antonym questions, which asked for the opposites of listed words, will not be on the new test.

In addition, TSWE (Test of Standard Written English) will no longer be given as part of the three-hour SAT I exam. TSWE was a multiple-choice test designed to test your knowledge of the elements of good composition and to give colleges an idea of your writing ability. It was one of the half-hour sections, but it was a separate test and its score was not part of the SAT scores. TSWE-type questions (plus some new multiple-choice questions and an essay) are included in a new Writing Test as part of the new SAT II.

The mix of questions—how many questions of each type—is quite different in the new SAT I. These tables should give you an idea of the new mix of questions.

Mix of Verbal Questions	Old SAT	New SAT I
Antonyms	25 Questions	None
Analogies	20 Questions	19 Questions
Sentence Completions	15 Questions	19 Questions
Reading Passage Questions	25 Questions	40 Questions
Total Questions	85 Questions	78 Questions

Mix of Math Questions	Old SAT	New SAT I
Multiple Choice	40 Questions	35 Questions
Quantitative Comparisons	20 Questions	15 Questions
Grid-ins	None	10 Questions
Total Questions	60 Questions	60 Questions

Understanding Your Scores

There's a lot of mystery and even misinformation about SAT scores. People—and this includes high school and college teachers, parents, and students—have all sorts of ideas about how the test is scored, what the scores mean, and how the scores can and should be used.

This chapter is designed to clear up a lot of these mysteries.

Scoring the SAT

The SAT I will continue to be scored in the same way as it has in the past. First, the number of questions answered right minus a fraction of the multiple-choice questions answered wrong is computed. (No points are earned or subtracted for unanswered questions, and nothing is subtracted from your score for incorrect answers to grid-in questions.) If the resulting score includes a fraction, the score is rounded to the nearest whole number—1/2 or more is rounded up; less than 1/2 is rounded down.

Your score is then converted into a 200 (lowest) to 800 (highest) scaled score using a statistical process called equating. Tests are equated to adjust for minor differences between test editions. Equating assures test takers and colleges that a score of, say, 450, on one edition of a test indicates the same level of ability as a score of 450 on another edition. The equating process also ensures that your score doesn't depend on how well others did on the same test. The tests are not marked on a curve, so you won't be marked down if other students do very well on the test.

Score Range No test can ever measure precisely what your skills are, but it can provide good estimates. If you took many editions of the test within a short time, your scores would tend to vary, but not too far above or below your actual abilities. The score range is an estimate of how your scores might vary if you were tested many times. The SAT score range is usually about 30 points above and below your specific numerical score, and it indicates the range in which your true abilities probably fall.

Percentiles

The SAT has no passing or failing scores. Your scores can be considered high or low only in comparison to the scores of other students. That's why, in addition to the scaled SAT score, you'll also get a percentile score. This compares your scores to the scores of other students who took the test. The comparison is given as a number between 1 and 99, and it tells what percentage of students earned a score lower than yours. For example, if your percentile is 53, it means that out of every 100 test takers in the comparison group, you performed better than 53 of them.

Your percentile permits you to make direct comparisons between yourself and other students. You might not know how "good" a score of 350, or 450, or 600 really is, but your percentile scores will give you a good idea of how you compare with others.

Your percentile changes depending on the group with which you are being compared. For the SAT I, your national percentile (all recently graduated college-bound seniors from across the nation who took the test) is often higher than your state percentile (all recently graduated college-bound seniors from your state who took the test). That's mainly because the national group contains a larger, more diverse group of test takers.

Using Your Scores

The new SAT I score report has been designed to help you understand how your score compares to the scores of similar groups of students. This is why, along with your score, your score range and percentile are also reported. Raw score information (the number you got right, wrong, or omitted) is also given for the different verbal and math questions. This information can help you analyze your performance.

Your score report will also provide the profiles of up to four colleges or universities to which you asked that your scores be sent. These profiles include institutional characteristics, high school preparation required, freshman admission policies, and cost/financial aid information. If you fill out the Student Descriptive Questionnaire, that information will also be included.

There's a lot more information you can get from your SAT I scores than just a pair of numbers. You may want to get an idea of how your abilities compare to the abilities of students already enrolled at the colleges you are considering. Guides such as *The College Handbook* often provide information about SAT I scores of enrolled freshmen. (Your score report will also contain this information.) If your scores are in the range of the scores at a campus you are interested in, you will probably be able to handle the academic challenge there. If your scores fall far below freshman scores, you may well be in for a struggle. If your scores are much higher, you'll want to make sure you will be academically challenged at that campus.

You should not, however, select a college simply because your scores match the profile of students already enrolled there. You may be the type of student who performs best under pressure and needs the challenge of a tough academic environment. Or, even though the freshman SAT I scores are below your score, a particular college may offer a unique major or social or cultural environment that makes it the right choice for you.

If you're a high school sophomore or junior or younger, you can also use your SAT scores to assess your own academic development. If you want to go to college but your scores are low, you should examine your study habits and interests, consult with parents, teachers, and counselors, and try to improve your academic performance.

Student Services

Question and Answer Service

You get it all. For the disclosed administrations (specified in the *Registration Bulletin* you receive) you can receive a computer-generated report that provides the question number, the correct answer, your answer, the type of question, and the difficulty level of that question. You will receive the questions from the form of the test you took as well.

Student Answer Service

This service is available if the Question and Answer Service is not offered because the test was not disclosed. The Student Answer Service provides your answers, the correct answer, the type of question, and difficulty level of that question.

You can order these services when you register for the test, or you can use the order form that is sent with your score report.

The New PSAT/NMSQT

The PSAT/NMSQT has always been made up of test questions taken from the pool of SAT questions. The same will be true in the new PSAT/NMSQT.

So, as in the past, the way you prepare for the PSAT/NMSQT should not be very different from the way you prepare for the SAT I.

The PSAT/NMSQT serves three purposes:

- It gives you practice for SAT I.
- It is the first step in qualifying for scholarships sponsored by the National Merit Scholarship Corporation and other scholarship programs.
- It gives you the opportunity to participate in the Student Search Service (SSS).

Practice for the SAT I

The PSAT/NMSQT is composed of test questions that have been used previously on the SAT I. But there are several differences between the PSAT/NMSQT and the SAT I:

- The PSAT/NMSQT is shorter than the SAT I: about 108 questions instead of 138 questions.
- The PSAT/NMSQT is not quite as difficult as the SAT I because of the mix of questions. The PSAT/NMSQT includes fewer of the most difficult questions.

Preparing for the New PSAT/NMSQT

The types of questions on the new PSAT/NMSQT are the same as on the new SAT I, so here's what you need to do to prepare:

1. Familiarize yourself with each type of SAT question.
2. Go over the sections in this book on each of the SAT question types.
3. Practice applying the hints and tips.
4. Carefully go through the math review section. If it's close to exam time, concentrate on the math skills and concepts that you already know. If you have plenty of time before the test, start learning some of the unfamiliar skills and concepts.
5. Make sure you're familiar with the basic test-taking tips outlined in Part III of this book—Improving Your Scores.

Recognize the differences between the two tests. The length and organization of the PSAT/NMSQT is different from the SAT.

- Make sure you're familiar with how the PSAT/NMSQT is laid out so that you aren't confused when you see the test.
- Set your target scores according to the PSAT/NMSQT score tables. If you are an average student, you can expect to score about 41 on the verbal and 45 on the math. The top 10 percent fall at 55 and above on the verbal and 61 and above on the math.

Check with your counselor and with specific scholarship programs to find out what scores are needed to qualify for specific scholarships. Most students are not taking the PSAT/NMSQT to compete for scholarships. So for the majority of test takers, the PSAT/NMSQT is practice for the SAT I.

Scholarships

The National Merit Scholarship Program uses PSAT/NMSQT scores to allow students to enter its scholarship programs. Many corporations and other scholarship programs also use the test scores as part of their criteria for selecting students for scholarships.

The two primary sources of information about these programs are the PSAT/NMSQT *Student Bulletin* and the counseling office in your high school. The *Bulletin* is available, free, from your high school counseling office. It contains test information as well as information on many of the scholarship programs that use the test scores.

Student Search Service

The Student Search Service helps colleges find prospective students. If you take the PSAT/NMSQT, you can ask to be included in this free Search. Here's how it works.

If you indicate that you want to be part of the Search (there's a check-box on the answer sheet), your name and other information you provide are put in a data base. The information includes address, high school grade-point average, social security number, intended college major, and projected career.

Colleges then use the Search to help them recruit students they are interested in. For instance, they may ask the Student Search Service for lists of students with test scores in certain ranges or who come from certain parts of the country or who are interested in certain majors. The colleges (and some scholarship programs, too) then get in touch with the students on the list.

Things to keep in mind about the Student Search Service:

- Your participation is voluntary. You may take the test without participating in the Search.
- Colleges do not receive your PSAT/NMSQT scores. They can ask for the names of students within certain score ranges, but your exact score is not reported.

- Being contacted by a college is not the same thing as getting admitted. You can only be admitted after you apply. The Student Search Service is a means by which colleges reach prospective students, that's all. Once they contact you, it is up to you to decide whether to apply and follow through with the college.
- You may also participate in the Student Search Service when you take the SAT or Advanced Placement (AP) Examinations.

CHAPTER 2

SAT II: Subject Tests

The SAT II: Subject Tests are designed to find out how well you have mastered specific subjects.

The subject tests may be used in the college admission process. They are helpful in counseling you about what college courses to take. They also can be used by colleges to place you in freshman courses appropriate to your ability.

Of particular interest here is the SAT II Writing Test, which replaces both the TSWE (Test of Standard Written English) that was given with the old SAT and the English Composition Achievement Test (ECT).

This chapter provides a general description of the SAT II testing program.

What Is the SAT II?

The SAT II subject-specific exams are designed to find out how well you have mastered a variety of high school subjects.

Unlike the SAT I (Reasoning) tests, the SAT II (Subject) tests assume that you have knowledge of specific subjects. You would not, for instance, take the SAT II Biology Test unless you had taken biology in high school.

The tests do not depend on any particular curriculum but reflect the expected outcome of a typical high school course.

Each SAT II test is based on a curriculum or course of study but not on any specific course. In other words, the French test is not based on the French course that is given at some particular high school. It is based on what a committee of high school and college French teachers think high school students should know. The same is true for mathematics, science, history, and all the other SAT II exams.

For this reason, you shouldn't expect to know everything on an SAT II exam. But you should expect to be familiar with most of what is presented.

What Exams Are Offered?

English

- Literature
- Writing (replaces English Composition); it always includes a writing sample.

History

- American History and Social Studies
- World History (replaces European History and World Cultures).

Foreign Language

- Chinese
- French
- German
- Italian
- Japanese
- Latin
- Modern Hebrew
- Spanish

Mathematics

- Math Level I: Assumes you have taken elementary and intermediate algebra and geometry.
- Math Level IIC: Assumes you have taken elementary and intermediate algebra, geometry, and either precalculus or trigonometry.

Science

- Biology
- Chemistry
- Physics

The subject areas and titles of the tests occasionally change to reflect changes in U.S. high school education. The content of individual tests is under continual review and new tests are planned.

Purpose of the SAT II

SAT II tests:

- Allow you to demonstrate mastery of specific subjects;
- Help colleges in their admission decisions and help you decide which college is best for you;
- Help in the choice of and placement in entry-level college courses.

Showing Your Strengths One of the purposes of the SAT II (Subject) tests is to let you show off because you can choose to take tests in your strongest subjects. (Some colleges do require certain SAT II tests, but that doesn't stop you from taking others.)

Taking an SAT II test can be a way for you to demonstrate your ability to do advanced work in your areas of interest.

Helping in the College Admission Process

The SAT II can be helpful to both you and the colleges to which you apply. For the colleges, the SAT II tests provide specific information about what you have learned in high school. They help colleges assess the quality of your high school program and your ability to achieve in college courses.

The SAT II tests can help you match your academic accomplishments with the colleges to which you are applying. If you do well on these tests, you can be confident that you are well prepared to tackle college-level work in your SAT II subjects. You can also make sure that your scores on the subject tests match the type of program you are considering. For instance, if you would like to be a doctor but score poorly in the science exams (especially biology and chemistry), you are likely to have a hard time in a rigorous premed program. Or if you don't do well in the Writing Test, you might expect to have to put in extra work in a college major that requires extensive writing.

These are not hard and fast rules. But they are things that you might want to discuss with your counselor, your parents, and even with the college admission officers before you make your application decisions.

The point here is to be active, not passive, in your college choices. The question is not whether you will get into some college or another. The question is, "Assuming you are admitted, are you likely to be successful?"

Choosing College Courses

The choice of freshman courses varies from college to college and even from program to program or major to major within a college. Sometimes your entire freshman year is set before you walk onto the campus. In other cases, you will have considerable choice about the courses you take.

Most colleges offer a combination of required courses and optional courses. The courses you are required to take ususally depend on two things:

- The major that you are considering: Most advanced courses have prerequisites—beginning or introductory courses you have to take before you can take the advanced classes.
- Certain basic skills that you demonstrate through testing: For instance, most colleges require that you either take an English composition course or show that you are already a competent writer.

The SAT II exams are one way that some colleges allow you to show that you can handle advanced work. If your tests show that you know the basics, you may be able to "place out" of introductory courses.

The Writing Test

The SAT II: Writing Test was born out of two of the old exams, the TSWE and the ECT with essay. The new test will always include a writing sample. It will also have three different types of multiple-choice questions that involve identifying errors in sentences and improving sentences (both of these types of questions appeared on the TSWE), and new questions that require improving paragraphs. With the essay and these three types of multiple-choice questions, colleges will have a single test that is appropriate for two major purposes—admission decisions and placement in English classes after admission.

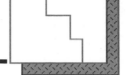

PART TWO

Test-Taking Strategies

- Chapter 3 Misconceptions about the SAT I
- Chapter 4 Test-Taking Strategies
- Chapter 5 Psyching Yourself Up

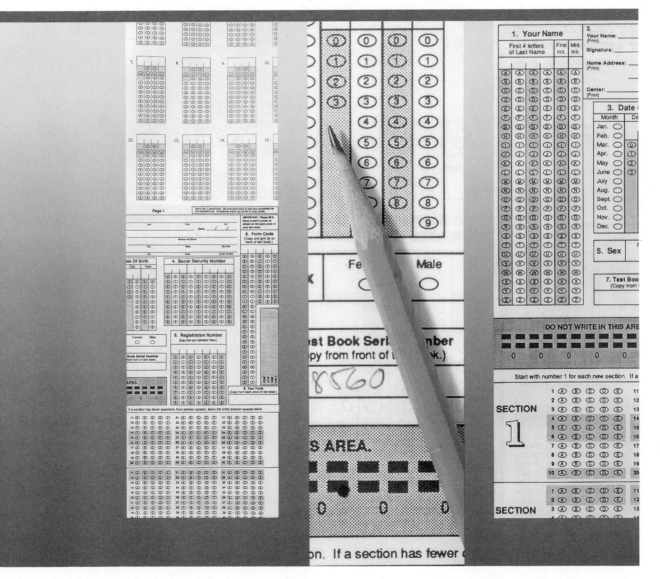

CHAPTER 3

Misconceptions about the SAT I

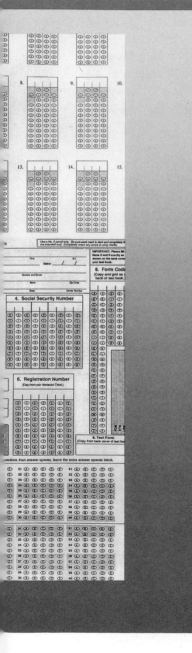

There's a lot of misunderstanding and misinformation about the SAT I, so before exploring some ways you can improve your scores, let's get the facts straight.

Myth: All Tests Aren't Alike

You may have heard that your score depends on when and where you take the test. This is really a myth. It is *NOT* true. Regardless of when and where you take the SAT I, all editions of the test are of comparable difficulty.

When the tests are produced, there are careful checks to make sure that each edition of the test contains as many hard and easy questions as the next. During the scoring process, the procedure used adjusts for any minor differences from one edition to the next. These adjustments make the 200 to 800 SAT score you get on one test comparable to the 200 to 800 SAT score you or anyone else gets on any other test taken any time, any place. One SAT may be *slightly* harder or easier than another, but the scoring procedure takes these differences into account.

Myth: You Should Never Guess

Totally random guessing on the SAT I (closing your eyes and picking an answer) is chancy. You do have one chance in five of picking the right answer. But remember, points are subtracted from your score for wrong answers.

Does that mean you shouldn't guess? Not always. On multiple-choice questions, if you can eliminate even one answer as being *definitely wrong*, you should make a guess among the other choices.

There are some exceptions to this simple rule. The details are in the chapter on guessing. That chapter even tells you how to experiment to find out whether you should guess.

Myth: It's a Hard Test

The SAT I is very different from most classroom tests. Consider the differences:

Most classroom tests

- Average score: 70 to 80 percent correct.
- Failing grade: 60 to 65 percent.
- You are expected to know everything on the test.
- You have recently studied all the things on the test.
- The test usually focuses on one subject area or only a part of one subject area.
- The test is designed so that everyone who has studied the material can get 100 percent or close to it.

The SAT I

- Average score: approximately 420 on the verbal section and 470 on the math.
- You aren't expected to be familiar with everything on the test. In fact, there will probably be things on the test that you aren't familiar with and have never studied.
- The test covers a wide range of material.
- There may be some things on the test that you learned outside of school, for example, when reading for fun.

So, is this a hard test? It's hard if you focus on the questions that you don't answer correctly. But the test isn't hard if you remember that you are doing better than average if you are getting about half the questions right! The SAT may seem a lot harder than the tests you take in class. What you have to fight against is the *feeling* that you are doing poorly when you're really doing OK.

Don't Let the Test "Psych" You Out

How you feel about the test can affect how well you do. Knowing what to expect can help you concentrate on each question and get a better score. There is more about how to get yourself ready for the test, psychologically, in the chapter on "Psyching Up."

Myth: Questions Are Tricky

Are SAT I questions purposely tricky? Do the test writers try to figure out ways to trap you? No! The questions are not designed to be tricky. Many are hard questions that require careful attention and some figuring out. Many have *incorrect* answers that look good at first glance or that will seem correct if you don't pay attention. But the questions are not designed to trap you.

Myth: There's More Than One Right Answer

Some people think you have to "psych out" which answer is *really* correct. Not true! All questions on the SAT are thoroughly tried out before they're used. The questions are constructed so that they have only one correct or best answer. (There is one exception: for some math Grid-in questions, there may be several correct answers.)

Myth: It Tests Intelligence

The SAT I Is Not an Intelligence Test

- It does not measure your inborn talents.
- It does measure abilities that do change as you study and learn.

The SAT I Is Not a Traditional Classroom Test

- It does not test what you know about a particular subject.
- It does not assume that you have taken any particular course or that you have gone through any particular curriculum.
- The SAT is not a test of creativity.

SAT I Tests Verbal and Mathematical Reasoning

The SAT I tests the skills and abilities that go into making you a successful student when you enter college. The SAT I tests verbal and mathematical reasoning. The test is based on certain assumptions about you and others taking it:

- That you can read, understand, and follow the logic of written material. The SAT I tests you on those skills and on how well you can reason based on written information.
- That you have a broad vocabulary.
- That you have the basic math skills that would be developed in arithmetic, elementary algebra, and geometry classes. It tests your ability to apply those skills in figuring out the answers to problems.

These abilities are developed throughout your school career. But many of these abilities can be built and enhanced outside of the classroom, too.

Myth: You Can't Prepare

This is definitely not true. There's a lot you can do to prepare for the SAT. Some preparation can help in a short period of time. Other things require a lot more time and effort to have any significant effect. But the fact remains that you do have just as much control over how well you do on the SAT as you do over your high school grade-point average. In fact, *how* to prepare for the SAT is the subject of the next section.

Preparing for the SAT I

Test preparation can be divided into two broad categories: short-term and long-term preparation. What you get from test preparation depends on what you do and on how much effort you put into it.

- Short-term preparation gets the quickest results.
- Long-term preparation has the biggest potential payoff.

Short-Term Preparation

Short-term preparation focuses on the test itself. It includes learning a number of specific test-taking tips and techniques, including:

- How to relax in order to beat test panic.
- What to expect from the test: what types of questions, how many questions, in what order.
- Getting familiar with test directions.
- Learning to pace yourself.
- When and how to guess.
- How to identify the easiest questions.
- Specific hints and approaches for each of the six types of test questions.

These are the types of tips and hints you'll find in the rest of this section. It also includes some of the techniques you'll find later in the book in Parts III and IV that deal specifically with the verbal and math sections of the SAT I.

This short-term preparation is designed to make sure that your score is as high as you deserve, based on the knowledge, skills, and abilities you have today. It's meant to keep you from getting a score that doesn't reflect all that you can do. It's designed to make sure that you identify and correctly answer every question that you currently have the ability to answer.

Short-term preparation can gain you some points on the test. But it's quite limited because it doesn't help you become a more able student.

Long-Term Preparation

Long-term preparation focuses on academic performance in general, not just on the test. It's designed to improve your abilities, to help you gain the skills necessary to answer more difficult questions. Long-term preparation includes things you can and should do all year. It is part and parcel of your overall education. It's what you're doing to prepare yourself academically for college. It focuses on such things as:

- Reading more effectively: giving you the ability to figure out what the author means as well as merely what the author says.
- Improving your vocabulary: giving you better tools to figure out new words from the context in which they are used.
- Developing your problem-solving abilities: helping you figure out what to do as well as how to do it and helping you get started on challenging problems when you seem to be stumped.

Remember, short-term preparation helps you make sure that you correctly answer all the questions you already have the ability to answer. Long-term preparation, on the other hand, can help you improve your abilities so that you can answer more questions. This general, long-term preparation can have the greatest effect on your scores and how well you'll do in college.

Your Chances of Gaining Points

Educational Testing Service (ETS) and the College Board keep statistics on what happens to the scores of students who take the SAT more than once. The *average* gains were, math: +15 points; verbal: +12 points. (Individual SAT scores only go up or down by 10 points. You can do 10 or 20 or 30 points better or worse, not 15 points or 12. The 15 points and 12 points are averages among all students included in the statistics.)

That doesn't mean a gain is guaranteed. The higher your score to begin with, the less likely you are to improve and the smaller the improvement is likely to be. In fact, the more your score exceeds 600 on either the verbal or math section, the more likely it is to go down (on average) rather than to go up when you take the test again.

- On average, about 5 of 100 students improve by 100 points or more in either the verbal or math section.
- On average, about 1 of 100 students loses 100 points or more the second time around.

Long-term preparation—preparation designed to improve your overall abilities, not just your test-taking skills—can pay off. If you start early and work consistently, your abilities will improve. And your test scores will come along for the ride.

Things You Should Do

1. Make sure you're familiar with the test.
2. Make sure you're familiar with the test-taking tips and techniques in this book.
3. Practice so you are comfortable with the test and the techniques.
4. Limit your test-specific preparation to 12 to 20 hours, at most. This can be done reasonably close to the time you take the test for the first time—say within a month or two.
5. Review the suggestions on long-term preparation and put them into practice. These are the strategies you should emphasize throughout your high school career.
6. Continue to work hard in school.

CHAPTER 4

Test-Taking Strategies

The Golden Rules of Test Taking

The following Golden Rules are designed to help you make sure that you don't throw away points unnecessarily. Their purpose is to stop you from stealing points from yourself.

1. Know the Directions

Make sure you're thoroughly familiar with the directions for every type of question on the SAT I before you actually take it.

2. Keep Moving

Never spend lots of time on any one question until you have tried all of the other questions in the section.

3. Check Your Answer Sheet

Always check the number of the question and the number on the answer sheet to be sure you're putting the answer in the right place. Check your sheet every few questions.

4. Don't Panic

Don't worry over questions that you can't answer. Feel good about each question you can answer.

5. Don't Throw Away Points to Carelessness

Never go so fast that you lose points on easy questions through careless errors.

6. Use Your Test Booklet As Scratch Paper

Make a mess of your test booklet—marking, noting, drawing, and scribbling as needed. But don't waste time.

7. Eliminate Choices

Before you give up on any question, try eliminating one or more choices.

Know the Directions

Take some time to carefully study the directions for answering the different types of questions. (The practice questions in Parts III and IV are a good place to begin.) That way, you won't spend time reading the directions on the day you take the SAT. You'll feel more confident and you'll be less likely to make careless errors because you didn't understand the instructions. This is particularly important in the math sections for the quantitative comparisons and the student-produced responses ("grid-ins").

Keep Moving

The biggest single time waster (and therefore the biggest single point stealer) is getting hung up on a single question.

If you can't answer a question without spending a long time figuring it out, go on to the next. You have to use your common sense on this. You should stop to think. But if you aren't sure about how to answer a question, or you don't know where to begin, stop working on that question. You'll probably have time to come back to it later.

An Important Technique

Don't just leave the question and go on. Put a mark in *your test booklet* (*not on your answer sheet*) next to any question that you don't answer. That way, you'll be able to find it easily when you go back.

A two-way marking system works well for many students:

? 1.

1. Put a question mark in the margin next to any question you didn't answer but that you have a reasonable chance of answering with some more time.

2. X

2. Put an X next to any question that you don't think you have much chance of answering correctly.

A small section of the test book might look like the one in the margin.

A simple system like this takes very little time, thought, or effort and can save lots of time when you go back through the test for questions you need to review or think more about.

Check Your Answer Sheet

Losing your place on the answer sheet is a major disaster that should never, ever happen, no matter how good or poor a test taker you think you are.

Here's how it happens:

Check the number of the question and the number on the answer sheet every few questions.

- You're moving through the test. You get stuck on a couple of questions, so you jump ahead.

Check them every time you skip a question.

- You're concentrating on the next question. (And you're congratulating yourself for being smart enough to find questions you can answer instead of wasting time on ones that you can't.)

- Then you get to the last question of the section, and there are still three spaces left on the answer sheet. *When you skipped the questions, you forgot to skip ahead on your answer sheet!*

A mistake like this one could mess up your SAT score, especially if you're not sure where the mistake happened, or if you don't catch the mistake until you've marked in 15 or 20 answers.

Just think about it. If you don't find the mistake, all the answers you marked in from the place where you skipped the question could be wrong. Even if you do find where you made the mistake, you're going to waste time erasing and re-marking your answer sheet. If you're in a hurry, you may not erase clearly. If you fill in the correct answer but don't fully erase the incorrect answer, you'll end up with two answers to the same question and no points. And you'll be rushing, so the chance of making an error is greater. And you'll be short on time for the section, so you'll have less time to check your work or to figure out the answers to tough questions.

It's very likely that you'll be worrying about the mistake as you work on other sections. So your performance on parts of the test that shouldn't even be affected by the mistake will probably suffer.

The really sad thing is that this particular error is completely avoidable. Just get into a few good habits.

Here's What to Do:

1. Fold your test booklet back so that you're looking at only one page at a time, not at the full two pages. (Of course, you wouldn't want to do this if you're working on a long reading passage or pair of passages that take more than one page.)
2. Keep your answer sheet close to the test booklet as you work.
3. Check that the number of the test question on your answer sheet and in the test booklet agree every few questions.
4. Check that the test question on your answer sheet and in the test booklet agree *every time* you skip a question.

Don't Panic

Getting panicky or depressed can be a subtle but very serious problem when you're taking the SAT. If you find that there are lots of questions you can't answer, you have to work hard to keep your focus on the ones that you can. If you aren't concentrating on the question you're working on, you are less likely to answer it correctly. Then you've got more questions you can't answer . . . then more worry, more distraction, more questions you can't do . . . . It's a vicious cycle.

Avoiding Test Panic

1. Remember that some questions are harder than most on the classroom tests you take. So it's all right to find there are more questions you can't answer than you are used to finding.

2. Remember that to get a good score, you don't have to answer every question. And you can miss a lot of questions and still get an average score.

3. Some students find it helpful to take a breather—or at least, take a breath. If you get that pit-in-your-stomach, sweaty-palm, I'm-getting-a-headache feeling:

- Stop
- Close your eyes
- Take two or three slow, controlled breaths, breathing in and out on a slow count of 5.
- Tell yourself that you're taking one question at a time.
- Tell yourself that every question you get right is worth points and you're not going to let any of those points get away.
- Then go on with the test.

4. Each time you find a question you *can* answer, congratulate yourself and start looking for the next one. Remind yourself that you got one and you're ready to find another.

Some of this advice may seem pretty simple, but it's very important. There's more like it in the chapter on "Psyching Up." It's too easy to get into a depressed spiral if you're not doing as well as you'd like or if you run into a bunch of questions you can't handle. Once that spiral begins, your energy drains and your ability to find easy questions (or dig out answers to tough questions) goes right down the tube.

One More Point

One thing that can happen if you get into an "I-can't-answer-these-questions" frame of mind is that you start passing over questions. If you rush by with that I-don't-know attitude, you're not giving yourself a chance to take a fresh look at each question. And you're bound to skip one or two that you really could answer. You've got to avoid getting into a no-answer rhythm.

So as hard as it is, take each question as it comes. And give yourself a chance to try each question as you read it.

Don't Throw Away Points

Don't rush! Don't let yourself go so fast that you lose points on easy questions through careless errors.

Of all the Golden Rules of test taking, this is the most important. There's nothing worse than losing points on questions you really do know how to answer.

In the anxiety of taking the test, it's easier than you think to make a mistake on a question you can answer. Marking the wrong answer is one way to do it. But it's just as easy to make an arithmetic error, read a question too quickly and miss an important point, forget to read all the answers, or just simply get caught by an inviting (but wrong) choice that you would have rejected if you had just taken a bit more time.

Here are a few things you can do to keep from losing points through carelessness:

1. After you fill in your answer on the answer sheet, check the answer you filled in against the choices in the test book. Read the answer and its letter to yourself (actually say the letter to yourself).

2. Do something to make sure that you don't rush. You might want to take a deep breath between questions. Or stop and take a deep breath after every five questions. Or put your pencil down, close your eyes, and count to 10 after every 10 questions. The idea is to work at an even, steady pace.

3. In math questions, especially word problems, check to see whether your answer makes common sense. Is a discount bigger than the original price? Is someone traveling too far too fast? Is someone making $150 an hour selling Girl Scout cookies? Is the average age of the students in a high school class 56 years old?

4. Again in math, when you review a question to check your work, start from the beginning. If you can, use a *different* method to check the answer than you used to get the answer the first time. If you use the *same* method, you may make the same mistake twice.

5. Always read all the answers to a verbal question before choosing the one you think is correct. (In math, you just need to look for the answer that agrees with your solution.)

6. With each of the verbal questions, there are specific pitfalls that catch students who are going just a bit too fast. These pitfalls will be covered in the sections on those questions.

In a nutshell: It's important to keep moving and to keep from wasting time, but it's never a good idea to rush.

Use Your Test Booklet

Your test booklet is not scored. It is collected, sent back to ETS, and eventually shredded and recycled.

While you have to keep your *answer sheet* clean and neat, your test booklet is yours to do with as you will. (There are limits. You *cannot* rip out pages, fold down corners to measure angles, use a highlighter, or take the test booklet home. You *can* write whatever you want, wherever you want, in the section of the booklet you're working on.)

How should you use your test booklet?

1. You know one suggestion already—mark each question using the **?, X** system described on page 31.
2. When you're working on a question, put a line through each choice as you eliminate it. (Don't make the choice unreadable; you may want to reconsider your decision. But make it clear that you think the choice is not correct.)
3. Feel free to use your pencil (remember—no highlighters!) to mark sections, sentences, or words in reading passages.
4. In math, make drawings to help you figure word problems. Mark key information on graphs. Add facts to drawings and diagrams as you figure.

Mark your booklet in any way that will help you work efficiently, find information, or figure out the answers.

Eliminate Choices

Don't give up right away if you can't answer a question. Take a shot at eliminating choices.

It's often easier to eliminate some choices than it is to find the one correct answer.

- On some questions, you can eliminate all the choices until you have only the one correct answer left.
- In some cases, eliminating some choices keeps you thinking about the question and helps you think your way through to the correct answer.
- As a last resort, if you can eliminate any choices as definitely wrong, it may pay to make a guess among the other choices.

RECAP: GOLDEN RULES

The Golden Rules are principles you should keep in mind throughout the test. They are sound test-taking techniques at any time and for anyone. Once again, they are:

1. Know the Directions. Don't lose time on test day reading the directions for the first time.
2. Keep moving: Don't get hung up on any one question.
3. Check your answer sheet: Don't mark answers in the wrong place.
4. Don't panic: Focus on what you can do, not on what you can't do.
5. Don't throw away points to carelessness: Keep moving but don't rush.
6. Use your test booklet as scratch paper: Write or mark anything that will help you.
7. Eliminate choices: If you can't answer the question, try to identify wrong answers.

Pacing

How Fast Do You Have to Go?

The question of pacing is based on the proposition that each question on the test takes a certain amount of time to read and answer. If you had unlimited time, or very few questions to answer, pacing would not be a problem.

So the question, "How fast do you have to go?" depends on how many questions you have to answer in the time allowed.

This may seem like a strange statement. But the number of questions on the test doesn't matter. What matters is the number of questions you need to answer. And, for most people, the two numbers are different. We'll assume for the moment that you're not one of those few students who's expecting to get a perfect score of 800 on each section.

Instead, let's take a very good verbal score of 600. A 600 would put you in about the top 5 percent of students taking the test. Question: How many verbal questions would you have to answer correctly to get a 600? Answer: on the practice test in this book, 62. Question: How many verbal questions are there on the new test? Answer: 78. That means you could leave out 16 questions and still get a 600 on this verbal test!

What about a 500? To get a 500 on the verbal SAT I, at most you need to answer 47 questions correctly. You could leave out at least

31 questions! To get an average score of 420 or 430, you need 35 correct answers. That means you have to answer fewer than half the questions correctly.

If you set reasonable expectations for yourself, you may be able to shorten the test you have to take. If you are shooting for a verbal 500, you shouldn't be worrying about answering every question on the test. You should think of the test as a 47-question test with 31 bonus questions. If you are shooting for an average score, *your* test is only about half as long as the test that's in the test booklet. If you are reaching for 600, you still don't have to think about all the questions—62 will do.

On the math sections the actual numbers are a little different, but the idea is the same.

You should set a reasonable target. Concentrate on the number of questions you should be able to answer correctly. If you have extra time, you can go after the "bonus" points.

IMPORTANT

The information about targets is meant to help you pace yourself when you take the SAT I. Knowing that you don't have to answer every question means you can skip ahead to questions you feel secure about answering and then go back to the ones that gave you problems if you have time. It also means that the world won't end if you don't answer every single question on the test.

However, it's not a good idea to decide that you're only going to answer a certain number of questions. For one thing, the examples are based on the number of questions you need to answer correctly. If you select the wrong answer to a question, it will lower your score because a fraction of a point is subtracted for each incorrect answer. Also, the number of right answers you need to "get" a certain score can vary from one test to another. It won't vary by much, but even one or two questions, plus a few incorrect answers you weren't counting on could make a difference!

Targets

Your targets are the scores that you expect to get when you take the SAT I. Targets are based on your current capabilities. They should reflect what you're able to do when you take the SAT I.

Be especially careful not to set targets based on what you believe (or what an admission officer or high school counselor tells you) is required to get into some college or another. That target might be unrealistically high or low. The targets that will help you on the test are based on what you can do, not on what someone else expects you to do.

It's very possible for you to do better than your target. Nothing in the techniques suggested in this book will keep you from overshooting your targets. In fact, the adjustments you make in your approach to the test may well have just that effect.

How Do You Set a Target?

Start with information you already have. If you have taken the PSAT/NMSQT or the SAT I itself, start with those scores. (Multiply the PSAT/NMSQT score by 10 to get an equivalent SAT I score.) Set your sights a little higher than your current score.

If you haven't taken either test before, take the test in this book and some of the tests in *10 SATs*. (The old tests are somewhat different, but the scores are comparable.)

Use the scores you get to figure out about how well you can expect to do when you take the SAT "for real." Be realistic—very few students will achieve 800 scores or even come close. And use the practice test to determine how many questions of each type you can expect to answer on the actual test. (Since the difficulty of each SAT is pretty much the same, this number won't vary by much.) If you know beforehand about how many questions you can comfortably answer, you should feel pretty relaxed about taking the SAT! And, since you'll be able to pace yourself, you should be able to go back and work on "bonus" questions in each section.

HINT:

Don't cheat yourself! Don't skip questions that you might be able to answer just because you don't "need" them to make your target. This is especially important in the first section of the test. Suppose you find you can answer more questions in that section than you expected. Of course answer them, because you may wind up answering fewer questions in the other sections. So be fair to yourself and tackle every question in every section that you can. Besides, if you answer *more* questions than you originally intended, and get a better score, no one will complain.

Finding "Your" Questions

When you take the test, first, go after the questions that are the easiest for you to answer quickly and feel confident you've answered correctly. Next, use your knowledge of the test and of your own abilities to find questions you can answer with some extra time and effort. When you have found all the questions you can handle and have checked your answers, then you can spend time digging out the hard stuff, working on really difficult questions that take more time and effort.

The Basic Steps

1. Go through the section you're working on, answering all the questions that come easily to you. Mark the ones that you'll probably be able to answer on a second try.
2. Then go back to the questions you think you can answer and work on them.
3. Go back and check your work to make sure you have not lost points due to careless errors, or try some of the bonus questions, the tough ones that can help push you past your target score.

Should You Skip Questions?

You shouldn't ignore any questions, especially questions that you might be able to answer. But you shouldn't worry about questions that fall beyond your target score.

> **HINT:**
>
> Focus on getting to your target, and you're likely to have the time you need to reach and even exceed it.

Another reason to set realistic targets is to help you psychologically. Many students get discouraged by the number of SAT questions they can't answer. Once they get discouraged, they start focusing on the problems they're having instead of on individual questions.

If you set appropriate targets, instead of being discouraged by what you aren't doing, you're more likely to be encouraged by what you are accomplishing. When your frame of mind is better, you're likely to perform better.

> **RECAP: FINDING THE QUESTIONS ON *YOUR* TEST**
>
> Know where you are.
>
> Make an honest assessment of your current abilities. Use the practice SAT as a gauge of where you are, today.
>
> Know what you want.
>
> Set the targets that you want to achieve and that you can reasonably attain.
>
> Know what you need.
>
> Use your target to help you set your pace through the test, and to help you stay positive, relaxed, and focused on the questions as you take the test.

Rules for Pacing

Here are some basic principles of pacing—strategies that will help ensure that you don't waste time on the SAT I and that you'll have time to consider all the questions you have the ability to answer.

Keep Moving

This is one of the Golden Rules of test taking, but it's so important that it bears repeating:

Keep moving. Don't stop to puzzle out hard questions before you have at least tried to find and answer all the easier ones.

Some Reminders:

- Mark the questions as you work on them, especially the ones you want to go back to, so you can find them later. It won't do you any good to save time by leaving a hard question if you lose that time looking for it later.

- If you can eliminate any choices on the way, put a *light* line through those you have eliminated. This will also save time when you come back to the question.

Easy to Hard

VERBAL. In general, it's best to work from easy to hard. Analogy and Sentence Completion questions are arranged in order of difficulty. The easier questions come first, followed by the more difficult ones. If you find that the Sentence Completions are getting too hard, look through the rest of the questions quickly, then jump ahead to the beginning of the Analogy questions to pick up the easy ones.

The Critical Reading questions are *not* necessarily arranged in easy-to-hard order.

HINT:

Work through a reading passage and all its questions completely before moving on.

More hints on pacing your way through the Reading Passages are given in "Handling the Critical Reading Questions" in Part III of this book and in the sample Critical Reading passages in Chapter 7.

MATH. Math questions generally go from easy to hard, but there's a little more variety in their arrangement. Still, the general advice is the same as with the Sentence Completion and Analogy questions: Look for the easiest math questions at the beginning of each section.

In general it's better to work through shorter questions (or questions that you can answer easily) before moving on to questions that are longer (or take longer to figure out).

You might think it's a good idea to tackle the tough questions first, when you're fresh, and go back to the quick, easy ones when there are still a few minutes left at the end of the section. For most students this is a mistake. The best advice is to answer what you can at the beginning of each section, then move to the questions that take longer.

The SAT is designed so that, in general, test takers have adequate time to reach each question. But since the more time-consuming questions tend to be at the end of each section, a student halfway through a section with one-half of the time already used is not likely to reach all of the questions.

An Example of Pacing

Say you're beginning to work on a verbal section that has 35 questions—23 Analogies and Sentence Completions and 12 questions based on a reading passage. Assume it takes about 30 to 40 seconds to do a short question and an average of 75 seconds per question for the reading questions. (This includes time to read the passage as well as answer all 12 questions.)

At this rate, you would have just about enough time to finish, if you don't get stuck on anything. Now, what happens if you decide that you want to start with the Critical Reading questions? *If everything goes exactly according to schedule,* you'll finish the section. No problem. If everything goes according to schedule. But what if you take an extra *three minutes* on the reading passage? That three minutes translates into *six* Sentence Completion or Analogy questions you never even get a chance to try.

It's harder to control the time you take with reading passages than the time you need for shorter questions. So starting with the Reading Passages may be risky. Try to get your "quick points" first.

Going after the Math You Know

Unless you're a math whiz, you'll probably find that some types of math questions are easier for you than others. Here's a tip for handling the math sections most efficiently:

- First, work on the questions that you're sure you know how to answer.
- Second, work on the questions that have familiar concepts and procedures.
- Save the real tough ones for last.

Critical Reading

Critical Reading questions take an investment in time. You can't begin to answer them until you've read the passage. Once you make the investment in reading the passage, don't throw it away.

1. Try to answer all the questions you can about one reading passage before you move on to another passage or back to the short-answer questions.

2. Keep moving. Don't spend 5 minutes digging out the answer to the second question on a reading passage until you have tried the others. If one question hangs you up, move on to the next question on that passage. But go back to the tough questions and give them a second shot before moving on.

There are two reasons for this strategy. First, you don't want to have to reread the passage to figure out the tough questions later. Second, you may pick up extra information from the passage that will help you answer one question when you are searching for the answers to others.

3. The fastest reading questions to answer are usually the vocabulary-in-context questions. Make sure you at least take a good look at those for every passage on the test.

Move on Quickly If:

- The question includes words that are unfamiliar.
- You don't know how to get started on a math question.

Keep Working When:

- You are working out a math problem and haven't run into any dead ends.
- You don't have an answer, but you're still moving forward. Perhaps you can eliminate some choices.

Stop Working and Move on If:

- You're down to two or three possible answers, but you're going to have to rethink the question before you make up your mind about which is correct.
- You haven't made your decision on the answer, and you start thinking the same thoughts about the question over and over again.
- You feel yourself getting angry or frustrated by the question.

Be sure to mark any questions you skip with a question mark before you move on. And watch your answer sheet!

Don't Lose Work You've Done

You don't want to have to start over when you come back to a question.

1. Make sure you mark (in the test booklet) all questions you want to come back to.
2. Lightly cross out answers you have been able to eliminate.
3. Always leave yourself a thought trail. What's a "thought trail"? It's notes about what you were thinking while you were working on the question. Good notes (a good thought trail) let you pick up from where you left off instead of having to start all over again.

➥ REMEMBER:

Always check that the question number in your test book and on your answer sheet agree *every time* you skip a question.

Rushing Loses You Time

- Rushing will get you into a tizzy. If you try to go too fast, you won't think clearly and you'll take extra time settling your mind down to work on challenging questions.
- Rushing promotes carelessness. Correcting careless errors takes time, and that's bad. Not correcting them is even worse.
- Rushing makes you concentrate on going fast instead of on answering questions. You should keep your pace even enough so you can concentrate on each question as you face it. You don't want to have half your mind on the clock and only half available for work.

Keep a Steady Pace

If you remember only one thing, it's this: Work steadily. Don't rush. Don't stop or slow down.

RECAP: PACING

Keep moving.
Work from easier to harder questions.
Work from shorter to longer questions.
Work on familiar types of math problems first.
Answer all the questions you can on one reading passage before
    moving on to the next.
Know when and how to move on.
Don't lose the work you have done.
Rushing loses you time and a lot more.
Keep a steady pace.

Guessing

There's a lot of misunderstanding about guessing on the SAT. The fact is, the scoring system for all the multiple-choice questions is set up so that you get one point for each correct answer and lose a fraction of a point for each wrong answer. Questions you omit neither gain nor lose points.

The deduction for a wrong answer is set to exactly offset the chance of getting the answer right by wild guessing.

Does that mean you should never guess? No! Sometimes guessing is a good idea.

Some Good Advice about Guessing

Don't

Wild guessing is not a good idea. The scoring system is set up so that, on average, taking the entire test by making only wild guesses will result in a *ZERO* raw score. As many points will be lost as will be gained.

Do

If you can eliminate some choices as definitely wrong, then it is to your advantage to guess among the choices that are left.

The more choices you can eliminate as definitely wrong, the better your odds of getting the correct answer.

There is one type of question on which there is no deduction for a wrong answer: the Grid-in math questions, for which you have to write in your own answer instead of choosing. If you worked out an answer but are not certain it is correct, go ahead and grid it in.

If you can eliminate some choices on multiple-choice questions, you can make an educated guess. This sample question and the answers following it show you how educated guessing works.

Which of the following is true of Hydra, the monster of Greek legend?
(A) It lured sailors with music.
(B) It had many heads.
(C) It shopped at the mall.
(D) It wrote Beethoven's 5th symphony.
(E) It is the lead singer for a punk-rock group.

You might not know exactly who/what Hydra is, but you should be able to eliminate some of the choices just using common sense. Generally speaking monsters—especially if they're legendary—don't shop at malls. Odds are, Beethoven wrote his own symphony. And to fit the description, the punk rocker would have to be both Greek and a legend—not to mention a monster. So that leaves you with choices A and B.

If you guess from among the two remaining choices, your chance of getting the question right is better than the penalty for getting it wrong. In other words, in a case like this, you *should* guess.

To see the difference between wild guessing and making an educated guess (where you can eliminate some answers), try the exercise at the end of this chapter.

The more choices you can eliminate, the better your odds. But even if you can only eliminate one choice, your odds of guessing correctly improve.

Should You Guess?

Remember, guessing has to do with odds, with chances. The more questions you guess on, the more likely you are to come out close to the way the odds say you will come out. If you guess on just one or two questions, there's really no telling how you will do. (Then again, there isn't too much risk either!)

> **REMEMBER:**
>
> There is no deduction for answering a Grid-in math question wrong. At the same time, it is unlikely that you can guess the answer correctly.
>
> So, with Grid-in questions on the Math sections, answer the question if you can work it out. But don't spend time guessing unless you've answered all of the questions you're certain of.

Guessing Experiment

Wild guessing

The answer grid below represents a set of wild guessing questions. To make sure that you're making wild guesses, you're not even going to get to see the questions!

Fill in the answer grid below to see how you do in a wild guessing situation:

Wild guessing score:

Number of right
  answers _____
Minus 1/4 point for each
  wrong answer _____
Total _____

1. Ⓐ Ⓑ Ⓒ Ⓓ Ⓔ
2. Ⓐ Ⓑ Ⓒ Ⓓ Ⓔ
3. Ⓐ Ⓑ Ⓒ Ⓓ Ⓔ
4. Ⓐ Ⓑ Ⓒ Ⓓ Ⓔ
5. Ⓐ Ⓑ Ⓒ Ⓓ Ⓔ
6. Ⓐ Ⓑ Ⓒ Ⓓ Ⓔ
7. Ⓐ Ⓑ Ⓒ Ⓓ Ⓔ
8. Ⓐ Ⓑ Ⓒ Ⓓ Ⓔ
9. Ⓐ Ⓑ Ⓒ Ⓓ Ⓔ
10. Ⓐ Ⓑ Ⓒ Ⓓ Ⓔ
11. Ⓐ Ⓑ Ⓒ Ⓓ Ⓔ
12. Ⓐ Ⓑ Ⓒ Ⓓ Ⓔ
13. Ⓐ Ⓑ Ⓒ Ⓓ Ⓔ
14. Ⓐ Ⓑ Ⓒ Ⓓ Ⓔ
15. Ⓐ Ⓑ Ⓒ Ⓓ Ⓔ
16. Ⓐ Ⓑ Ⓒ Ⓓ Ⓔ
17. Ⓐ Ⓑ Ⓒ Ⓓ Ⓔ
18. Ⓐ Ⓑ Ⓒ Ⓓ Ⓔ
19. Ⓐ Ⓑ Ⓒ Ⓓ Ⓔ
20. Ⓐ Ⓑ Ⓒ Ⓓ Ⓔ

Now score your wild guessing test. The answers are on page 48. Give yourself 1 point for each correct answer.

Most people will come out pretty close to zero.

If you don't . . . well, remember, wild guessing is about odds. Have a couple of family members or friends try. Overall, the results will be close to zero.

Educated guessing

To test educated guessing, two choices on each question have been eliminated, just as you would eliminate any choices that you decided were *definitely wrong.* Remember, even when you're making educated guesses, you're choosing randomly among the choices that remain.

Fill in the answer grid below. Then check how you did against the answer key on page 48. Unless you are very unlucky (and some of you will be), you should end up with a positive score.

Educated guessing score:

Number of right answers _____

Minus 1/4 point for each wrong answer _____

Total _____

1. (B) (C)   (E)
2. (B) (C)   (E)
3. (B) (C)   (E)
4. (B) (C)   (E)
5. (B) (C)   (E)
6. (B) (C)   (E)
7. (B) (C)   (E)
8. (B) (C)   (E)
9. (B) (C)   (E)
10. (B) (C)   (E)
11. (B) (C)   (E)
12. (B) (C)   (E)
13. (B) (C)   (E)
14. (B) (C)   (E)
15. (B) (C)   (E)
16. (B) (C)   (E)
17. (B) (C)   (E)
18. (B) (C)   (E)
19. (B) (C)   (E)
20. (B) (C)   (E)

RECAP: GUESSING

1. If you have no idea about the correct answer, it's a waste of time to guess.

2. If you can eliminate even one answer as definitely wrong, it will probably pay to guess among the rest of the choices.

Answers for the Guessing Experiment

Wild Guessing: Question	Answers	Educated Guessing: Question	Answers
1	D	1	C
2	B	2	B
3	E	3	E
4	C	4	E
5	A	5	B
6	C	6	C
7	D	7	B
8	D	8	E
9	A	9	C
10	C	10	C
11	E	11	B
12	B	12	E
13	A	13	C
14	E	14	B
15	D	15	B
16	B	16	B
17	E	17	C
18	A	18	E
19	C	19	C
20	B	20	E

CHAPTER 5

Psyching Yourself Up

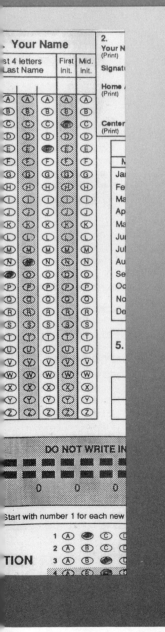

Your SAT I results depend on how much you know and on how well you can put what you know to work. But your results can also depend on how you feel. Nerves, distractions, poor concentration, or a negative attitude can pull down your performance.

Relaxation Techniques

Being nervous is natural. Being nervous, by itself, isn't really a problem. A bit of a nervous edge can keep you sharp and focused. Too much nervousness, however, can work in just the opposite direction—keeping you from concentrating and working effectively.

Here are some techniques you can use to keep your nerves in check.

Before the Test

Don't cram.

Do something enjoyable and relaxing.

Get a good night's sleep.

Have everything that you need for the test ready the night before.

You can start your psychological preparation the day before the test. Here's how:

Don't cram. The SAT I isn't the sort of test where jamming another fact or two into your head the day before will do you much good.

Try to relax. Do something you really enjoy the day before the test. You want to take your mind off the test for a while. And you want to go into the test feeling good.

Whatever you do to relax and enjoy yourself, try not to stay up too late. The test is going to make you use your brains, so getting a good night's sleep is important.

Use the list below for a starter, but make your own personal list as well. Make sure you have:

- The appropriate ID, which must include your photo, or a brief description of you. The description must be on school stationery or a school ID form, and you must sign it in front of your principal or guidance counselor, who must also sign it.
- Admission Ticket
- #2 pencils
- Calculator with charged batteries

Make sure you know the way to the test center and any special instructions for finding the entrance on Saturday or Sunday.

Leave yourself plenty of time for mishaps and emergencies.

If you haven't been to the test center before, check the directions. It's a good idea to take a dry run to the location, so you'll know the way and won't get lost and arrive late.

Check your Admission ticket for special instructions. For example, because the tests are given on weekends, some test center entrances can be locked.

Get up early. Figure out how much time you need to get to the test center, then give yourself an extra 15 minutes. It will make the morning more relaxed. And, if something does go wrong, you'll have

50

extra time to deal with the problem. There may be as many as 400,000 students taking the test on the same day. Some of them will get caught in traffic or spill their orange juice in their laps and have to change their clothes. If one of these disasters is yours, you want to be able to shrug it off and still get to the test on time.

Why all this worry about lateness?

- If you're not there when the test starts, you can't take the test.
- If you're late and rushing to get to the center, getting there will be the focus of your attention instead of the test itself. If you just make it, chances are it's going to take you some time to settle down and start focusing on the test questions.
- The extra nervous energy you spend getting to the test center will take the edge off your performance. The "Whew, I made it!" feeling will probably be followed by a little letdown, just when you should be gearing up.

Think Positively

Getting down on yourself during the test does more than make you feel bad. It can keep you from doing as well as you could. It can rob you of the confidence you need to solve problems. It can distract you. If you're thinking that you aren't doing well, you aren't thinking about the question in front of you. Think positive thoughts that will help you keep up your confidence and focus on each question. Try telling yourself things like:

- "This test is going to seem harder than tests I usually take, so it's OK if I can't answer as many questions as usual. What's important is to do the questions I can do and can get right."
- "I've already answered 10 questions right, and there are other easy questions that I have yet to find."
- Each time you get a question right, say: "There's another bunch of points I've put in the bank."

Keep Yourself Focused

Be aware of your own thoughts. If you find your mind wandering, stop yourself right away. Some test takers find it helpful to close their eyes and take a deep breath and remind themselves to get back to answering questions.

Remember:

- Try not to think about anything except the question in front of you.
- If you catch yourself thinking about something else, bring your focus back to the test, but congratulate yourself. Remind yourself that you are in control. You can feel good that you've stopped yourself from wasting time and losing points.

Concentrate on Yourself

The first thing a lot of students do when they get stuck on a question or find themselves running into a batch of tough questions is to look around to see how everyone else is doing. What they usually see is that others are filling in their answer sheets. That's when the fear and the negative thoughts start building:

"Look at how well everyone else is doing. . . . I must be the stupidest one here. . . . What's wrong with me?"

Those thoughts won't do you any good. If you start thinking that way, try to remember:

- It's probably not true. You're probably not the worst one in the room.

- Just because others are working away happily on their answer sheets doesn't mean that they are filling in the correct answers.

- Finally, and this is most important, thinking about what someone else is doing doesn't help you answer even a single question. In fact, it takes away time you should be using on your test.

Use Targets to Help

Remind yourself of how long *your* test really is.

Remember that you have *your* questions and bonus questions in each section.

Focusing on *your* test can help you avoid thinking, "Others are doing so much better."

Remind yourself that you're in control.

Your target scores can be a major psychological help when you take the test if you set ones that are reasonable. Here's how to use them to your advantage:

When you realize that you don't have to answer every question, you should be able to stay more relaxed, more positive, and more focused.

If you set your target accurately, you'll only face tough questions among the bonus ones. You should be able to do quite well with the questions that are on *your* test.

The others are working away because their tests are different from yours. Even better, they're struggling away and they may not even realize that they may be wasting time on questions they won't be able to answer and leaving no time for the questions they can answer.

To take psychological advantage of your targets, work out the number of questions you need to answer correctly. That way you'll know which are the questions on your test and which are the bonus ones.

Consider all the things you did to put and keep yourself in control:

- You have a plan for finding all the questions that you can answer.
- You have targets that put you in charge of the test you are taking. And that is a test on which you should be able to do well.
- You know how to keep yourself focused.
- You can work efficiently and confidently, knowing that you have a good technique for taking the test.

By reminding yourself of these things, you will be able to keep relaxed, keep your attitude positive, and keep yourself focused and effective.

Stay Physically Relaxed

Staying relaxed helps keep you focused. Some relaxation techniques were covered in the Pacing section and in the Golden Rules, but they are worth reviewing:

Don't rush. Keep an even pace.

Check question numbers on the answer sheet and test booklet. This will eliminate one source of possible concern. It is also an easy process to remember and do right. And each thing that you do right helps your sense of control and confidence. Finally, checking numbers will help keep you from rushing.

Remind yourself that you have a sound plan that will help you do as well as possible on the test.

If you find that you are tensing up, some test takers find it helps to

- Put the pencil down.
- Close their eyes.
- Take three or four measured, even breaths, counting slowly to four or five as they breathe in and out.
- Congratulate themselves for having gained control.
- Get to work on the next question.

Put the Test in Perspective

The SAT is important, but how you do on one test will not determine whether you get into college.

- The test is only one factor in the college admission decision.
- High school grades are considered more important than the SAT by most college admission officers.
- Nonacademic admission criteria are important, too. These include things like extracurricular activities and personal recommendations. College admission officers at individual colleges will usually be glad to discuss the admission policies at their institutions with you.
- And if you don't do as well as you wanted to, you can take the test again.

Remember You're in Control

If you create a good plan for taking the test—set target scores, practice each type of question, know where and how to find all the questions you can answer, remember some relaxation techniques and use them— you'll stay in control as you take the SAT. And if you're in control, you'll have a good chance of getting all the points you deserve.

PART THREE

SAT I: Verbal Reasoning

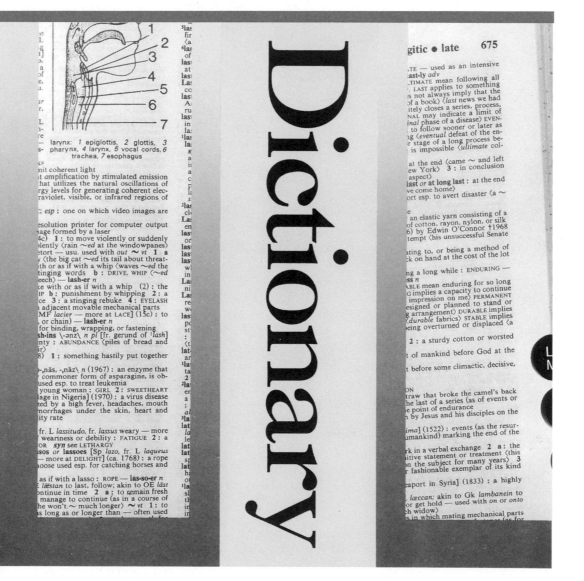

CHAPTER 6

Introduction to the Verbal Sections

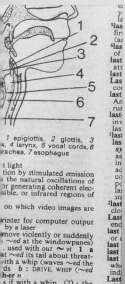

The verbal sections of SAT I contain three types of questions:

- Analogies
- Sentence Completions
- Critical Reading

Analogies focus on the relationships between pairs of words; they measure your reasoning ability as well as the depth and breadth of your vocabulary. Sentence Completions are fill-in questions that test your vocabulary and your ability to understand fairly complex sentences. Critical Reading questions are based on passages 400 to 850 words long. The content of the passages is drawn from the Humanities, the Social Sciences, and the Natural Sciences. Narrative passages (usually prose fiction) also are used in the test.

The three types of verbal questions are designed to test how well you understand the written word. Your ability to read carefully and to think about what you read is crucial to your success in college. In college, you will have to learn a great deal on your own from your assigned reading. And that's just as true in mathematics and science and technical courses as it is in "reading" courses like literature, philosophy, and history. Verbal skills are fundamental building blocks of academic success.

Analogies

Analogies focus on the relationships between pairs of words.

Analogy questions present a pair of words. Your job is to figure out the relationship between the two words and then identify the pair of words among the five answer choices that has the same relationship. These are the directions that will appear on the test.

> **Each question below consists of a related pair of words or phrases, followed by five pairs of words or phrases labeled A through E. Select the pair that <u>best</u> expresses a relationship similar to that expressed in the original pair.**
>
> **Example:**
>
> **CRUMB:BREAD::**
> (A) **ounce:unit**
> (B) **splinter:wood**
> (C) **water:bucket**
> (D) **twine:rope**
> (E) **cream:butter**

The correct answer is (B). An explanation of the answer to this question is given in Chapter 7.

Sentence Completions

Sentence Completion questions test both reasoning and vocabulary skills.

Sentence Completion questions are fill-in questions consisting of a sentence with either one or two words left out. Your job is to find the answer with the word or words that best fill in the blank(s). These are the directions that will appear on the test.

> **Each sentence below has one or two blanks, each blank indicating that something has been omitted. Beneath the sentence are five words or sets of words labeled A through E. Choose the word or set of words that, when inserted in the sentence, best fits the meaning of the sentence as a whole.**
>
> **Example:**
>
> **Medieval kingdoms did not become constitutional republics overnight; on the contrary, the change was ----.**
> **(A) unpopular**
> **(B) unexpected**
> **(C) advantageous**
> **(D) sufficient**
> **(E) gradual**

The correct answer is (E). An explanation of how to answer this question is given in Chapter 7.

Critical Reading

Critical Reading requires going beyond what the author says and figuring out what the author means.

Critical Reading on the SAT involves reading a passage and then answering questions about what you have read. All the information you will need to answer the questions can be found in the passage. The following are sample directions for this type of question.

> **Each passage below is followed by questions based on its content. Answer the questions on the basis of what is <u>stated</u> or <u>implied</u> in each passage and in any introductory material that may be provided.**

Notice the <u>underlined</u> words in the directions: <u>stated</u> or <u>implied</u>. The word "implied" indicates that, while something might not be stated directly, you can make an inference or draw a conclusion about it from what is stated.

Paired Passages   Some of the reading selections will consist of a *pair* of related passages. The two passages will have a common theme or subject. Some of the Critical Reading questions associated with paired passages will ask you to compare and contrast significant elements of the two passages.

Strategies for Tackling the Questions

Get your quick points first

About half of the Verbal questions are Analogies and Sentence Completions. Take your best shot first at these questions in any section that includes all three types of Verbal questions. But don't spend half your time on them, because the Critical Reading passages take a lot more time. As you work on one of the 30-minute Verbal sections, you may want to use the following strategy:

- Begin with the first set of Sentence Completions. Answer as many as you can. Mark the others with a question mark (?) or an X. You'll recall from Chapter 4 that a question mark means you have a good chance of answering the question with a little more time. An X means you don't think you'll have much chance of answering the question correctly.

- Move on next to the Analogy questions and work through them the same way you worked through the Sentence Completions.

- Go back and take a second, quick look at the questions you marked with a question mark. Answer the ones you can without spending lots of time.

- Then move on to the Critical Reading passages and questions.

- **Important:** one 15-minute Verbal section includes *only* Critical Reading questions.

Take a Look at All the Sentence Completions and Analogies

Even when questions of one type become difficult to answer, give the rest of them a quick read before you skip ahead to the next type. All of these questions are based in part on your knowledge of vocabulary, and you never can tell when you might hit on a word that you know. It doesn't take long to read these questions and you may pick up a correct answer or two.

Eliminate Choices on Tough Questions

If you have time to go back to some of the more difficult questions that you skipped, try eliminating choices. Sometimes you can get to the correct answer that way. If not, eliminating choices will at least allow you to make educated guesses.

If You Don't Know a Word . . . Attack!

Consider related words, familiar sayings and phrases, roots, prefixes, and suffixes. If you don't know what a word means right away, stop for a moment to think about whether you have heard or seen a word that might be related to it.

You might get help from common sayings and phrases. If you don't know a word but are familiar with a phrase that uses it, you might be able to figure the word out.

For instance, you might not immediately remember what the words **ovation** and **annul** mean. But you probably would recognize them in the phrases **a standing ovation** and **annul a marriage.** If you can recall a phrase or saying in which a word is used, you may be able to figure out what it means in another context.

Building Vocabulary Skills

Building vocabulary takes time, but it doesn't take magic. The single most effective thing you can do to build your vocabulary, over time, is to read a lot. Your teachers and librarians will be more than happy to recommend a variety of helpful and often enjoyable reading materials for you.

In addition to reading, there are many other things you can do to improve your vocabulary. The suggestions offered here are presented in outline form, but vocabulary building is a long-term effort. If you succeed, the results will go a long way toward helping you reach your academic goals, including and beyond getting good SAT I verbal scores.

Focus on how words are used, not just on what they mean.

- Memorizing lists of words and their definitions is not particularly useful.
- When you see a word you don't know, first try to figure out what it means from its context (from the way it is used).
- When you look up a word in the dictionary, pay attention to the different definitions and the contexts in which each is appropriate.
- Practice your expanding vocabulary by using the new words you have learned in your reading with your friends and in your school writing assignments.

Pay close attention to roots, prefixes, and suffixes.

- Most dictionaries include the etymologies of words as well as their definitions. The etymology is the history of the word—what word(s) it is derived from, what the parts of the word mean, and how those parts relate. Get in the habit of reading the etymologies along with the definitions.
- Check your school or local library and/or bookstore for vocabulary-building books. Almost all of them include lists of common roots, prefixes, and suffixes.
- Memorizing the meanings of roots, prefixes, and suffixes will be more helpful than memorizing individual words.

Knowing foreign languages can help—even if you're just a beginner.

- Apply your knowledge of foreign languages, especially those related to Latin, such as Spanish, French, and Italian. English has many cognates, or words with similar meanings, from these languages.
- You don't have to be an expert linguist to take advantage of your knowledge of a foreign language. Even if you have studied for only a few months, you have probably learned a number of English cognates. *Ami* in French, *amicus* in Latin, and *amigo* in Spanish all mean "friend." They show up in English as amicable, which means friendly. *Puer* in Latin means "boy." In English it appears as the word puerile, which means childish.

Target some of your reading toward vocabulary building.

- When you read to improve your vocabulary, have a dictionary and a pencil handy. Each time you encounter a word you don't know, stop. Try to figure out what it means from the context. If you can't figure the word out, look it up and make a note of it.

Make and use vocabulary index cards.

- Make a series of index cards for vocabulary words—one word per card. On the card, write a sentence or context in which the word is used, its definition(s), and its derivation.
- Don't make a card for every new word you encounter. Instead, use the "dictionary dot" method. Every time you look up a word in your dictionary, put a small dot in pencil next to the word. If you look up a word that already has one or two dots, make a card for it. It's obviously a word that's used a lot and that you haven't learned yet.
- Carry the cards with you. Read through them in your spare time—waiting for the bus, while the microwave is heating dinner, standing in line at the supermarket.

- You want to become familiar with the words, but you don't have to memorize all the definitions. If you keep running through the cards, you'll remember enough about the words so that you'll probably have a good idea of what they mean and how they are used when you see them again.

> **HINT**
>
> If you take the time to do vocabulary building work every time you read, you may not get much reading done or enjoy your reading as fully as you should. So set aside a reasonable amount of time, perhaps half an hour, for vocabulary building two or three times a week. If you keep it up week-in and week-out, month after month, you'll be surprised at how much you will add to your vocabulary in a year's time.

Play word games.

- Work crossword puzzles.
- Play Scrabble or Boggle.
- Play word-find games but not the kind where you circle words in a grid of letters. What you want to do is see how many short words you can make using the letters from a long word. For instance, how many words of four or more letters can you make out of the letters in *archaeoastronomy* or *ethnological*?

Special words, ordinary meanings

Whenever you learn a word as part of the specialized vocabulary of a subject, look it up in the dictionary to see whether it has a more general meaning. See if you can figure out how the meanings relate. Here are some words to start with: meter (in music or poetry), reduction (in chemistry), axis (in graphs or math), application (in computer programming), distill (in chemistry), symmetry (in mathematics and science).

63

CHAPTER 7

Sample Verbal Questions and Answers

Analogy Questions

Analogies are vocabulary questions, but they require more than just knowing the definitions of words. Analogies ask you to figure out the relationship between pairs of words. They challenge you to think about why it makes sense to put two words together. So, you have to know the definitions of words, but you also have to know how the words are used.

To return to the directions and the sample question from the previous chapter:

> **Each question below consists of a related pair of words or phrases, followed by five pairs of words or phrases labeled A through E. Select the pair that <u>best</u> expresses a relationship similar to that expressed in the original pair.**
>
> **Example:**
>
> **CRUMB:BREAD::**
> **(A) ounce:unit**
> **(B) splinter:wood**
> **(C) water:bucket**
> **(D) twine:rope**
> **(E) cream:butter**

The correct answer is (B).

Explanation:

To answer Analogy questions, you must first figure out the relationship between the two words in CAPITAL LETTERS. Then look for the pair of words among the answers that has the same relationship.

In the sample, the words in capital letters are CRUMB and BREAD. What is the relationship between these two words? A CRUMB *is a very small piece that falls off or breaks off of a piece of* BREAD.

What makes (B) splinter:wood the right answer? A *splinter is a very small piece that breaks off or splits away from a piece of wood.* You can use almost the very same words to describe the relationships between CRUMB and BREAD, on the one hand, and *splinter* and *wood,* on the other. That is what makes the relationships *analogous,* what makes them similar.

None of the relationships between the two words in the other choices is similar to the relationship between CRUMB and BREAD:

- An **ounce** is a type of **unit;** it is not a small piece of a **unit.**
- **Water** can be carried in a **bucket;** it is not a piece of a **bucket.**
- **Twine** is thinner and less strong than **rope,** but it is not a small piece that breaks off of a **rope.**
- **Cream** is what **butter** is made from, but **cream** is not a small piece of **butter.**

Hints

Look for similar *relationships*, not similar *meanings*.

Learn the basic approach to Analogy questions.

With analogies, you are looking for similar *relationships*, not similar *meanings*. Analogy questions do not ask you to look for words that have the same meaning as the word in capital letters.

In the preceding example, (B) is the correct answer because the relationship between **splinter** and **wood** is similar to the relationship between CRUMB and BREAD. The word CRUMB does not mean the same thing as the word **splinter,** and the word BREAD does not have the same meaning as the word **wood.**

The explanation of the preceding example gives you two clues: first, you can express the relationship between the two words in capital letters in a sentence that explains how they are related. Second, you can express the relationship between the two words in the correct answer by using almost the *same sentence* and substituting the words in the answer for the words in capitals.

To answer Analogy questions, start by making up a "test sentence" that explains how the two words in capital letters are related. Then try the words from each answer in your test sentence to see which pair makes the most sense.

Here's a question to practice on.

ALBUM:PHOTOGRAPHS::
(A) trial:briefs
(B) board:directors
(C) meeting:agendas
(D) scrapbook:clippings
(E) checkbook:money

Make up a sentence that expresses the relationship between the two words in capital letters. That sentence will become your test sentence for the answers:

An ALBUM is a place for saving PHOTOGRAPHS.
A _____ is a place for saving _____.

67

Try the words in each choice in your test sentence and eliminate any choices that don't make sense. The pair that makes the most sense in the test sentence is the correct answer.
(A) A **trial** is a place for saving **briefs.**
(B) A **board** is a place for saving **directors.**
(C) A **meeting** is a place for saving **agendas.**
(D) A **scrapbook** is a place for saving **clippings.**
(E) A **checkbook** is a place for saving **money.**

Only choice (D) makes sense. It's analogous to the words in capital letters.

Be flexible

If you don't get a single correct answer right away, you'll have to revise your test sentence. Many English words have more than one meaning. And pairs of words can have more than one relationship. So you may have to try a couple of test sentences before you find one that gives you a single correct answer. Some test sentences will state a relationship that is so broad or general that more than one answer makes sense. Other test sentences may be so narrow or specific that none of the choices fits.

Practice is the key here. You may have to try several test sentences before you find one that gives you a single correct answer. Don't worry about writing style when making up your test sentences. You're just trying to state the relationship between the pair of words in a way that will help you choose the correct answer. And you don't get any points for making up grammatically correct test sentences. You get points for choosing correct answers. The sentences are only a technique. Once you make up a test sentence, you still have to think about how the choices work in it.

Analogy questions use words consistently.

If you can't tell how a word in capital letters is being used (if it is a word that can represent more than one part of speech), look at the answers. The words in the answer can sometimes help you make sense of the two words in capital letters.

Comparing individual words

Don't be distracted by the relationships between individual words in the answers and individual words in capital letters. Remember that you are looking for analogous relationships between *pairs* of words.

Reversing word order

It's okay to reverse the order of the words in capital letters when you make up your test sentence. But if you do, remember to reverse the order of the words in the answers, too, when you try them in your test sentence.

Handling abstract questions

Although abstract words may be more challenging than concrete words, the same strategies are applicable to answering both kinds of analogy questions. Identify the relationship between the two words, then express that relationship in a test sentence. Finally, use the test sentence to identify the correct answer.

68

Sample Questions

1 ACT:PLAY::
   (A) song:music
   (B) rhyme:poem
   (C) page:novel
   (D) chapter:book
   (E) scenery:performance

Your test sentence:

Your answer:

2 BOLD:FOOLHARDY::
   (A) lively:enthusiastic
   (B) natural:synthetic
   (C) generous:spendthrift
   (D) wise:thoughtful
   (E) creative:childlike

Your test sentence:

Your answer:

3 CHILL:COLD::
   (A) parch:dry
   (B) crush:soft
   (C) freeze:white
   (D) feed:hungry
   (E) scrub:hard

Your test sentence:

Your answer:

4 LAWYER:CLIENT::
   (A) doctor:surgeon
   (B) admiral:sailor
   (C) judge:defendant
   (D) musician:audience
   (E) tutor:student

Your test sentence:

Your answer:

5 IRON:BLACKSMITH::
   (A) gold:miser
   (B) clay:potter
   (C) food:gourmet
   (D) steel:industrialist
   (E) silver:miner

Your test sentence:

Your answer:

6 ILLOGICAL:CONFUSION::
   (A) profound:laughter
   (B) revolting: sympathy
   (C) astounding:amazement
   (D) obscure:contrast
   (E) deliberate:vitality

Your test sentence:

Your answer:

Answers and Explanations

1 ACT:PLAY::
(A) song:music
(B) rhyme:poem
(C) page:novel
(D) chapter:book
(E) scenery:performance

The correct answer is (D).
Test sentence:

> An ACT is a large section of a PLAY.
> A _____ is a large section of a _____.

Explanation:

Your first test sentence may have stated a more general relationship, such as an ACT is a *part of* a PLAY. But this test sentence works for several answers because *part of* is too broad. It can refer to elements of some larger entity—like chapters and pages. It can also refer to anything that is related to something else—like scenery in a performance. But an ACT is the way the content of a play is divided up, just as a *chapter* is the way the content of a *book* is divided up. However you may word your test sentence, it must be precise and detailed enough to yield only one correct answer.

HINT

If more than one answer makes sense in your test sentence, revise your sentence so it states a more specific relationship.

2 BOLD:FOOLHARDY::
(A) lively:enthusiastic
(B) natural:synthetic
(C) generous:spendthrift
(D) wise:thoughtful
(E) creative:childlike

The correct answer is (C).
Test sentence:

> To be overly BOLD is to be FOOLHARDY.
> To be overly _____ is to be _____.

Explanation:

The relationship between BOLD and FOOLHARDY expresses a positive quality turning into a negative quality. Even though these terms are abstract, the basic approach is still the same: establish the relationship between the capitalized words in a test sentence and then try each of the choices in the test sentence until you figure out which choice fits best.

HINT

Whether the words are hard or easy, abstract or concrete, solve analogies by establishing the relationship between the words in capitals first and then looking for a similar or parallel relationship in the answers.

 CHILL:COLD::
(A) parch:dry
(B) crush:soft
(C) freeze:white
(D) feed:hungry
(E) scrub:hard

The correct answer is (A).
Test sentence:

To CHILL something is to make it COLD.
To _____ something is to make it _____.

Explanation:

The word CHILL can be used as several different parts of speech. It can be used as a verb (as it is in the test sentence), as an adjective (a CHILL wind), or as a noun (I caught a CHILL).

In this question, if you used the word CHILL as anything but a verb, your test sentence wouldn't work for any of the answer choices. If you're unsure of how to state the relationship between the words in capital letters, try working your way through the answers to establish relationships.

HINT

Pay attention to the way you are using the words in capital letters in your test sentence. They should be used the same way (be the same parts of speech) as the words in the answers.

---

4 LAWYER:CLIENT::
(A) doctor:surgeon
(B) admiral:sailor
(C) judge:defendant
(D) musician:audience
(E) tutor:student

The correct answer is (E).
Test sentence:

A LAWYER is hired to help a CLIENT.
A _____ is hired to help a _____.

Explanation:

Some students get distracted by the relationships between the individual words in the answers and the individual words in capital letters. There is a close relationship between a *judge* and a LAWYER, but the relationship between a *judge* and a *defendant* is not similar to the relationship between a LAWYER and a CLIENT.

Of course, tutors mostly teach (which lawyers do only rarely), and lawyers represent their clients in courtrooms (which tutors never do). Every analogy has some dissimilarities as well as similarities. The correct answer is the one that *"best* expresses" a similar relationship with the pair in capital letters.

HINT

Remember that you are looking for analogous relationships between pairs of words. Don't be distracted by individual words in the answers that have relationships to individual words in capital letters.

---

5 IRON:BLACKSMITH::
(A) gold:miser
(B) clay:potter
(C) food:gourmet
(D) steel:industrialist
(E) silver:miner

The correct answer is (B).
Test sentence:

A BLACKSMITH shapes things out of IRON.
A _____ shapes things out of _____.

Explanation:

You may initially have expressed the relationship with the test sentence A BLACKSMITH *deals with* IRON, but *deals with* is a very general statement and would not have eliminated many choices. The phrase *shapes things out of* is more precise because it specifies what the BLACKSMITH does with IRON.

You might also have thought of the sentence A BLACK-SMITH *hammers* IRON. But *hammers* is too specific. It is only one of the things that the BLACKSMITH does while working with IRON. None of the choices would have worked using *hammers* as the key to the relationship.

HINT

Be flexible when establishing relationships. If your first test sentence yields no possible answers, try a different or more general approach. If it yields several possible answers, try a more specific approach. And remember: it's okay to switch the order of the words in capitals when you make up your test sentence, but make sure that you also switch the order of the words in the answer choices when you test them.

6 ILLOGICAL:CONFUSION::
(A) profound:laughter
(B) revolting:sympathy
(C) astounding:amazement
(D) obscure:contrast
(E) deliberate:vitality

The correct answer is (C).
Test sentence:

If something is ILLOGICAL, it leads to CONFUSION.
If something is ＿＿＿＿＿, it leads to ＿＿＿＿＿.

Explanation:
CONFUSION is usually thought of as negative or undesirable, and amazement is more positive. But the dissimilarity between these words doesn't matter as long as the *relationship* between the words in capitals is parallel to the *relationship* between the words in the correct answer.

HINT

In Analogy questions, always look for similar *relationships* between words, NOT for similar meanings or similar connotations of words.

RECAP: HINTS ON ANALOGY QUESTIONS

1. Look for *analogous relationships* between pairs of words, *not* for words that have *similar meanings*.

2. Learn the basic approach to Analogy questions. First state the relationship between the pair of words in capital letters as a sentence. Then try the pair of words in each answer in your test sentence, one at a time. Eliminate choices that don't make sense. If necessary, revise your test sentence until you can identify a single correct answer. Very general statements of the relationship often need to be made more specific. Overly specific relationships may need to be broadened.

3. Be flexible. Words can have more than one meaning, and pairs of words different relationships. So you may have to try a few test sentences before you come up with the right relationship.

4. Analogy questions use words consistently. If you can't tell how a word in capital letters is being used (if it is a word that can represent more than one part of speech), check the answer. The words in capital letters will be used in the same way as the words in the answers are used.

5. Remember that you are looking for analogous relationships between pairs of words. Don't compare individual words in the answers to one of the words in capital letters.

6. You can reverse the order of the words in capital letters when you make up your test sentence. But if you do, remember to reverse the order of the words in the answers, too, when you try them in your test sentence.

7. You should use the same strategy for answering abstract questions that you use for concrete questions.

Sentence Completion Questions

Sentence Completion questions challenge both reasoning and vocabulary skills.

Sentence Completion questions require a broad vocabulary plus the ability to understand the logic of sentences that are sometimes quite complex. There is no short, simple approach to Sentence Completions. But there are a number of strategies that will help you through even the toughest questions.

To return to the directions and the sample question from the previous chapter:

> **Each sentence below has one or two blanks, each blank indicating that something has been omitted. Beneath the sentence are five words or sets of words labeled A through E. Choose the word or set of words that, when inserted in the sentence, *best* fits the meaning of the sentence as a whole.**
>
> **Example:**
>
> **Medieval kingdoms did not become constitutional republics overnight; on the contrary, the change was - - - -.**
> **(A) unpopular**
> **(B) unexpected**
> **(C) advantageous**
> **(D) sufficient**
> **(E) gradual**

The correct answer is (E).

Explanation:

The first part of the sentence says that the kingdoms did not change *overnight*. The second part begins with *on the contrary* and explains the change. So the correct answer will be a word that describes a change that is *contrary* to an *overnight* change. *Gradual* change is contrary to *overnight* change.

• Sentence Completion questions can have one or two blanks, but each sentence, as a whole, still counts as only **one** question.

• Some of the questions with one blank are straightforward vocabulary questions. Others require that you know more than just the meanings of the words involved. They also require that you understand the logic of fairly complicated sentences.

• Most Sentence Completions involve compound or complex sentences, that is, sentences made up of several clauses. In many cases, to answer the question correctly you have to figure out how the parts of the sentence—the different clauses—relate to each other.

Here are some examples of the different types of Sentence Completion questions you will see:

Example 1: A one-blank vocabulary-based question

This type of question depends more on your knowledge of vocabulary than on your ability to follow the logic of a complicated sentence. You still need to know how the words are used in the context of the sentence, but if you know the definitions of the words involved, you almost certainly will be able to select the correct answer.

These one-blank vocabulary-based questions tend to be relatively short, usually not more than 20 words.

Ravens appear to behave - - - -, actively
helping one another to find food.

(A) mysteriously
(B) warily
(C) aggressively
(D) cooperatively
(E) defensively

The correct answer is (D).

Explanation:
This sentence asks you to look for a word that describes how the ravens behave. The information after the comma restates and defines the meaning of the missing word. You are told that the ravens *actively help one another*. There is only one word among the choices that accurately describes this behavior—*cooperatively*.

Example 2: A two-blank vocabulary-based question

You will also find some two-blank sentences with rather straightforward logic but challenging vocabulary.

Both - - - - and - - - -, Wilson seldom spoke
and never spent money.

(A) vociferous..generous
(B) garrulous..stingy
(C) effusive..frugal
(D) taciturn..miserly
(E) reticent..munificent

The correct answer is (D).

Explanation:

In this sentence, the logic is not difficult. You are looking for two words that describe Wilson. One of the words has to mean that he *seldom spoke* and the other that he *never spent money*. The correct answer is *taciturn..miserly*. *Taciturn* means "shy, unwilling to talk." *Miserly* means "like a miser, extremely stingy."

Example 3: A one-blank logic-based question

Success in answering these questions depends as much on your ability to reason out the logic of the sentence as it does on your knowledge of vocabulary.

After observing several vicious territorial fights, Jane Goodall had to revise her earlier opinion that these particular primates were always - - - - animals.

(A) ignorant
(B) inquisitive
(C) responsive
(D) cruel
(E) peaceful

The correct answer is (E).

Explanation:

To answer this question, you have to follow the logical flow of the ideas in the sentence. A few key words reveal that logic:

- First, the introductory word *After* tells you that the information at the beginning of the sentence is going to affect what comes later. The word *After* also gives an order to the events in the sentence.

- Second, the word *revise* tells you that something is going to change. It is going to change *after* the events described at the beginning of the sentence. So the events at the beginning really cause the change.

- Finally, the end of the sentence—*her earlier opinion that these particular primates were always - - - - animals*—tells you what is changing. The word filling the blank should convey a meaning you would have to revise after seeing the animals fight. *Peaceful* is the only such word among the five choices.

Example 4: A two-blank logic-based question

The following question requires you to know the meanings of the words, know how the words are used in context, and understand the logic of a rather complicated sentence.

Although its publicity has been
- - - -, the film itself is intelligent, well-acted,
handsomely produced, and altogether - - - -.

(A) tasteless..respectable
(B) extensive..moderate
(C) sophisticated..amateur
(D) risqué..crude
(E) perfect..spectacular

The correct answer is (A).

Explanation:

The first thing to notice about this sentence is that it has two parts or clauses. The first clause begins with *Although*, the second clause begins with *the film*.

The logic of the sentence is determined by the way the two clauses relate to each other. The two parts have contrasting or conflicting meanings. Why? Because one of the clauses begins with *Although*. The word *Although* is used to introduce an idea that conflicts with something else in the sentence: *Although* something is true, something else that you would expect to be true is not.

The answer is *tasteless..respectable*. You would not expect a film with *tasteless publicity* to be *altogether respectable*. But the introductory word *Although* tells you that you should expect the unexpected.

Hints

Read the entire sentence.

Know your vocabulary.

Small words make a big difference.

Start out by reading the entire sentence saying *blank* for the blank(s). This gives you an overall sense of the meaning of the sentence and helps you figure out how the parts of the sentence relate to each other.

Always begin by trying to pin down the standard dictionary definitions of the words in the sentence and the answers. To answer Sentence Completion questions, you usually don't have to know a nonstandard meaning of a word.

Introductory and transitional words are extremely important.

They can be the key to figuring out the logic of a sentence. They tell you how the parts of the sentence relate to each other. Consider the following common introductory and transitional words: *but, although, however, yet, even though*. These words indicate that the two parts of the sentence will contradict or be in contrast with each other. There are many other introductory and transitional words that you should watch for when working on Sentence Completion questions. Always read the sentences carefully and don't ignore any of the details.

Watch out for negatives.

Some of the most difficult Sentence Completion questions contain negatives, which can make it hard to follow the logic of the sentences. Negatives in two clauses of a sentence can be even more of a challenge:

> According to Burgess, a novelist **should not** preach, for sermonizing **has no place** in good fiction.

A negative appears in each clause of this sentence. The transitional word "for" indicates that the second part of the sentence will explain the first.

Try answering the question without looking at the choices.

Figure out what sort of word(s) should fill the blank(s) before looking at the choices, then look for a choice that is similar to the one(s) you thought up. For many one-blank questions, especially the easier ones, you'll find the word you made up among the choices. Other times, a close synonym for your word will be one of the choices.

Try answering the following Sentence Completion question without looking at the choices.

> Once Murphy left home for good, he wrote
> no letters to his worried mother; he did not,
> therefore, live up to her picture of him as her
> - - - - son.

The transitional word **therefore** indicates that the information in the second part of the sentence is a direct, logical result of the information in the first part. What words might fit in the blank?

_____   _____

_____   _____

The second part of the sentence includes a negative (**he did not . . .live up to her picture. . .**), so the blank must be a positive term. Words like **perfect, sweet, respectful, favorite**—all could fit in the blank. Now, look at the actual choices:

(A) misunderstood
(B) elusive
(C) destructive
(D) persuasive
(E) dutiful

(E) **dutiful** is the only choice that is even close to the ones suggested. (E) is the correct answer.

You can also try this technique with two-blank questions. You are less likely to come up with as close a word match, but it will help you get a feel for the meaning and logic of the sentence.

Try answering two-blank questions one blank at a time.

With two-blank questions, try eliminating some answers based on just one blank. If one word in an answer doesn't make sense in the sentence, then you can reject the entire choice.

Try approaching two-blank questions like this:

- Work on the first blank, alone. Eliminate any choices for which the first word doesn't make sense.
- Work on the second blank, alone. Eliminate any choices for which the second word doesn't make sense. If there is only one choice left, that choice is the correct answer. If more than one choice remains, go on to the next step.
- Work on both blanks together only for those choices that are left. Always read the complete sentence with both words in place to make sure your choice makes sense.

Example 4, discussed previously, shows how this approach works.

Work on the first blank.

The first words in all the choices could make sense:

> its publicity has been tasteless
> its publicity has been extensive
> its publicity has been sophisticated
> its publicity has been risqué
> its publicity has been perfect

Work on the second blank.

The second blank is part of a list that includes **intelligent, well-acted, handsomely produced,** and _____. The word **and** indicates that the last word in the list (the blank) should be a positive word, in general agreement with the others. With that in mind, examine the second words in the choices:

> intelligent, well-acted. . .and altogether respectable
> intelligent, well-acted. . .and altogether moderate
> ~~intelligent, well-acted. . .and altogether amateur~~
> ~~intelligent, well-acted. . .and altogether crude~~
> intelligent, well-acted. . .and altogether spectacular

Amateur and **crude** are definitely not complementary. No matter what the rest of the sentence says, neither of these words makes sense in the second blank. So you can eliminate the answers that contain **amateur** and **crude**. With two choices eliminated, the question becomes much easier to deal with.

Always check all of the choices.

Remember that the instructions for all the verbal questions ask you to choose the *best* answer. One choice may seem to make sense, but it still might not be the *best* of the five choices. Unless you read all the choices, you may select only the *second best* and thus lose points.

Check your choice.

Check your choice by reading the entire sentence with the answer you have selected in place to make sure the sentence makes sense. This step is extremely important, especially if you have used short-cuts to eliminate choices.

Sample Questions

1 A judgment made before all the facts are known must be called - - - -.

(A) harsh
(B) deliberate
(C) sensible
(D) premature
(E) fair

2 Despite their - - - - proportions, the murals of Diego Rivera give his Mexican compatriots the sense that their history is - - - - and human in scale, not remote and larger than life.

(A) monumental..accessible
(B) focused..prolonged
(C) vast..ancient
(D) realistic..extraneous
(E) narrow..overwhelming

3 The research is so - - - - that it leaves no part of the issue unexamined.

(A) comprehensive
(B) rewarding
(C) sporadic
(D) economical
(E) problematical

4 A dictatorship - - - - its citizens to be docile and finds it expedient to make outcasts of those who do not - - - -.

(A) forces. .rebel
(B) expects. .disobey
(C) requires. .conform
(D) allows. .withdraw
(E) forbids. .agree

5 Alice Walker's prize-winning novel exemplifies the strength of first-person narratives; the protagonist tells her own story so effectively that any additional commentary would be - - - -.

(A) subjective
(B) eloquent
(C) superfluous
(D) incontrovertible
(E) impervious

6 The Supreme Court's reversal of its previous ruling on the issue of State's rights - - - - its reputation for - - - -.

(A) sustained..infallibility
(B) compromised..consistency
(C) bolstered..doggedness
(D) aggravated..inflexibility
(E) dispelled..vacillation

Answers and Explanations

1 A judgment made before all the facts are known must be called - - - -.

(A) harsh
(B) deliberate
(C) sensible
(D) premature
(E) fair

The correct answer is (D).

Explanation:

Getting the correct answer to this question depends almost entirely on your knowing the definitions of the five words you must choose from. Which of the choices describes a judgment made before *all the facts are known?* Such a judgment, by definition, is not *deliberate,* and the sentence doesn't tell us whether the judgment was *harsh* or lenient, *sensible* or dumb, *fair* or unfair. *Premature* means hasty or early. It fits the blank perfectly.

HINT

Know your vocabulary. Think carefully about the meanings of the words in the answer choices.

---

2 Despite their - - - - proportions, the murals of Diego Rivera give his Mexican compatriots the sense that their history is - - - - and human in scale, not remote and larger than life.

(A) monumental. .accessible
(B) focused. .prolonged
(C) vast. .ancient
(D) realistic. .extraneous
(E) narrow. .overwhelming

The correct answer is (A).

Explanation:

The keys to this sentence are the word *Despite,* the words *human in scale,* and the words *not remote and larger than life.* The word filling the first blank has to be one that would relate closely to something that seems *larger than life.* The word filling the second blank has to fit with *human in scale.* If you focus on just one of the two blanks, you will be able to eliminate several choices before you even think about the other blank.

HINT

Watch for key introductory and transitional words that determine how the parts of the sentence relate to each other. Then try answering two-blank questions one blank at a time. If you can eliminate one word in a choice, the entire choice can be ruled out.

---

3 The research is so - - - - that it leaves no part of the issue unexamined.

    (A) comprehensive
    (B) rewarding
    (C) sporadic
    (D) economical
    (E) problematical

The correct answer is (A).

Explanation:
    Try filling in the blank without reading the answer choices. What kind of words would fit? Words like *complete, thorough,* or *extensive* could all fit. Now look at the answer choices. *Comprehensive* is very similar to the words suggested, and none of the other choices fits at all.

HINT

Try thinking about the logic of the sentence without looking at the choices. Then look for the choice that has a similar meaning to the words you thought up.

---

4 A dictatorship - - - - its citizens to be docile and finds it expedient to make outcasts of those who do not - - - -.

    (A) forces. .rebel
    (B) expects. .disobey
    (C) requires. .conform
    (D) allows. .withdraw
    (E) forbids. .agree

The correct answer is (C).

Explanation:

Answering this question depends in part on your knowledge of vocabulary. You have to know what the words *dictatorship, docile,* and *expedient* mean. You also have to watch out for key words such as *not.* If you leave out the word *not* then answer choices like (A) and (B) make sense.

HINT

Think carefully about the standard dictionary definitions of the important words in the sentence. And remember that small words such as *not* can make a big difference. When you pick your answers, read the entire sentence with the blank(s) filled in to be sure that it makes sense.

---

5 Alice Walker's prize-winning novel exemplifies the strength of first-person narratives; the protagonist tells her own story so effectively that any additional commentary would be - - - -.

(A) subjective
(B) eloquent
(C) superfluous
(D) incontrovertible
(E) impervious

The correct answer is (C).

Explanation:

Words like *prize-winning, strength,* and *effectively* tell you that the writer thinks Alice Walker's novel is well written. So would *additional commentary* be necessary or unnecessary? Once you've figured out that it is unnecessary, you can look for an answer with a similar meaning. That way, you may be able to answer the question more quickly, since you won't have to plug in each choice one by one to see if it makes any sense.

⚬━► HINT

Think about the meaning of the sentence before you look at the choices. Get a sense of what you're looking for *before* you start looking.

---

6 The Supreme Court's reversal of its previous ruling on the issue of State's rights - - - - its reputation for - - - -.

(A) sustained. .infallibility
(B) compromised. .consistency
(C) bolstered. .doggedness
(D) aggravated. .inflexibility
(E) dispelled. .vacillation

The correct answer is (B).

Explanation:
Getting the correct answer to this question depends in large part on your knowledge of the meanings of the words offered as choices. You have to know the definitions of the words before you can try the choices one by one to arrive at the correct pair.

You also need to think about the central idea in the sentence: the court's *reversal* blank *its reputation for* blank. The logic is complicated and the vocabulary in the choices is hard: but, if you stick with it, you'll figure out that only (B) makes sense.

⚬━► HINT

When you read the sentence to yourself, substitute the word *blank* for each blank. Try to figure out what the sentence is saying before you start plugging in the choices.

> ### RECAP: HINTS ON SENTENCE COMPLETION QUESTIONS
>
> 1. Read the sentence, substituting the word *blank* for each blank. This helps you figure out the meaning of the sentence and how the parts of the sentence relate to each other.
> 2. Know your vocabulary. Always begin by trying to pin down the dictionary definitions of the key words in the sentence and the answer choices.
> 3. Small words make a big difference. Watch for the key introductory and transitional words. These determine how the parts of the sentence relate to each other. Also watch carefully for negatives.
> 4. Try figuring out words to fill in the blank or blanks without looking at the answers. Then look for the choice that is similar to the one you thought up.
> 5. Try answering two-blank questions one blank at a time. If you can eliminate one word in an answer, the entire choice can be eliminated.
> 6. Always check all of the answer choices before making a final decision. A choice may seem ok, but still not be the best answer. Make sure that the answer you select is the best one.
> 7. Check your answer to make sure it makes sense by reading the entire sentence with your choice in place.

Critical Reading Questions

Of the three types of verbal questions, the Critical Reading questions give you the best shot at getting the right answers. Why? Because all the information you need to answer the questions is in the passages.

Success in answering Critical Reading questions depends less on knowledge you already have and more on your ability to understand and make sense of the information given to you in the passages. The passages are drawn from a wide variety of subject areas. You may find that you are familiar with the topics of some of the passages, but you will probably not be familiar with most of them. The passages are selected so that you can answer the questions without any prior study or in-depth knowledge of the subjects.

Answering most of the Critical Reading questions will take more than just looking back at the passage to see what it says. You'll also have to *think* about the content of each passage, analyze and evaluate the ideas and opinions in it, figure out the underlying assumptions, and follow the author's argument. You'll have to make inferences, which means drawing conclusions from what the author *says* so you can figure out what the author really *means*. You'll also have to relate parts of the passage to each other, compare and contrast different theories and viewpoints, understand cause and effect, and pay attention to the author's attitude, tone, and overall purpose.

Like a lot of college-level reading, the passages will be thoughtful and sophisticated discussions of important issues, ideas, and events. A few questions in each test will ask you to simply demonstrate that you have understood what the author is saying at some point in the passage. And a few other questions will ask you to figure out the meaning of a word as it is used in the passage. But the great majority of the Critical Reading questions will require "extended reasoning." You'll have to do more than just absorb information and then recognize a restatement of it. You'll have to be an *active* reader and think carefully about what you're reading.

Hints

The answers come from the passage.

Details in a passage are there because they mean something. And those details determine the answers to some of the Critical Reading questions.

Every single answer to the Critical Reading questions can be found in or directly inferred from the passage. So be sure to read the passages carefully. If the author mentions that it's a rainy day, he or she has probably done so for a reason. The author did not have to talk about the weather at all. Rainy days suggest a certain mood, or reflect certain feelings, or set up certain situations—slippery roads, for instance—that the author wants you to know about or feel.

Every word counts.

The same goes for words describing people, events, and things. If someone's face is described as *handsome* or *scarred*, if an event is *surprising*, or a word is *whispered* or *shouted* or *spoken with a smile*, pay attention. Details like these are mentioned to give you an understanding about how the author wants you to feel or think.

When you are faced with a question about the mood or tone of a passage, or when you are asked about the author's attitude or intent or whether the author might agree or disagree with a statement, you have to think about the details the author has provided.

Mark the passages or make short notes.

It may help you to mark important sections or words or sentences. But be careful that you don't mark too much. The idea of marking the passage is to help you find information quickly. If you have underlined or marked three-quarters of it, your marks won't help.

Some students jot a short note—a few words at most—in the margin that summarizes what a paragraph or key sentence is about. Just be careful not to spend more time marking the passage than you will save. And remember, you get points for answering the questions, not for marking your test booklet.

Read the questions and answers carefully.

This is as important as reading the passage carefully.

Most Critical Reading questions require three things: You have to think about what the question is asking. You have to look back at the passage for information that will help you with the question. Then you have to think again about how you can use the information to answer the question correctly. Unless you read the question carefully, you won't know what to think about, and you won't know where to look in the passage.

An answer can be true and still be wrong.

The correct choice is the one that best answers the question, not any choice that makes a true statement. An answer may express something that is perfectly true and still be the wrong choice. The only way you're going to keep from being caught by a choice that is true but wrong is to make sure you read the passage, the questions, and the answer choices carefully.

The passage must support your answer.

There should always be information or details in the passage that provide support for your answer—specific words, phrases, and/or sentences that help to prove your choice is correct. Remember that Critical Reading questions depend on the information in the passage and your ability to *interpret* it correctly. Even with the inference, tone, and attitude questions—the ones in which you have to do some reading between the lines to figure out the answers—you can find evidence in the passage supporting the correct choice.

Try eliminating choices.

Compare each choice to the passage and you'll find that some choices can be eliminated as definitely wrong. Then it should be easier to choose the correct answer from the remaining choices.

Double-check the other choices.
Pace yourself.

When you have made your choice, read quickly (again) through the other choices to make sure there isn't a better one.

You will spend a lot of time reading a passage before you're ready to answer even one question. So take the time to answer as many questions as you can about each passage before you move on to another.

- Jump around within a set of questions to find the ones you can answer quickly, but don't jump from passage to passage.
- Don't leave a reading passage until you are sure you have answered all the questions you can. If you return to the passage later, you'll probably have to reread it.

Go back to any questions you skipped.

When you've gone through all the questions on a passage, go back and review any you left out or weren't sure of. Sometimes information you picked up while thinking about one question will help you answer another.

Pick your topic.

Some verbal sections contain more than one reading passage. Students often find it easier to read about familiar topics or topics that they find interesting. So if you have a choice, you may want to look for a passage that deals with a familiar or especially interesting subject to work on first. If you skip a passage and set of questions, be sure that you don't lose your place on the answer sheet.

Questions Involving Two Passages

One of the reading selections will involve a *pair* of passages. The two passages will have a common theme or subject. One of the passages will oppose, support, or in some way relate to the other. If one of the paired passages seems easier or more interesting than the other, you may want to start with that one and answer the questions specific to it first. Then go back and wrestle with the questions specific to the other passage and with the questions that refer to both passages.

In most cases, you'll find that the questions are grouped: first, questions about Passage 1, then questions about Passage 2, finally questions comparing the two passages.

When a question asks you to compare two passages, don't try to remember everything from both passages. Take each choice one at a time. Review the relevant parts of each passage before you select your answer.

If a question asks you to identify something that is true in *both* passages, it is often easiest to start by eliminating choices that are *not* true for one of the passages.

Don't be fooled by a choice that is true for one passage but not for the other.

Vocabulary-in-Context Questions

Some Critical Reading questions will ask about the meaning of a word as it is used in the passage. When a word has several meanings, a vocabulary-in-context question won't necessarily use the most common meaning.

Even if you don't know the word, you can sometimes figure it out from the passage and the answers. This is why the questions are called *vocabulary-in-context*. The context in which the word is used determines the meaning of the word. You can also use the context to figure out the meaning of words you're not sure of.

Vocabulary-in-context questions usually take less time to answer than other types of Critical Reading questions. Sometimes, but *not* always, you can answer them by reading only a sentence or two around the word, without reading the entire passage.

If you can't answer a vocabulary-in-context question right away, or if you don't know the meaning of the word, pretend that the word is a blank. Read the sentence substituting *blank* for the word. Look for an answer that makes sense with the rest of the sentence.

Sample Passages

Sample directions and a sample pair of passages and questions are followed by discussions of the correct answers and some hints.

In Passage 1, the author presents his view of the early years of the silent film industry. In Passage 2, the author draws on her experiences as a mime to generalize about her art. (A mime is a performer who, without speaking, entertains through gesture, facial expression, and movement.)

Passage 1

Talk to those people who first saw films when they were silent, and they will tell you the experience was
Line magic. The silent film had extraordinary powers to draw members of an audience into the story, and an equally
(5) potent capacity to make their imaginations work. It required the audience to become engaged—to supply voices and sound effects. The audience was the final, creative contributor to the process of making a film.

The finest films of the silent era depended on two
(10) elements that we can seldom provide today—a large and receptive audience and a well-orchestrated score. For the audience, the fusion of picture and live music added up to more than the sum of the respective parts.

The one word that sums up the attitude of the silent
(15) filmmakers is *enthusiasm*, conveyed most strongly before formulas took shape and when there was more room for experimentation. This enthusiastic uncertainty often resulted in such accidental discoveries as new camera or editing techniques. Some films experimented
(20) with players; the 1915 film *Regeneration*, for example, by using real gangsters and streetwalkers, provided startling local color. Other films, particularly those of Thomas Ince, provided tragic endings as often as films by other companies supplied happy ones.

(25) Unfortunately, the vast majority of silent films survive today in inferior prints that no longer reflect the care that the original technicians put into them. The modern versions of silent films may appear jerky and flickery, but the vast picture palaces did not attract four to six
(30) thousand people a night by giving them eyestrain. A silent film depended on its visuals; as soon as you degrade those, you lose elements that go far beyond the image on the surface. The acting in silents was often very subtle, very restrained, despite legends to the contrary.

Passage 2

(35) Mime opens up a new world to the beholder, but it does so insidiously, not by purposely injecting points of interest in the manner of a tour guide. Audiences are not unlike visitors to a foreign land who discover that the modes, manners, and thoughts of its inhabitants are not
(40) meaningless oddities, but are sensible in context.

I remember once when an audience seemed perplexed at what I was doing. At first, I tried to gain a more immediate response by using slight exaggerations. I soon realized that these actions had nothing to do with the
(45) audience's understanding of the character. What I had believed to be a failure of the audience to respond in the manner I expected was, in fact, only their concentration on what I was doing; they were enjoying a gradual awakening—a slow transference of their understanding
(50) from their own time and place to one that appeared so unexpectedly before their eyes. This was evidenced by their growing response to succeeding numbers.

Mime is an elusive art, as its expression is entirely dependent on the ability of the performer to imagine a
(55) character and to re-create that character for each performance. As a mime, I am a physical medium, the instrument upon which the figures of my imagination play their dance of life. The individuals in my audience also have responsibilities—they must be alert collabora-
(60) tors. They cannot sit back, mindlessly complacent, and wait to have their emotions titillated by mesmeric musical sounds or visual rhythms or acrobatic feats, or by words that tell them what to think. Mime is an art that, paradoxically, appeals both to those who respond
(65) instinctively to entertainment and to those whose appreciation is more analytical and complex. Between these extremes lie those audiences conditioned to resist any collaboration with what is played before them; and these the mime must seduce despite themselves. There
(70) is only one way to attack those reluctant minds—take them unaware! They will be delighted at an unexpected pleasure.

1 The author of passage 1 uses the phrase "enthusiastic uncertainty" in line 17 to suggest that the filmmakers were

(A) excited to be experimenting in a new field
(B) delighted at the opportunity to study new technology
(C) optimistic in spite of the obstacles that faced them
(D) eager to challenge existing conventions
(E) eager to please but unsure of what the public wanted

2 In Passage 1, the statement "but the . . . eyestrain" (lines 29-30) conveys a sense of

(A) irony regarding the incompetence of silent film technicians
(B) resentment at the way old silent films are now perceived
(C) regret that the popularity of picture palaces has waned
(D) pleasure in remembering a grandeur that has passed
(E) amazement at the superior quality of modern film technology

3 In lines 20-24, *Regeneration* and the films of Thomas Ince are presented as examples of

(A) formulaic and uninspired silent films
(B) profitable successes of a flourishing industry
(C) suspenseful action films drawing large audiences
(D) daring applications of an artistic philosophy
(E) unusual products of a readiness to experiment

4 In line 34, "legends" most nearly means

(A) ancient folklore
(B) obscure symbols
(C) history lessons
(D) famous people
(E) common misconceptions

5 The author of Passage 2 most likely considers the contrast of mime artist and tour guide appropriate because both

(A) are concerned with conveying factual information
(B) employ artistic techniques to communicate their knowledge
(C) determine whether others enter a strange place
(D) shape the way others perceive a new situation
(E) explore new means of self-expression

6 In lines 41-52, the author most likely describes a specific experience in order to

(A) dispel some misconceptions about what a mime is like
(B) show how challenging the career of a mime can be
(C) portray the intensity required to see the audience's point of view
(D) explain how unpredictable mime performances can be
(E) indicate the adjustments an audience must make in watching mime

7 In lines 60-63, the author's description of techniques used in other types of performances is

(A) disparaging
(B) astonished
(C) sorrowful
(D) indulgent
(E) sentimental

8 Both passages are primarily concerned with the subject of

(A) shocking special effects
(B) varied dramatic styles
(C) visual elements in dramatic performances
(D) audience resistance to theatrical performances
(E) nostalgia for earlier forms of entertainment

9 The incident described in lines 41-52 shows the author of Passage 2 to be similar to the silent filmmakers of Passage 1 in the way she

(A) required very few props
(B) used subtle technical skills to convey universal truths
(C) learned through trial and error
(D) combined narration with visual effects
(E) earned a loyal audience of followers

10 What additional information would reduce the apparent similarity between these two art forms?

(A) Silent film audiences were also accustomed to vaudeville and theatrical presentations.
(B) Silent films could show newsworthy events as well as dramatic entertainment.
(C) Dialogue in the form of captions was integrated into silent films.
(D) Theaters running silent films gave many musicians steady jobs.
(E) Individual characters created for silent films became famous in their own right.

11 Both passages mention which of the following as being important to the artistic success of the dramatic forms they describe?

(A) Effective fusion of disparate dramatic elements
(B) Slightly exaggerated characterization
(C) Incorporation of realistic details
(D) Large audiences
(E) Audience involvement

Answers and Explanations

1 The author of Passage 1 uses the phrase "enthusiastic uncertainty" in line 17 to suggest that the filmmakers were

(A) excited to be experimenting in a new field
(B) delighted at the opportunity to study new technology
(C) optimistic in spite of the obstacles that faced them
(D) eager to challenge existing conventions
(E) eager to please but unsure of what the public wanted

The correct answer is (A).

Explanation:

Look at the beginning of the third paragraph of Passage 1. The filmmakers were *enthusiastic* about a new kind of art form in which they could experiment. And experimentation led to *accidental discoveries* (line 18), which suggests *uncertainty*.

The other choices

Choice (B) is wrong because the filmmakers were **delighted** with *using* the new technology rather than with studying it.

Choice (C) can be eliminated because the passage does not talk about **obstacles** faced by the filmmakers.

Choice (D) is specifically contradicted by the words in line 16 that refer to the fact that these filmmakers were working **before formulas took shape**. The word **formulas** in this context means the same thing as **conventions**.

Choice (E) is not correct because the **uncertainty** of the filmmakers was related to the new technology and how to use it, not to **what the public wanted**.

HINT

Read each choice carefully and compare what it says to the information in the passage.

---

2 In Passage 1, the statement "but the . . . eyestrain" (lines 29-30) conveys a sense of

(A) irony regarding the incompetence of silent film technicians
(B) resentment at the way old silent films are now perceived
(C) regret that the popularity of picture palaces has waned
(D) pleasure in remembering a grandeur that has passed
(E) amazement at the superior quality of modern film technology

The correct answer is (B).

Explanation:

The author draws a distinction between the way silent films look when viewed today—*jerky and flickery* (line 28)—and the way they looked when they were originally shown. He implies that thousands of people would not have come to the movie houses if the pictures had given them *eyestrain*. The author suggests that the perception of silent films today is unfair. This feeling can be described as resentment.

The other choices

Choice (A) can be eliminated because there is no indication in the passage that silent film technicians were **incompetent.** The author even mentions "the care" taken by "the original technicians" (lines 26–27).

Both choices (C) and (D) are wrong because they do not answer this question. Remember, the question refers to the statement about **eyestrain.** The remark about eyestrain concerns the technical quality of the films, not the **popularity of picture palaces** or **a grandeur that has passed.**

Choice (E) is incorrect for two reasons. First, no sense of **amazement** is conveyed in the statement about eyestrain. Second, the author does not say that modern films are **superior** to silent films, only that the **prints** of silent films are **inferior** to what they once were (lines 25–26).

HINT

Try eliminating choices that you know are wrong. Rule out choices that don't answer the question being asked or that are contradicted by the information in the passage.

3 In lines 19-24, *Regeneration* and the films of Thomas Ince are presented as examples of

(A) formulaic and uninspired silent films
(B) profitable successes of a flourishing industry
(C) suspenseful action films drawing large audiences
(D) daring applications of an artistic philosophy
(E) unusual products of a readiness to experiment

The correct answer is (E).

Explanation:

The author's argument in the third paragraph is that there was lots of *room for experimentation* (line 17) in the silent film industry. Both *Regeneration* and Ince's films are specifically mentioned as examples of that readiness to experiment.

The other choices

Choice (A) is directly contradicted in two ways by the information in the passage. First, line 16 says that the filmmakers worked **before formulas took shape,** so their work could not be **formulaic.** Second, the author refers to **Regeneration** as having some **startling** effects and indicates that the endings of Ince's films were different from other films of the time. So it would not be correct to describe these films as **uninspired.**

Choices (B), (C), and (D) are wrong because the author does not argue that these films were **profitable, suspenseful,** or **applications of an artistic philosophy.** He argues that they are examples of a willingness to **experiment.**

HINT

As you consider the choices, think of the words, phrases, and sentences in the passage that relate to the question you are answering. Be aware of how the ideas in the passage are presented. What is the author's point? How does the author explain and support important points?

---

4 In line 34, "legends" most nearly means

(A) ancient folklore
(B) obscure symbols
(C) historic lessons
(D) famous people
(E) common misconceptions

The correct answer is (E).

Explanation:

A *legend* is an idea or story that has come down from the past. A secondary meaning of *legend* is anything made up rather than based on fact. Throughout the final paragraph of Passage 1, the author emphasizes that people today have the wrong idea about the visual quality of silent films. In the last sentence, the author states that the acting was *often very subtle* and *very restrained,* and then he adds, *despite legends to the contrary.* So, according to the author, silent film acting is today thought of as unsubtle and unrestrained, but that is a misconception, an idea not based on fact, a *legend.*

The other choices

Choice (A) is the most common meaning of **legend,** but it doesn't make any sense here. There is no reference to or suggestion about **ancient folklore.**

Choice (B) has no support at all in the passage.

Choice (C) can be eliminated because the author does not refer to **historic lessons** in this sentence, but to mistaken notions about the performances in silent films.

Choice (D) simply doesn't make sense. In line 34, the word **legends** refers to acting, not to **people.**

> **HINT**
>
> This is a vocabulary-in-context question. Even if you don't know the meaning of the word, try to figure it out from the passage and the choices. Examine the context in which the word is used.
>
> Think of some word(s) that would make sense in the sentence, then look at the answers to see if any choice is similar to the word(s) you thought of.

5 The author of Passage 2 most likely considers the contrast of mime artist and tour guide appropriate because both

(A) are concerned with conveying factual information
(B) employ artistic techniques to communicate their knowledge
(C) determine whether others enter a strange place
(D) shape the way others perceive a new situation
(E) explore new means of self-expression

The correct answer is (D).

Explanation:

To answer this question, you have to find a choice that describes a similarity between the performances of a mime and the work of a tour guide. The author begins Passage 2 by saying that a mime *opens up a new world to the beholder,* but in a *manner* (or way) different from that of a tour guide. Thus the author assumes that contrasting the mime and the tour guide is appropriate because both of them *shape the way others perceive a new situation.*

The other choices

Choice (A) may correctly describe a tour guide, but it doesn't fit the mime. Nowhere in the passage does the author say the mime conveys **factual information.**

Choice (B) is true for the mime but not for the tour guide.

Choice (C) is wrong because the author of Passage 2 contrasts how mimes and tour guides introduce others to "a new world," not how they **determine** entrance to **a strange place.**

Choice (E) is incorrect because the author does not discuss **self-expression** as a tour guide's work, and because she indicates that, as a mime, she expresses a particular character, not her own personality.

HINT

Pay close attention when authors make connections, comparisons, or contrasts. These parts of passages help you identify the authors' point of view and assumptions.

---

6 In lines 41-52, the author most likely describes a specific experience in order to

(A) dispel some misconceptions about what a mime is like
(B) show how challenging the career of mime can be
(C) portray the intensity required to see the audience's point of view
(D) explain how unpredictable mime performances can be
(E) indicate the adjustments an audience must make in watching mime

The correct answer is (E).

Explanation:

The correct answer must explain why the author described a particular experience in lines 41–52. The author's point is that she learned the audience was "enjoying a gradual awakening." Only choice (E) indicates that the story shows the *adjustments* the audience had to make to appreciate her performance.

The other choices

Choice (A) can be eliminated because the only **misconception** that is dispelled is the author's **misconception** about the audience.

Choice (B) is wrong because, while the story might suggest that mime is a **challenging career,** that is not the author's point in describing the experience.

Choice (C) can't be correct because there is no reference to *intensity* on the part of the mime.

Choice (D) is wrong because the emphasis of lines 41–52 is not on how **unpredictable** mime performance is but on what the author learned from her failure to understand the audience's initial reaction.

◖ HINT

Every word counts. When you're asked about the author's intent in describing something, you have to pay close attention to how the author uses details to explain, support, or challenge the point being made.

---

7 In lines 60-63, the author's description of techniques used in other types of performances is

(A) disparaging
(B) astonished
(C) sorrowful
(D) indulgent
(E) sentimental

The correct answer is (A).

Explanation:
The beginning of the sentence in line 60 says that when viewing mime, the audience *cannot sit back, mindlessly complacent.* The author then says that other types of performances *titillate* audience emotions by *mesmeric musical sounds* or *acrobatic feats*. The author uses these kinds of words to belittle other techniques—her tone is *disparaging*.

The other choices

Choices (B), (C), and (E) can be eliminated because no **astonishment, sorrow,** or **sentimentalism** is suggested in lines 60-63.

Choice (D) is almost the opposite of what the author means. She is not at all **indulgent** toward these other types of performance.

HINT

To figure out the author's attitude or tone, or how the author feels about something, think about how the author uses language in the passage.

---

8 Both passages are primarily concerned with the subject of

(A) shocking special effects
(B) varied dramatic styles
(C) visual elements in dramatic performances
(D) audience resistance to theatrical performances
(E) nostalgia for earlier forms of entertainment

The correct answer is (C).

Explanation:

This question asks you to think about *both* passages. Notice that the question asks you to look for the main subject or focus of the pair of passages, not simply to recognize that one passage is about silent film and the other about mime.

The discussion in Passage 1 is most concerned with the effectiveness of silent films for audiences of that era. The discussion in Passage 2 is most concerned with what makes a mime performance effective for the audience. The main subject for *both* passages is ways that a silent, visual form of entertainment affects an audience. Choice (C) is correct because it refers to performance in a visual art form.

The other choices

Choice (A) can be eliminated because shocking special effects is not a main subject of either passage.

Choice (B) is wrong because, although **varied dramatic styles** (used by film performers and in mime) is briefly touched on in both passages, it is not the main subject of the *pair* of passages.

In Choice (D), **audience resistance to theatrical performances** is too specific: both authors are making points about the overall role of audiences in the performance. Choice (D) is also incorrect because that topic is primarily addressed only in Passage 2.

Choice (E) can be eliminated because a tone of nostalgia appears only in Passage 1.

●← HINT

This question involves a comparison of two reading passages. Review the relevant parts of *each* passage as you make your way through the choices.

---

9 The incident described in lines 41-52 shows the author of Passage 2 to be similar to the silent filmmakers of Passage 1 in the way she

(A) required very few props
(B) used subtle technical skills to convey universal truths
(C) learned through trial and error
(D) combined narration with visual effects
(E) earned a loyal audience of followers

The correct answer is (C).

Explanation:

The question focuses on the story related in lines 41-52 and already examined in question 6. This question asks you to explain how that story shows that the mime is similar to silent filmmakers. So the correct answer has to express a point made about the mime in lines 41–52 that is also true for the filmmakers described in Passage 1. Lines 41–52 show the mime changing her performance when she found something that did not work. Passage 1 says that filmmakers learned through *experimentation* and *accidental discoveries*. So all of these people *learned through trial and error.*

The other choices

Choices (A), (B), (D), and (E) are not correct answers because they don't include traits both *described in lines 41–52* and *shared with the filmmakers.*

Choice (A) is wrong because **props** aren't mentioned in either passage.

Choice (B) is wrong because **conveying universal truths** is not discussed in Passage 1.

Choice (D) is wrong because a mime performs without speaking or **narration.**

Choice (E) is wrong because Passage 1 describes loyal audiences but lines 41–52 do not.

HINT

When a question following a pair of passages asks you to identify something that is common to both passages or true for both passages, eliminate any answer that is true for only one of the two passages.

10 What additional information would reduce the apparent similarity between these two art forms?

(A) Silent film audiences were also accustomed to vaudeville and theatrical presentations.

(B) Silent film could show newsworthy events as well as dramatic entertainment.

(C) Dialogue in the form of captions was integrated into silent films.

(D) Theaters running silent films gave many musicians steady jobs.

(E) Individual characters created for silent films became famous in their own right.

The correct answer is (C).

Explanation:

This question asks you to do two things: first, figure out a similarity between silent films and mime; second, choose an answer with information that isn't found in either passage but would make mime performance and silent films seem *less* similar.

If you think about the art forms discussed in the two passages, you should realize that neither uses *speech*. And this is an important similarity. Silent films include music but not spoken words. As stated in the Introduction to the two passages, a mime entertains *without speaking*. Choice (C) adds the information that *dialogue* between characters was part of silent films. Characters "spoke" to each other even though audiences read captions instead of hearing spoken words. So silent film indirectly used speech and was different from mime, which relies on *gesture, facial expression, and movement.*

The other choices

Choices (A), (B), (D) and (E) are wrong because they don't deal with the fundamental **similarity** between the two art forms—the absence of words. These may all be interesting things to know about silent film, but **vaudeville** performances, **newsworthy events, steady jobs** for musicians, and fame of **individual characters** have nothing to do with mime. None of these things is related to an apparent similarity between mime and silent films.

> ○→ HINT
>
> This question asks you to think about the two reading passages together. Remember that you should also consider the information in the Introduction when you compare passages.

11 Both passages mention which of the following as being important to the artistic success of the dramatic forms they describe?

(A) Effective fusion of disparate dramatic elements
(B) Slightly exaggerated characterization
(C) Incorporation of realistic details
(D) Large audiences
(E) Audience involvement

The correct answer is (E).

Explanation:

Passage 1 very clearly states in lines 5-8 that audience involvement was important to the success of silent films. In lines 58-60 of Passage 2, the author makes a similarly strong statement about how important it is for the audience to be involved in mime performance.

The other choices

Choices (A)–(D) are wrong because they don't refer to ideas mentioned in *both* passages as **important to the artistic success of the dramatic forms.** Choice (A) can be eliminated because Passage 1 talks about the **fusion** of pictures and music, but Passage 2 is not concerned at all with **disparate dramatic elements.**

Choice (B) refers to something mentioned in Passage 2 (line 43), but it is *not* something important to the success of a mime performance. And Passage 1 says that the **acting in silents was often very subtle, very restrained** (lines 33–34), which is the opposite of **exaggerated.**

Choice (C) is mentioned only in Passage 1 (lines 20–22), and *not* as an element **important to the artistic success** of silent films in general.

Choice (D) is not correct because the author of Passage 1 says that silent films did enjoy **large audiences,** but he doesn't say that **large audiences** were critical to the **artistic success** of the films. Passage 2 doesn't mention the size of the audiences at all.

HINT

When comparing two passages, focus on the specific subject of the question. Don't try to remember everything from both passages. Refer to the passages as you work your way through the five choices.

RECAP: HINTS ON CRITICAL READING QUESTIONS

1. The information you need to answer each question is *in the passage(s)*. All questions ask you to base your answer on what you read in the passages, introductions, and (sometimes) footnotes.
2. Every word counts. Details in a passage help you understand how the author wants you to feel or think.
3. Try marking up the passages or making short notes in the sample test and practice questions in this book. Find out whether this strategy saves you time and helps you answer more questions correctly.
4. Reading the questions and answers carefully is as important as reading the passage carefully.
5. An answer can be true and still be the wrong answer to a particular question.
6. There should always be information in the passage(s) that support your choice—specific words, phrases, and/or sentences that help to prove your choice is correct.
7. If you're not sure of the correct answer, try eliminating choices.
8. When you have made your choice, double-check the other choices to make sure there isn't a better one.
9. For some passages, you might want to read the questions before you read the passage so you get a sense of what to look for. If the content of the passage is familiar, looking at the questions before you read the passage might be a waste of time. So try both methods when you take the sample test and do the practice questions in this book to see if one approach is more helpful than the other.
10. Don't get bogged down on difficult questions. You might want to skim a set of questions and start by answering those you feel sure of. Then concentrate on the harder questions. Don't skip between *sets* of reading questions, because when you return to a passage you'll probably have to read it again.
11. When you have gone through all the questions associated with a passage, go back and review any you left out or weren't sure about.
12. If a verbal section contains more than one reading passage, you may want to look for one that deals with a familiar or especially interesting topic to work on first. If you skip a set of questions, however, be sure to fill in your answer sheet correctly.

A Final Note on Critical Reading Questions

There's no shortcut to doing well on Critical Reading questions. The best way to improve your reading skills is to practice—not just with specific passages and multiple-choice test questions but with books, magazines, essays, and newspapers that include complex ideas, challenging vocabulary, and subjects that make you think.

There are some things to keep in mind as you tackle the actual test questions. The most important is to always go back to the passages and look for the specific words, phrases, sentences, and ideas that either support or contradict each choice.

You may not have time to go back to the passage for every answer to every question. If you remember enough from what you have read to answer a question quickly and confidently, you should do so, and then go on to the next question. But the source for the answers is the passages. And when you're practicing for the test, it's a good idea to go back to the passage after answering a question and prove to yourself that your choice is right and the other choices are wrong. This will help you sharpen your reading and reasoning skills and give you practice in using the information in the passages to figure out the correct answers.

CHAPTER 8

Practice Questions

Independent Practice The following questions are meant to give you a chance to practice the test-taking skills and strategies you've developed so far. Use them to try out different hints and ways of approaching questions before you take the practice test in the last section of this book. If you have trouble with any of the questions, be sure to review the material in Chapters 6 and 7. Keep in mind that this chapter is intended to give you practice with the different types of questions, so it isn't arranged the way the questions will actually appear on the SAT.

Analogies

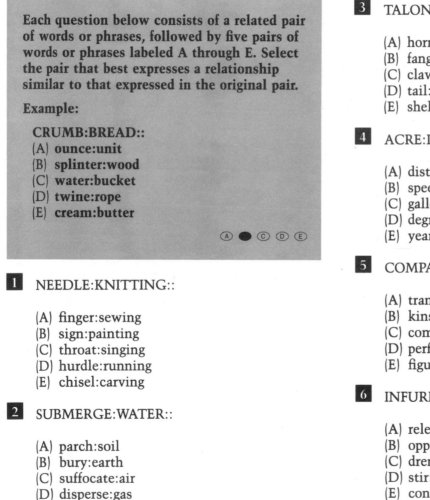

Each question below consists of a related pair of words or phrases, followed by five pairs of words or phrases labeled A through E. Select the pair that best expresses a relationship similar to that expressed in the original pair.

Example:

CRUMB:BREAD::
(A) ounce:unit
(B) splinter:wood
(C) water:bucket
(D) twine:rope
(E) cream:butter

Ⓐ ● Ⓒ Ⓓ Ⓔ

1 NEEDLE:KNITTING::

(A) finger:sewing
(B) sign:painting
(C) throat:singing
(D) hurdle:running
(E) chisel:carving

2 SUBMERGE:WATER::

(A) parch:soil
(B) bury:earth
(C) suffocate:air
(D) disperse:gas
(E) extinguish:fire

3 TALON:HAWK::

(A) horn:bull
(B) fang:snake
(C) claw:tiger
(D) tail:monkey
(E) shell:tortoise

4 ACRE:LAND::

(A) distance:space
(B) speed:movement
(C) gallon:liquid
(D) degree:thermometer
(E) year:birthday

5 COMPATRIOTS:COUNTRY::

(A) transients:home
(B) kinsfolk:family
(C) competitors:team
(D) performers:audience
(E) figureheads:government

6 INFURIATE:DISPLEASE::

(A) release:drop
(B) oppress:swelter
(C) drench:moisten
(D) stir:respond
(E) conceive:imagine

7 STRATAGEM:OUTWIT::

   (A) prototype:design
   (B) variation:change
   (C) decoy:lure
   (D) riddle:solve
   (E) charade:guess

8 WANDERLUST:TRAVEL::

   (A) fantasy:indulge
   (B) innocence:confess
   (C) ignorance:know
   (D) digression:speak
   (E) avarice:acquire

9 DEFECTOR:CAUSE::

   (A) counterfeiter:money
   (B) deserter:army
   (C) critic:book
   (D) advertiser:sale
   (E) intruder:meeting

10 TACIT:WORDS::

   (A) visible:scenes
   (B) inevitable:facts
   (C) colorful:hues
   (D) suspicious:clues
   (E) unanimous:disagreements

Sentence Completions

Each sentence below has one or two blanks, each blank indicating that something has been omitted. Beneath the sentence are five lettered words or sets of words labeled A through E. Choose the word or set of words that, when inserted in the sentence, best fits the meaning of the sentence as a whole.

Example:

Medieval kingdoms did not become constitutional republics overnight; on the contrary, the change was—.

(A) **unpopular**
(B) **unexpected**
(C) **advantegous**
(D) **sufficient**
(E) **gradual**

(A) (B) (C) (D) ●

1 Investigation of the epidemic involved determining what was ---- about the people who were affected, what made them differ from those who remained well.

(A) chronic
(B) unique
(C) fortunate
(D) misunderstood
(E) historical

2 Because management ---- the fact that employees find it difficult to work alertly at repetitious tasks, it sponsors numerous projects to ---- enthusiasm for the job.

(A) recognizes . . generate
(B) disproves . . create
(C) respects . . quench
(D) controls . . regulate
(E) surmises . . suspend

3 They did their best to avoid getting embroiled in the quarrel, preferring to maintain their ---- as long as possible.

(A) consciousness
(B) suspense
(C) interest
(D) decisiveness
(E) neutrality

4 The strong affinity of these wild sheep for mountains is not ----: mountain slopes represent ---- because they effectively limit the ability of less agile predators to pursue the sheep.

(A) useful . . peril
(B) accidental . . security
(C) instinctive . . attainment
(D) restrained . . nourishment
(E) surprising . . inferiority

5 Even those who do not ---- Robinson's views ---- him as a candidate who has courageously refused to compromise his convictions.

(A) shrink from . . condemn
(B) profit from . . dismiss
(C) concur with . . recognize
(D) disagree with . . envision
(E) dissent from . . remember

6 The alarm voiced by the committee investigating the accident had a ---- effect, for its dire predictions motivated people to take precautions that ---- an ecological disaster.

(A) trivial . . prompted
(B) salutary . . averted
(C) conciliatory . . supported
(D) beneficial . . exacerbated
(E) perverse . . vanquished

7 At the age of forty-five, with a worldwide reputation and an as yet unbroken string of notable successes to her credit, Carson was at the ---- of her career.

(A) paradigm
(B) zenith
(C) fiasco
(D) periphery
(E) inception

8 The fact that they cherished religious objects more than most of their other possessions ---- the ---- role of religion in their lives.

(A) demonstrates . . crucial
(B) obliterates . . vital
(C) limits . . daily
(D) concerns . . informal
(E) denotes . . varying

9 Mary Cassatt, an Impressionist painter, was the epitome of the ---- American: a native of Philadelphia who lived most of her life in Paris.

(A) conservative
(B) provincial
(C) benevolent
(D) prophetic
(E) expatriate

10 In the nineteenth century many literary critics saw themselves as stern, authoritarian figures defending society against the ---- of those ---- beings called authors.

(A) depravities . . wayward
(B) atrocities . . exemplary
(C) merits . . ineffectual
(D) kudos . . antagonistic
(E) indictments . . secretive

Critical Reading

Fear of communism swept through the United States in the years following the Russian Revolution of 1917. Sev-
Line *eral states passed espionage acts that restricted political*
discussion, and radicals of all descriptions were rounded
(5) *up in so-called Red Raids conducted by the attorney gen-*
eral's office. Some were convicted and imprisoned; others
were deported. This was the background of a trial in
Chicago involving twenty men charged under Illinois's
espionage statute with advocating the violent overthrow
(10) *of the government. The charge rested on the fact that*
all the defendants were members of the newly formed
Communist Labor party.
The accused in the case were represented by Clarence
Darrow, one of the foremost defense attorneys in the
(15) *country. Throughout his career, Darrow had defended the*
poor and the despised against exploitation and prejudice.
He defended the rights of labor unions, for example, at a
time when many sought to outlaw the strike, and he was
resolute in defending constitutional freedoms. The fol-
(20) *lowing are excerpts from Darrow's summation to the jury.*

Members of the Jury . . . If you want to convict these twenty men, then do it. I ask no consideration on behalf of any one of them. They are no better than any other twenty men or women; they are no better than the mil-
(25) lions down through the ages who have been prosecuted and convicted in cases like this. And if it is necessary for my clients to show that America is like all the rest, if it is necessary that my clients shall go to prison to show it, then let them go. They can afford it if you members of
(30) the jury can; make no mistake about that . . .
The State says my clients "dare to criticize the Consti-tution." Yet this police officer (who the State says is a fine, right-living person) twice violated the federal Consti-tution while a prosecuting attorney was standing by. They
(35) entered Mr. Owen's home without a search warrant. They overhauled his papers. They found a flag, a red one, which he had the same right to have in his house that you have to keep a green one, or a yellow one, or any other color, and the officer impudently rolled it up and put another
(40) flag on the wall, nailed it there. By what right was that done? What about this kind of patriotism that violates the Constitution? Has it come to pass in this country that officers of the law can trample on constitutional rights and then excuse it in a court of justice? . . .
(45) Most of what has been presented to this jury to stir up feeling in your souls has not the slightest bearing on proving conspiracy in this case. Take Mr. Lloyd's speech in Milwaukee. It had nothing to do with conspiracy.

Whether that speech was a joke or was serious, I will not
(50) attempt to discuss. But I will say that if it was serious it was as mild as a summer's shower compared with many of the statements of those who are responsible for work-ing conditions in this country. We have heard from people in high places that those individuals who express sympa-
(55) thy with labor should be stood up against a wall and shot. We have heard people of position declare that individuals who criticize the actions of those who are getting rich should be put in a cement ship with leaden sails and sent out to sea. Every violent appeal that could be conceived
(60) by the brain has been used by the powerful and the strong. I repeat, Mr. Lloyd's speech was gentle in comparison . . .
My clients are condemned because they say in their platform that, while they vote, they believe the ballot is secondary to education and organization. Counsel
(65) suggests that those who get something they did not vote for are sinners, but I suspect you the jury know full well that my clients are right. Most of you have an eight-hour day. Did you get it by any vote you ever cast? No. It came about because workers laid down their tools and said we
(70) will no longer work until we get an eight-hour day. That is how they got the twelve-hour day, the ten-hour day, and the eight-hour day—not by voting but by laying down their tools. Then when it was over and the victory won . . . then the politicians, in order to get the labor vote,
(75) passed legislation creating an eight-hour day. That is how things changed; victory preceded law . . .
You have been told that if you acquit these defendants you will be despised because you will endorse everything they believe. But I am not here to defend my clients'
(80) opinions. I am here to defend their right to express their opinions. I ask you, then, to decide this case upon the facts as you have heard them, in light of the law as you understand it, in light of the history of our country, whose institutions you and I are bound to protect.

1 Which best captures the meaning of the word "consideration" in line 22?

(A) Leniency
(B) Contemplation
(C) Due respect
(D) Reasoned judgment
(E) Legal rights

2 By "They can afford it if you members of the jury can" (lines 29-30), Darrow means that

(A) no harm will come to the defendants if they are convicted in this case
(B) the jurors will be severely criticized by the press if they convict the defendants
(C) the defendants are indifferent about the outcome of the trial
(D) the verdict of the jury has financial implica-tions for all of the people involved in the trial
(E) a verdict of guilty would be a potential threat to everyone's rights

3 Lines 31-44 suggest that the case against Owen would have been dismissed if the judge had interpreted the constitution in which of the following ways?

(A) Defendants must have their rights read to them when they are arrested.
(B) Giving false testimony in court is a crime.
(C) Evidence gained by illegal means is not admissible in court.
(D) No one can be tried twice for the same crime.
(E) Defendants cannot be forced to give incriminating evidence against themselves.

4 In line 46, the word "bearing" most nearly means

(A) connection
(B) posture
(C) endurance
(D) location
(E) resemblance

5 In lines 45-61, Darrow's defense rests mainly on convincing the jury that

(A) a double standard is being employed
(B) the prosecution's evidence is untrustworthy
(C) the defendants share mainstream American values
(D) labor unions have the right to strike
(E) the defendants should be tried by a federal rather than a state court

6 The information in lines 45-61 suggests that the prosecution treated Mr. Lloyd's speech primarily as

(A) sarcasm to be resented
(B) propaganda to be ridiculed
(C) criticism to be answered
(D) a threat to be feared
(E) a bad joke to be dismissed

7 Darrow accuses "people in high places" (lines 53-54) of

(A) conspiring to murder members of the Communist party
(B) encouraging violence against critics of wealthy business owners
(C) pressuring members of the jury to convict the defendants
(D) advocating cruel and unusual punishment for criminals
(E) insulting the public's intelligence by making foolish suggestions

8 The word "education" (line 64) is a reference to the need for

(A) establishing schools to teach the philosophy of the Communist Labor party
(B) making workers aware of their economic and political rights
(C) teaching factory owners about the needs of laborers
(D) creating opportunities for on-the-job training in business
(E) helping workers to continue their schooling

9 The statement "victory preceded law" (line 76) refers to the fact that

(A) social reform took place only after labor unions organized support for their political candidates
(B) politicians need to win the support of labor unions if they are to be elected
(C) politicians can introduce legislative reform only if they are elected to office
(D) politicians did not initiate improved working conditions but legalized them after they were in place
(E) politicians have shown that they are more interested in winning elections than in legislative reform

10 Judging from lines 77-79, the jury had apparently been told that finding the defendants innocent would be the same as

(A) denying the importance of the Constitution
(B) giving people the right to strike
(C) encouraging passive resistance
(D) inhibiting free speech
(E) supporting communist doctrine

11 In order for Darrow to win the case, it would be most crucial that the jurors possess

(A) a thorough understanding of legal procedures and terminology
(B) a thorough understanding of the principles and beliefs of the Communist Labor party
(C) sympathy for labor's rights to safe and comfortable working conditions
(D) the ability to separate the views of the defendants from the rights of the defendants
(E) the courage to act in the best interests of the nation's economy

Answer Key

	ANALOGIES		SENTENCE COMPLETIONS		CRITICAL READING
1.	E	1.	B	1.	A
2.	B	2.	A	2.	E
3.	C	3.	E	3.	C
4.	C	4.	B	4.	A
5.	B	5.	C	5.	A
6.	C	6.	B	6.	D
7.	C	7.	B	7.	B
8.	E	8.	A	8.	B
9.	B	9.	E	9.	D
10.	E	10.	A	10.	E
				11.	D

PART FOUR

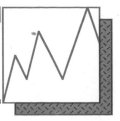

SAT I: Mathematical Reasoning

- Chapter 9   Mathematics Review
- Chapter 10   Sample Mathematics Questions and Answers

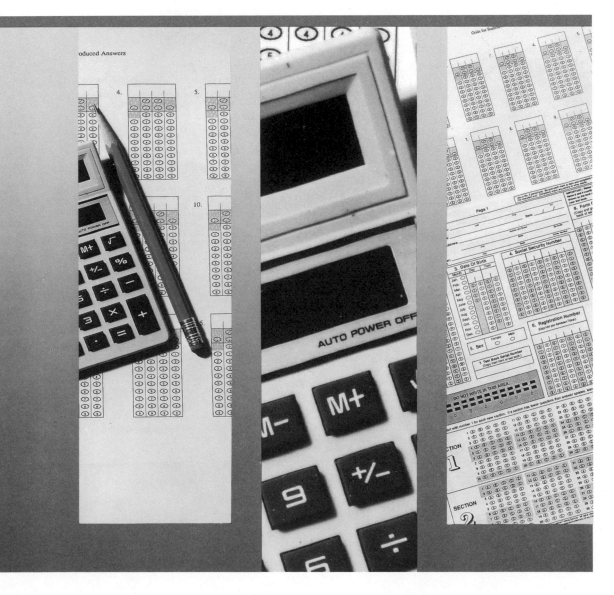

CHAPTER 9

Mathematics Review

Introduction to the Mathematics Sections

These sections of the SAT emphasize mathematical reasoning. They evaluate how well you can think through mathematics problems.

The test does require that you know some specific math concepts and that you have learned some math skills. But the point of the test is not how many math facts or procedures you know. The test evaluates how well you can use what you know to solve problems.

This chapter presents many of the skills and concepts that will appear on the test and shows you how to use those skills and concepts.

Concepts You Need to Know

There are four broad categories of problems in the math test: Arithmetic, Algebra, Geometry, and Miscellaneous.

The following table lists the basic skills and concepts with which you need to be familiar in each of the four categories. Remember, *be familiar with* means that you understand them and can apply them to a variety of math problems.

Arithmetic
<ul><li>Problem solving that involves simple addition, subtraction, multiplication, and division</li><li>Conceptual understanding of arithmetic operations with fractions</li><li>Averages (arithmetic mean), median, and mode</li><li>Properties of integers: odd and even numbers, prime numbers, positive and negative integers, factors, divisibility, and multiples</li><li>Word problems involving such concepts as: rate/time/distance, percents, averages</li><li>Number line: order, betweenness, and consecutive numbers</li><li>Ratio and proportion</li></ul>**Not included**<ul><li>Tedious or long computations</li></ul>

Algebra

- Operations involving signed numbers
- Word problems: translating verbal statements into algebraic expressions
- Substitution
- Simplifying algebraic expressions
- Elementary factoring
- Solving algebraic equations and inequalities
- Manipulation of positive integer exponents and roots
- Simple quadratic equations

Not included
- Complicated manipulations with radicals and roots
- Solving quadratic equations that require the use of the quadratic formula
- Exponents that are NOT whole numbers

Geometry

- Properties of parallel and perpendicular lines
- Angle relationships—vertical angles and angles in geometric figures
- Properties of triangles: right, isosceles, and equilateral; 30°-60°-90° and other "special" right triangles; total of interior angles; Pythagorean theorem; similarity
- Properties of polygons: perimeter, area, angle measures
- Properties of circles: circumference, area, radius, diameter
- Solids: volume, surface area
- Simple coordinate geometry, including: slope, coordinates of points

Not included
- Formal geometric proofs
- Volumes other than rectangular solids and those given in the reference material or in individual questions

Miscellaneous
• Probability
• Data interpretation
• Counting and ordering problems
• Special symbols
• Logical analysis

Math Reference Material

Reference material is included in the math test. You may find these facts and formulas helpful in answering some of the questions on the test. To get an idea of what's included, take a look at the practice test in Part Five of this book.

Don't let the Reference Material give you a false sense of security. It isn't going to tell you how to solve math problems. To do well on the math test, you have to be comfortable working with these facts and formulas. If you haven't had practice using them before the test, you will have a hard time using them efficiently during the test.

For instance, if you forgot whether the ratio of the sides of a 45°-45°-90° triangle is $1:1:\sqrt{2}$, then the Reference Material will help you. If you don't know that there is a specific ratio for sides of a 45°-45°-90° triangle, or you don't know how to look for and recognize a 45°-45°-90° triangle, then the Reference Material isn't likely to help very much.

Doing well on the math test depends on being able to apply your math skills and knowledge to many different situations. Simply knowing formulas will not be enough.

Types of Questions

There are three types of questions on the math test: five-choice Multiple-Choice questions, Quantitative Comparison questions, and Student-Produced Responses ("Grid-in" questions).

Five-Choice Multiple-Choice Questions

Here's an example of a Multiple-Choice question with five choices:

If $2x + 2x + 2x = 12$, what is the value of $2x - 1$?

(A) 2
(B) 3
(C) 4
(D) 5
(E) 6

We'll return to this example later in the section; for now, we'll just tell you the correct answer is (B). Hints for answering specific kinds of five-choice Multiple-Choice questions are presented in Chapter 10.

Quantitative Comparison Questions

Quantitative Comparison questions are quite different from regular five-choice Multiple-Choice questions. Instead of presenting a problem and asking you to figure out the answer, Quantitative Comparison questions give you two quantities and ask you to compare them.

You'll be given one quantity on the left in Column A, and one quantity on the right in Column B. You have to figure out whether:

- The quantity in Column A is greater.
- The quantity in Column B is greater.
- The quantities are equal.
- You cannot determine which is greater from the information given.

Here are the directions you'll see on the test.

Directions for Quantitative Comparison Questions

The <u>questions</u> each consist of two quantities in boxes, one in Column A and one in Column B. You are to compare the two quantities and on the answer sheet fill in oval

A if the quantity in Column A is greater;
B if the quantity in Column B is greater;
C if the two quantities are equal;
D if the relationship cannot be determined from the information given.

AN E RESPONSE WILL NOT BE SCORED.

<u>Notes:</u>

1. In some questions, information is given about one or both of the quantities to be compared. In such cases, the given information is centered above the two columns and is not boxed.
2. In a given question, a symbol that appears in both columns represents the same thing in Column A as it does in Column B.
3. Letters such as x, n, and k stand for real numbers.

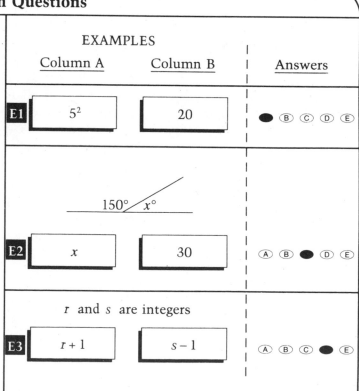

Specific hints on Quantitative Comparison questions are presented in Chapter 10.

All you are asked to do is make a comparison between two quantities. Frequently, you don't have to finish your calculations or determine an exact answer. You just have to know enough about the quantities to determine which one is greater.

Memorize the four choices for Quantitative Comparison questions:

- (A) if the column A quantity is greater;
- (B) if the column B quantity is greater;
- (C) if they are equal;
- (D) if you cannot tell from the information given.

The four choices are printed at the top of each page of every Quantitative Comparison section, but you can save some time if you memorize them.

If any two of the relationships (A), (B), or (C) can be true for a particular Quantitative Comparison question, then the answer to that question is (D).

Think of the columns as a balanced scale. You are trying to figure out which side of the scale is heavier. Before you make your measurement, you can eliminate any quantities that are the same on both sides of the scale. In other words, look for ways to simplify expressions and remove equal quantities from both columns before you make your comparison. For example:

Column A	**Column B**
34 + 43 + 58	36 + 43 + 58

You don't have to add up all the numbers to compare these two quantities. You can eliminate numbers 43 and 58, which appear in both columns. Now your comparison is much easier to make.

If you have a question in which quantities containing variables must be compared, try substituting values for the variables.

- Make sure you check above the columns for any information about what the values can be.
- And check the information centered above the columns (if any) to see whether any values have been ruled out for that question.

When substituting values to answer a Quantitative Comparison question, make sure you check the special cases: 0, 1, at least one number between 0 and 1, a number or numbers greater than 1, and a few negative numbers.

Grid-in Questions

The Grid-in format is being introduced for the first time, so make sure you read this discussion carefully and study and review the Grid-in questions and answers presented in Chapter 10.

In contrast to the Multiple-Choice question format, the student-produced response format requires you to figure out the correct answer and grid it on the answer sheet rather than just be able to recognize the correct answer among the choices.

Grid-in questions emphasize the importance of active problem solving and critical thinking in mathematics. Grid-in questions are solved just like any other math problems, but you have to figure out the correct answer exactly and fill it in on the grid. Here's the same question presented in the discussion of five-choice Multiple-Choice questions, but as a Grid-in question:

If $2x + 2x + 2x = 12$, what is the value of $2x - 1$?

The answer is still 3, and the explanation of the solution is the same, but instead of filling in Choice (A), (B), (C), (D), or (E), you have to write 3 at the top of the grid and fill in 3 below.

One of the most important rules to remember about Grid-in questions is that **only answers entered on the grid are scored. Your handwritten answer at the top of the grid is not scored.** However, writing your answer at the top of the grid may help you avoid gridding errors.

In many cases, the Grid-in format allows you to provide your answer in more than one form. Here is an example of how you can use the grid to express the same answer as either a decimal or a fraction:

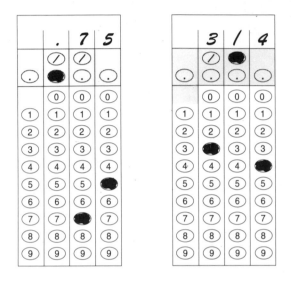

Here is an example of how you can enter the same answer in different ways on the grid. (Both are correct.)

Some fractions can't be entered due to space limitations. An answer of 2 1/4 would not fit because the grid cannot accommodate the space between the integer and the fraction.

Wrong!
Grid error!

The grid scoring system cannot distinguish between 2 1/4 and 21/4, so this answer would have to be entered as 2.25 or 9/4.

IMPORTANT!!!

Remember that only the answer entered on the grid, and not the answer handwritten at the top of the grid, is scored. You must decide whether to first write your answer in at the top of the grid and then transfer it to the grid or to transfer your answer directly from notes in your test book, or in your head, to the grid. You might practice both approaches and see which one works best for you. You want to make sure you enter your answer correctly. While it might be more time-consuming to first write your answer in at the top of the grid, you may find this approach helps you avoid errors.

Grid-in Scoring

Answers to Grid-in questions are either completely correct and given full credit or completely wrong and given no credit. No partial credit is given, and *no* points are deducted for wrong answers.

You have to figure out the correct answer (or one of the correct answers on questions where more than one answer is possible), and correctly grid that answer to get credit for the question. **Remember,** you *won't* be penalized for a wrong answer in a Grid-in question. So it's better to put in an answer you're not sure of than to leave it blank.

HINTS: GRID-IN QUESTIONS

The slash mark (/) is used to indicate a fraction bar.

You do not have to reduce fractions to their lowest terms, unless your answer will not fit in the grid.

You may express an answer as a fraction or a decimal: You can grid 1/2 as 1/2 or .5.

Mixed numbers must be expressed as improper fractions or decimals: You **must** express 1 3/5 as 8/5 or 1.6.

You don't have to grid in a zero in front of a decimal less than 1; 1/2 can be gridded as .5 or 0.5.

Grid as much of a repeating decimal as will fit in the grid. You may need to round a repeating decimal, but round only the last digit: grid 2/3 as 2/3, or as .666, or as .667. Do not grid the value 2/3 as .66 or .67 because these decimals don't fill the grid and aren't as accurate as .666 or .667.

Since you don't have choices provided to help avoid careless errors on Grid-in questions:
• Carefully check your calculations.
• Always double-check your answers. Make sure the answer you enter makes sense.

Make sure you have gridded your answer accurately and according to all the Grid-in rules.

Important: If you change your answer, erase your old gridded answer completely.

Practice a few Grid-in questions with a variety of answer types—whole numbers, fractions, and decimals. Get familiar with the mechanics of gridding.

Some Grid-in questions have more than one correct answer. You can grid any one of the correct answers and get full credit for the question.

Calculators Are Recommended

It is recommended that you bring a calculator to use on the math sections of the test. Although no question will require a calculator, field trials of the New SAT have shown that, on average, students who used calculators did slightly better on the test than students who did not.

While a number of factors influence your performance on the math sections, students with solid math preparation who use calculators on a regular basis are likely to do better on the test than students without this preparation.

Although math scores may improve on average with the use of calculators, there is no way of generalizing about the effect of calculator use on an individual student's score. It is likely that different students' scores will be affected in different ways.

Bring Your Own Calculator

You are expected to provide your own calculator, which can be any basic four-function, scientific, or graphing model (programmable or non-programmable).

You won't be permitted to use pocket organizers, handheld mini-computers, laptop computers, calculators with a typewriter type of keypad, calculators with paper tape, calculators that make noise, or calculators that require an external power source like an outlet. In addition, calculators can't be shared.

●⟵ HINTS: CALCULATORS

Bring a calculator with you when you take the test, whether you think you will use it or not.

Only bring a calculator that you're comfortable using. Don't rush out to buy a sophisticated new calculator just for the test.

Don't try to use your calculator on every question.

First decide how you will solve each problem—then decide whether to use the calculator. The best way to learn which types of questions can be solved with a calculator is to practice on a variety of problems with and without the calculator. You'll learn when to turn to the calculator, and you'll be much more comfortable using your calculator during the actual test.

The calculations you are likely to do will usually involve simple arithmetic. If the arithmetic of a question gets so complicated or difficult that you need a calculator to figure it out, you are probably doing something wrong.

Make sure your calculator is in good working order and has fresh batteries. If it breaks down during the test, you'll have to go on without it.

Enter numbers very carefully. The calculator doesn't leave any notes, so if you enter the wrong numbers, you may not realize it.

Some General Tips

Don't rush. Make notes in your test book.

- Draw figures to help you think through problems that involve geometric shapes, segment lengths, distances, proportions, sizes, etc.
- Write out calculations so that you can check them later.
- When a question contains a figure, note any measurements or values you calculate right on the figure.

If you have time to check your work, try to redo your calculations in a different way from the way you did them the first time. This may take a bit more time, but it may help you catch an error.

Use the choices to your advantage:

- If you can't figure out how to approach a problem, the form of the choices may give you a hint.
- You may find that you can eliminate some choices so you can make an educated guess, even if you aren't sure of the correct answer.

If you decide to try all the choices, start with choice (C). *This is not because (C) is more likely to be the correct answer.*

Start with (C) because, if the choices are numbers, they are usually listed in ascending order, from lowest to highest value. Then, if (C) turns out to be too high, you don't have to worry about (D) or (E). If (C) is too low, you don't have to worry about (A) or (B).

Even though the questions generally run from easy to hard, always take a quick look at all of them. You never know when one of the "hard" ones just happens to involve a concept that you have recently learned or reviewed.

Arithmetic Concepts You Should Know

Properties of Integers

You will need to know the following information for a number of questions on the math test:

- Integers include negative whole numbers, positive whole numbers, and zero (0).

$$-3, -2, -1, 0, 1, 2, 3, 4$$

- Integers extend indefinitely in both negative and positive directions.
- Integers *do not* include fractions or decimals.

The following are negative integers:
$$-4, -3, -2, -1$$

The following are positive integers:
$$1, 2, 3, 4$$

The integer zero (0) is neither positive nor negative.

Odd Numbers

$$-5, -3, -1, 1, 3, 5$$

Even Numbers

$$-4, -2, 0, 2, 4$$

The integer zero (0) is an even number.

Consecutive Integers

Integers that follow in sequence, where the positive difference between two successive integers is 1, are consecutive integers.

$$-1, 0, 1, 2, 3$$
$$1001, 1002, 1003, 1004$$
$$-14, -13, -12, -11$$

The following is a general mathematical notation for representing consecutive integers:

$$n, n + 1, n + 2, n + 3 \ldots, \text{ where } n \text{ is any integer.}$$

Prime Numbers

A prime number is any number that has exactly two whole number factors—itself and the number 1. The number 1 itself *is not* prime.
Prime numbers include:

$$2, 3, 5, 7, 11, 13, 17, 19$$

Addition of Integers

$$\text{even} + \text{even} = \text{even}$$
$$\text{odd} + \text{odd} = \text{even}$$
$$\text{odd} + \text{even} = \text{odd}$$

Multiplication of Integers

$$\text{even} \times \text{even} = \text{even}$$
$$\text{odd} \times \text{odd} = \text{odd}$$
$$\text{odd} \times \text{even} = \text{even}$$

Number Lines

A number line is used to geometrically represent the relationships between numbers: integers, fractions, and/or decimals.

$$-6 \quad -5 \quad -4 \quad -3 \quad -2 \quad -1 \quad 0 \quad 1 \quad 2 \quad 3 \quad 4 \quad 5$$

- Numbers on a number line always increase as you move to the right.
- Negative numbers are always shown with a minus sign (−). The plus sign (+) is usually not shown.
- Number lines are drawn to scale. You will be expected to make reasonable approximations of positions between labeled points on the line.

Number-line questions generally require you to figure out the relationships among numbers placed on the line. Number-line questions may ask:

- Where a number should be placed in relation to other numbers;
- The differences between two numbers;
- The lengths and the ratios of the lengths of line segments represented on the number line.

Sample Question

Here is a sample number-line question:

On the number line above, the ratio of the length of *AC* to the length of *AG* is equal to the ratio of the length of *CD* to the length of which of the following?

(A) *AD*
(B) *BD*
(C) *CG*
(D) *DF*
(E) *EG*

In this question, the number line is used to determine lengths: AC = 2, AG = 6, CD = 1. Once you have these lengths, the question becomes a ratio and proportion problem.

- The ratio of AC to AG is 2 to 6.
- AC is to AG as CD is to what?

- $\frac{2}{6} = \frac{1}{x}$
- $x = 3$

Now you have to go back to the number line to find the segment that has the length of 3. The answer is (A).

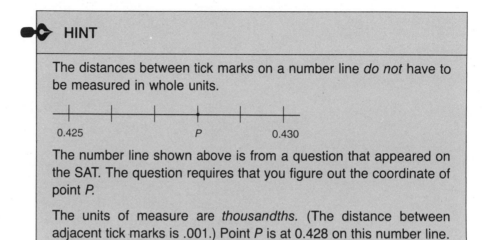

HINT

The distances between tick marks on a number line *do not* have to be measured in whole units.

0.425   P   0.430

The number line shown above is from a question that appeared on the SAT. The question requires that you figure out the coordinate of point *P*.

The units of measure are *thousandths*. (The distance between adjacent tick marks is .001.) Point *P* is at 0.428 on this number line.

Squares and Square Roots

Squares of Integers

Although you can always figure them out with paper and pencil or with your calculator, it's helpful if you know or at least can recognize the squares of integers between -12 and 12. Here they are:

x	1	2	3	4	5	6	7	8	9	10	11	12
x^2	1	4	9	16	25	36	49	64	81	100	121	144

x	-1	-2	-3	-4	-5	-6	-7	-8	-9	-10	-11	-12
x^2	1	4	9	16	25	36	49	64	81	100	121	144

Your knowledge of common squares and square roots may speed up your solution to some math problems. The most common types of problems for which this knowledge will help you will be those involving:

- Factoring and/or simplifying expressions;
- Problems involving the Pythagorean theorem ($a^2 + b^2 = c^2$);
- Areas of circles or squares.

Squares of Fractions

Remember that if a positive fraction whose value is less than 1 is squared, the result is always *smaller* than the original fraction:

$$\text{If } 0 < n < 1$$
$$\text{Then } n^2 < n.$$

Try it.
What are the values of the following fractions?

$$\left(\frac{2}{3}\right)^2$$
$$\left(\frac{1}{8}\right)^2$$

The answers are 4/9 and 1/64, respectively. Each of these is less in value than the original fraction. For example, 4/9 < 2/3.

Fractions

You should know how to do basic operations with fractions:

- Adding, subtracting, multiplying, and dividing fractions;
- Reducing to lowest terms;
- Finding the least common denominator;
- Expressing a value as a mixed number (2 1/3) and as an improper fraction (7/3);
- Working with complex fractions—ones that have fractions in their numerators or denominators.

Decimal/Fraction Equivalents

You may have to work with decimal/fraction equivalents. That is, you may have to be able to recognize common fractions as decimals and vice versa.

To change any fraction to a decimal, divide the denominator into the numerator.

Although you can figure out the decimal equivalent of any fraction (a calculator will help here), you'll be doing yourself a favor if you know the following:

Fraction	$\frac{1}{4}$	$\frac{1}{3}$	$\frac{1}{2}$	$\frac{2}{3}$	$\frac{3}{4}$
Decimal	0.25	0.3333*	0.50	0.6666*	0.75

* These fractions don't convert to terminating decimals— the 3 and 6 repeat indefinitely.

Factors, Multiples, and Remainders

In most math tests, you'll find several questions that require you to understand and work with these three related concepts.

Factors

The factors of a number are integers that can be divided into the number without any remainders.

For instance, consider the number 24:

The numbers 24, 12, 8, 6, 4, 3, 2, and 1 are all factors of the number 24.

Common Factors

Common factors are factors that two numbers have in common. For instance, 3 is a common factor of 6 and 15.

Prime Factors

Prime factors are the factors of a number that are prime numbers. That is, the prime factors of a number cannot be further divided into factors.

The prime factors of the number 24 are:
2 and 3.

The term "divisible by" means divisible by *without any remainder* or *with a remainder of zero*. For instance, 12 is divisible by 4 because 12 divided by 4 is 3 with a remainder of 0. Twelve is not divisible by 5 because 12 divided by 5 is 2 with a remainder of 2.

Multiples

The multiples of any given number are those numbers that can be divided by that given number *without a remainder*.

For instance: 16, 24, 32, 40, and 48 are all multiples of 8. They are also multiples of 2 and 4. Remember: The multiples of any number will always be multiples of all the factors of that number.

For instance:

- 30, 45, 60, and 75 are all multiples of the number 15.
- Two factors of 15 are the numbers 3 and 5.
- That means that 30, 45, 60, and 75 are all multiples of 3 and 5.

Sample Questions

Example 1:

What is the *least* positive integer divisible by the numbers 2, 3, 4, and 5?

- To find *any* number that is divisible by several other numbers, multiply those numbers together. You could multiply $2 \times 3 \times 4 \times 5$ and the result would be divisible by all those factors.

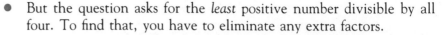

- But the question asks for the *least* positive number divisible by all four. To find that, you have to eliminate any extra factors.
- Any number divisible by 4 will also be divisible by 2. So you can eliminate 2 from your initial multiplication. If you multiply $3 \times 4 \times 5$, you will get a smaller number than if you multiply $2 \times 3 \times 4 \times 5$. And the number will still be divisible by 2.
- Because the remaining factors (3, 4, and 5) have no common factor, the result of $3 \times 4 \times 5$ will give you the answer.

Example 2:

Which of the following could be the remainders when four consecutive positive integers are each divided by 3?

(A) 1,2,3,1
(B) 1,2,3,4
(C) 0,1,2,3
(D) 0,1,2,0
(E) 0,2,3,0

Remember, the question asks only for the remainders.

- When you divide *any* positive integer by 3, the remainder must be less than or equal to 2.
- All the choices except (D) include remainders greater than 2. So (D) is the correct answer.

Averages

The word "average" can refer to several different measures.

Arithmetic Mean

- **Arithmetic mean**
- **Median**
- **Mode**

Arithmetic mean is what is usually thought of when talking about averages. If you want to know the arithmetic mean of a set of values, the formula is:

$$\frac{\text{The sum of a set of values}}{\text{The number of values in the set}}$$

For example, if there are three children, aged 6, 7, and 11, the arithmetic mean of their ages is:

$$\frac{6 + 7 + 11}{3}$$

or 8 years.

Median

The median is the middle value of a group. To find the median, place the values in ascending (or descending) order and select the middle value.

For instance:
What is the median of the following values?

$$1, 2, 667, 4, 19, 309, 44, 6, 200$$

- Place the values in ascending order:

$$1, 2, 4, 6, 19, 44, 200, 309, 667$$
- Select the value in the middle.
- There are nine values listed. The middle value is the fifth.
- The median of these values is 19.

The Median of an Even Set of Values

When you have an even set of values, the median is the average (arithmetic mean) of the two middle values.

Mode

The mode of a set of values is the value or values that appears the greatest number of times.

In the list used to illustrate the median, there was no mode, because all the values appeared just once. But consider the following list:

$$1, 5, 5, 7, 276, 4, 100, 276, 89, 4, 276, 1, 8$$

- The number 276 appears three times, which is more times than any other number appears.
- The **mode** of this list is 276.

Multiple Modes

It is possible to have more than one mode in a set of numbers:

$$1, 5, 5, 7, 276, 4, 10004, 89, 4, 276, 1, 8$$

In the set above, there are four modes: 1, 4, 5, and 276.

Weighted Average

A weighted average is the average of two or more groups in which there are more members in one group than there are in another. For instance:

15 members of a class had an average (arithmetic mean) SAT I: Math score of 500. The remaining 10 members of the class had an average of 550. What is the average score of the entire class?

You can't simply take the average of 500 and 550 because there are more students with 500s than with 550s. The correct average has to be weighted toward the group with the greater number.

To find a weighted average, multiply each individual average by its weighting factor. The weighting factor is the number of values that correspond to a particular average. In this problem, you multiply each average by the number of students that corresponds to that average. Then you divide by the total number of students involved:

$$\frac{(500 \times 15) + (550 \times 10)}{25} = 520$$

So the average score for the entire class is 520.

CALCULATOR HINT

You might find that a calculator will help you find the answer to this question more quickly.

Average of Algebraic Expressions

Algebraic expressions can be averaged in the same way as any other values:

What is the average (arithmetic mean) of $3x + 1$ and $x - 3$?

There are two expressions, $3x + 1$ and $x - 3$, to be averaged. Take the sum of the values and divide by the number of values:

$$\frac{1}{2}[(3x + 1) + (x - 3)]$$
$$= \frac{(4x - 2)}{2}$$
$$= 2x - 1$$

Using Averages to Find Missing Numbers

You can use simple algebra in the basic average formula to find missing values when the average is given:

- The basic average formula is:

$$\frac{\text{The sum of a set of values}}{\text{The number of values in the set}}$$

- If you have the average and the number of values, you can figure out the sum of the values:

$$(\text{average})(\text{number of values}) = \text{sum of values}$$

Sample Question

Try putting this knowledge to work with a typical question on averages:

The average (arithmetic mean) of a set of 10 numbers is 15. If one of the numbers is removed, the average of the remaining numbers is 14. What is the value of the number that was removed?

- You know the average and the number of values in the set, so you can figure out the sum of all values in the set.
- The difference between the sum before you remove the number and after you remove the number will give you the value of the number you removed.
- The sum of all the values when you start out is the average times the number of values: $10 \times 15 = 150$.
- The sum of the values after you remove a number is $9 \times 14 = 126$.
- The difference between the sums is $150 - 126 = 24$.
- You only removed one number, so the value of that number is 24.

Ratio and Proportion

Ratio

A ratio expresses a mathematical relationship between two quantities. Specifically, a ratio is a quotient of those quantities. The following are all relationships that can be expressed as ratios:

- My serving of pizza is 1/4 of the whole pie.
- There are twice as many chocolate cookies as vanilla cookies in the cookie jar.
- My brother earns $5 for each $6 I earn.

These ratios can be expressed in several different ways. They can be stated in words:

- The ratio of my serving of pizza to the whole pie is one to four.
- The ratio of chocolate to vanilla cookies is two to one.
- The ratio of my brother's earnings to mine is five to six.

They can be expressed as fractions:

- $\frac{1}{4}$

- $\frac{2}{1}$

- $\frac{5}{6}$

Or they can be expressed with a colon (:) as follows:

- 1:4
- 2:1
- 5:6

Sample Question

The weight of the tea in a box of 100 identical tea bags is 8 ounces. What is the weight, in ounces, of the tea in 3 tea bags?

Start by setting up two ratios. Remember, a proportion is nothing but two ratios set equal to each other.

- The ratio of 3 tea bags to all of the tea bags is 3 to 100 (3/100).
- Let x equal the weight, in ounces, of the tea in 3 tea bags.
- The ratio of the weight of 3 tea bags to the total weight of the tea is x ounces to 8 ounces (x/8).

The relationship between x ounces and 8 ounces is equal to the relationship between 3 and 100:

$$\frac{x}{8} = \frac{3}{100}$$
$$100x = 24$$
$$x = 24/100 \text{ or } .24$$

Sample Question

You may find questions that involve ratios in any of the following situations:

- Lengths of lines;
- Sizes of angles;
- Areas and perimeters;
- Rate/time/distance;
- Numbers on a number line.

You may be asked to combine ratios with other mathematical concepts. For instance:

The ratio of the length of a rectangular floor to its width is 3:2. If the length of the floor is 12 meters, what is the perimeter of the floor, in meters?

The ratio of the length to the width of the rectangle is 3:2, so set that ratio equal to the ratio of the actual measures of the sides of the rectangle:

$$\frac{3}{2} = \frac{\text{length}}{\text{width}}$$

$$\frac{3}{2} = \frac{12}{x}$$

$$3x = 24$$

$$x = 8 = \text{the width}$$

Now that you have the width of the rectangle, it is easy to find the perimeter: 2(length + width). The perimeter is 40 meters.

Algebra

Many math questions require a knowledge of algebra, so the basics of algebra should be second nature to you. You have to be able to manipulate and solve a simple equation for an unknown, simplify and evaluate algebraic expressions, and use algebraic concepts in problem-solving situations.

Factoring

The types of factoring included on the math test are:

- Difference of two squares:

$$a^2 - b^2 = (a + b)(a - b)$$

- Finding common factors, as in:

$$x^2 + 2x = x(x + 2)$$
$$2x + 4y = 2(x + 2y)$$

- Factoring quadratics:

$$x^2 - 3x - 4 = (x - 4)(x + 1)$$
$$x^2 + 2x + 1 = (x + 1)(x + 1) = (x + 1)^2$$

You are not likely to find a question instructing you to "factor the following expression." You may see questions that ask you to evaluate or compare expressions that require factoring. For instance, here is a Quantitative Comparison question:

Column A **Column B**

$$x \neq -1$$

$$\frac{x^2 - 1}{x + 1} \qquad\qquad x - 1$$

The numerator of the expression in Column A can be factored:

$$x^2 - 1$$
$$= (x + 1)(x - 1)$$

The $(x + 1)(x - 1)$ cancels with the $(x + 1)$ in the denominator, leaving the factor $(x - 1)$. So the two quantities—the one in Column A and the one in Column B—are equal.

138

Exponents

Three Points to Remember

1. When multiplying expressions with the same base, *add* the exponents:

$$a^2 \cdot a^5$$
$$= (a \cdot a)(a \cdot a \cdot a \cdot a \cdot a)$$
$$= a^7$$

2. When dividing expressions with the same base, subtract exponents:

$$\frac{r^5}{r^3} = \frac{r \cdot r \cdot r \cdot r \cdot r}{r \cdot r \cdot r} = r^2$$

3. When raising one power to another power, *multiply* the exponents:

$$(n^3)^6 = n^{18}$$

Solving Equations

Most of the equations that you will need to solve are linear equations. Equations that are not linear can usually be solved by factoring or by inspection.

Working with "Unsolvable" Equations

At first, some equations may look like they can't be solved. You will find that although you can't solve the equation, you can answer the question. For instance:

If $a + b = 5$, what is the value of $2a + 2b$?

You can't solve the equation $a + b = 5$ for either a or b. But you can answer the question:

- The question doesn't ask for the value of a or b. It asks for the value of the entire quantity ($2a + 2b$).
- $2a + 2b$ can be factored:
  $2a + 2b = 2(a + b)$
- $a + b = 5$

You are asked what 2 times $a + b$ is. That's 2 times 5, or 10.

Solving for One Variable in Terms of Another

You may be asked to solve for one variable in terms of another. Again, you're not going to be able to find a specific, numerical value for all of the variables.

139

For example:

If $3x + y = z$, what is x in terms of y and z?

You aren't asked what x equals. You are asked to manipulate the expression so that you can isolate x (put it by itself) on one side of the equation. That equation will tell you what x is *in terms of* the other variables:

- $3x + y = z$
- Subtract y from each side of the equation.
  $3x = z - y$
- Divide both sides by 3 to get the value of x.
  $x = \dfrac{(z - y)}{3}$

The value of x in terms of y and z is $\dfrac{(z - y)}{3}$.

Direct Translations of Mathematical Terms

Many word problems require that you translate the description of a mathematical fact or relationship into mathematical terms.

Always read the word problem carefully and double-check that you have translated it exactly.

A number is 3 times the quantity (4x + 6)
translates to $3(4x + 6)$

A number y decreased by 60 translates to $y - 60$

5 less than a number k translates to $k - 5$

A number that is x less than 5 translates to $5 - x$

20 divided by n is $\dfrac{20}{n}$

20 divided into a number y is $\dfrac{y}{20}$

See the Word Problem tips in this chapter.

HINT

Be especially careful with subtraction and division because the order of these operations is important:

$5 - 3$ is not the same as $3 - 5$.

Inequalities

An inequality is a statement that two values are *not* equal, or that one value is greater than or equal to or less than or equal to another. Inequalities are shown by four signs:

- Greater than: $>$
- Greater than or equal to: $\geq$
- Less than: $<$
- Less than or equal to: $\leq$

Most of the time, you can work with simple inequalities in exactly the same way you work with equalities.

Consider the following:

$$2x + 1 > 11$$

If this were an equation, it would be pretty easy to solve:

$$2x + 1 = 11$$
$$2x = 11 - 1$$
$$2x = 10$$
$$x = 5$$

You can use a similar process to solve inequalities:

$$2x + 1 > 11$$
$$2x > 11 - 1$$
$$2x > 10$$
$$x > 5$$

HINT

Remember that multiplying both sides of an inequality by a negative number reverses the direction of the inequality.

If $-x < 3$, then $x > -3$

Number Sequences

A number sequence is a sequence of numbers that follows a specific pattern. For instance, the sequence

$$3, 7, 11, 15, \ldots$$

follows the pattern, **add** 4. That is, each term in the sequence is 4 more than the one before it. The three dots (. . .) indicate that this sequence goes on forever.

Not all sequences go on indefinitely. The sequence

$$1, 3, 5, \ldots, 21, 23$$

contains odd numbers only up to 23, where the sequence ends. The three dots in the middle indicate that the sequence continues according to the pattern as shown, but it ends with the number 23.

The math test *does not* usually ask you to figure out the rule for determining the numbers in a sequence. When a number sequence is used in a question, you will usually be told what the rule is.

Number sequence questions might ask you for:

- The sum of certain numbers in the sequence;
- The average of certain numbers in the sequence;
- The value of a specific number in the sequence.

Word Problems

Some math questions are presented as word problems. They require you to apply math skills to everyday situations. With word problems you have to:

- Read and interpret what is being asked.
- Determine what information you are given.
- Determine what information you need to know.
- Decide what mathematical skills or formulas you need to apply to find the answer.
- Work out the answer.
- Double-check to make sure the answer makes sense.

Hints on Solving Word Problems

Translate as You Read

As you read word problems, translate the words into mathematical expressions:

- When you read **Jane has three dollars more than Tom,** translate $J = T + 3$.
- When you read **the average (arithmetic mean) of the weights of three children is 80 pounds,** translate to $(a + b + c)/3 = 80$.
- When you read **Jane buys one clown fish and two guppies for $3.00,** translate $c + 2g = \$3.00$.

When you've finished reading the problem, you will have already translated it into mathematical expressions.

The following table will help you with some of the more common phrases and mathematical translations:

Words	Operation	Translation
Is, was, has:	$=$	
Jane's son is as old as Tom's daughter.	$=$	$S = D$ or $J = T$
More than, older than, further than, greater than, sum of:	$+$	Addition
Jane has 2 dollars more than Tom.	$+$	$J = 2 + T$ or $J = T + 2$
Tom ran 10 miles further than Jane.		$T = 10 + J$ or $T = J + 10$
The sum of two integers is 36.		$x + y = 36$
Less than, difference, younger than, fewer:	$-$	Subtraction
Tom has 5 fewer marbles than twice the number Jane has.	$-$	$T = 2J - 5$ (Don't make the "$5 - 2J$" mistake!)
The difference between Tom's height and Jane's height is 22 centimeters.		$T - J = 22$ (or maybe $J - T = 22$)
Of:	$\times$	Multiplication
20% of Tom's socks are red.	$\%$	$R = .2 \times T$
Jane ate 3/4 of the candy.		$J = 3/4 \times C$
For, per:	ratio	Division
Jane won 3 games for every 2 that Tom won	$\div$	$J/T = 3/2$
50 miles per hour		50 miles/hour
2 bleeps per revolution		2 bleeps/revolution

Sample Questions

Figuring out these problems takes more than just knowing a bunch of math formulas. You have to think about what math skills and tools you will apply to the questions in order to reason your way through to the correct answer.

1. The price of a sweater went up 20% since last year. If last year's price was x, what is this year's price in terms of x?

- Last year's price $= 100\%$ of x
- This year's price is 100% of x plus 20% of x.
  $(100/100)x + (20/100)x = 1.2x$

2. One year ago an average restaurant meal cost $12.00. Today, the average restaurant meal costs $15.00. By what percent has the cost of the meal increased?

You can figure percent increase by taking the difference in prices first and then expressing it as a percentage of the original price:

$15 − $12 = $3 difference.
What percentage of the original price is $3?

$$\left(\frac{x}{100}\right)12 = 3$$
$$\frac{x}{100} = \frac{3}{12}$$
$$12x = 300$$
$$x = 25\%$$

Or you can figure what percent the new price is of the old price:

15 is what percent of 12?

$$15 = \left(\frac{x}{100}\right)12.$$
$$\frac{15}{12} = \frac{x}{100}$$
$$x = 125\%$$

This tells you what percent the current price ($15) is of the old price ($12). But the question asks for the percent increase. So you have to subtract 100 percent from 125 percent.

$$125 − 100 = 25\% \text{ increase.}$$

3. The average height of four members of a six-person volleyball team is 175 cm. What does the average height in centimeters of the other 2 players have to be if the average height of the entire team equals 180 cm?

Start with the formula for average:

$$\frac{\text{sums of values}}{\text{number of values}} = \text{average}$$

Use what you know to find out the sum of the heights of the 4 members whose average is 175 cm.

$$\frac{\text{sum}}{4} = 175$$
$$\text{sum} = \frac{4}{(175)} = 700$$

The average of all 6 players is 180 cm.

$$\text{Average of } 6 = \frac{(\text{sum of } 4 + \text{sum of } 2)}{6}$$

$$180 = \frac{(700 + \text{sum of } 2)}{6}$$

$$1080 = 700 + \text{sum of } 2$$
$$1080 - 700 = \text{sum of } 2$$
$$380 = \text{sum of } 2$$

What is the average of the heights of the 2 players?
Average = sum/number of players
Average = 380/2 = 190 cm.

4. A car traveling at an average rate of 55 kilometers per hour made a trip in 6 hours. If it had traveled at an average rate of 50 kilometers per hour, the trip would have taken how many <u>minutes</u> longer?

- How long was the trip?
  Distance = rate $\times$ time
  Distance = 55 kph $\times$ 6 hours
  Distance = 330 km.

- How long does the 330-kilometer trip take if the car is traveling at 50 kilometers per hour?

  $$\text{Time} = \frac{\text{distance}}{\text{rate}}$$

  $$\text{Time} = \frac{330}{50}$$

  $$\text{Time} = 6\frac{3}{5} \text{ hours}$$

- What does the question ask?
  The difference <u>in minutes</u> between the two trips.

  $$\text{Difference} = \frac{3}{5} \text{ hour}$$

  $$\text{Difference} = ? \text{ minutes}$$

  $$\frac{3}{5} = \frac{x}{60}$$
  $$5x = 180$$
  $$x = 36 \text{ minutes}$$

Geometry

The geometry questions focus on your ability to recognize and use the special properties of many geometric figures. You will find questions requiring you to know about:

- Triangles, in general;
- Special triangles—right triangles, isosceles and equilateral triangles;
- Rectangles, squares, and other polygons;
- Areas and perimeters of simple figures;
- The angles formed by intersecting lines and angles involving parallel and perpendicular lines;
- Area, circumference, and arc degrees in a circle.

Triangles

Equilateral Triangles

The three sides of an equilateral triangle (a, b, c) are equal in length. The three angles (x, y, z) are also equal and they each measure 60 degrees ($x = y = z = 60$).

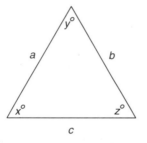

Isosceles Triangles

An isosceles triangle is a triangle with two sides of equal length ($m = n$). The angles opposite the equal sides are also equal ($x = y$).

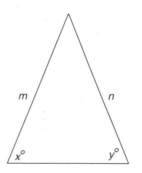

Right Triangles and the Pythagorean Theorem

You can get a lot of information out of figures that contain right triangles. And this information frequently involves the Pythagorean theorem:

> The square of the hypotenuse of a right triangle is equal to the sum of the squares of the other two sides.

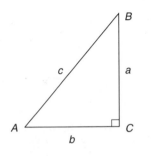

The hypotenuse is the longest side of the triangle and is opposite the right angle. The other two sides are usually referred to as legs. In the figure above:

- AB is the hypotenuse with length c.
- BC and AC are the two legs with lengths a and b, respectively.
- The Pythagorean theorem leads to the equation:

$$a^2 + b^2 = c^2$$

30°–60°–90° Right Triangles

The lengths of the sides of a 30°–60°–90° triangle are in the ratio of $1:\sqrt{3}:2$, as shown in the figure:

- Short leg $= x$
- Long leg $= x\sqrt{3}$
- Hypotenuse $= 2x$

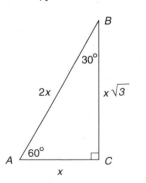

If you know the lengths of any two sides, the Pythagorean theorem will help you to find the length of the third.

For instance, if you know the length of the short leg is 1 and the length of the hypotenuse is 2, then the theorem gives you the length of the longer leg:

$$c^2 = a^2 + b^2$$
$$c = 2, b = 1$$
$$2^2 = 1^2 + a^2$$
$$4 = 1 + a^2$$
$$3 = a^2$$
$$\sqrt{3} = a$$

45°–45°–90° Triangle

The lengths of the sides of a 45°–45°–90° triangle are in the ratio of 1:1:$\sqrt{2}$, as shown in the figure below. If the equal sides are of length 1, apply the Pythagorean theorem to find the length of the hypotenuse:

$$c^2 = a^2 + b^2$$
$$a = 1, b = 1$$
$$c^2 = 1^2 + 1^2$$
$$c^2 = 1 + 1$$
$$c^2 = 2$$
$$c = \sqrt{2}$$

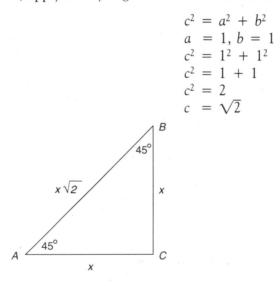

3–4–5 Triangle

The sides of a 3–4–5 right triangle are in the ratio of 3:4:5. In the figure below, if $x = 1$, then:

$$c^2 = a^2 + b^2$$
$$5^2 = 3^2 + 4^2$$
$$25 = 9 + 16$$
$$25 = 25$$

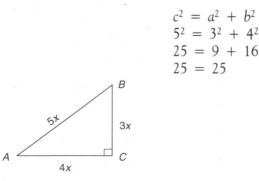

Quadrilaterals, Lines, and Angles

As with some triangles, you can figure out some things about the sides of quadrilaterals from their angles and some things about their angles from the lengths of their sides. In some special quadrilaterals—parallelograms, rectangles, and squares—there are relationships among the angles and sides that can help you solve geometry problems.

Parallelograms

In a parallelogram, the opposite angles are equal and the opposite sides are of equal length.

Angles BAD and BCD are equal; and angles ABC and ADC are equal. $AB = CD$ and $AD = BC$.

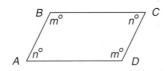

Rectangles

A rectangle is a special case of a parallelogram. In rectangles, all the angles are right angles.

Squares

A square is a special case of a rectangle in which all the sides are equal.

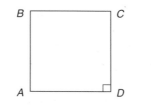

Notice that if you know the length of any side of a square, you also know the length of the diagonal.

The diagonal makes two 45°–45°–90° triangles with the sides of the square. So you can figure out the length of the sides from the length of the diagonal or the length of the diagonal from the length of a side.

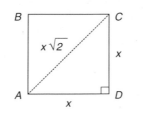

Areas and Perimeters

Rectangles and Squares

The formula for the area of any rectangle is:

$$\text{Area} = \text{length} \times \text{width}$$

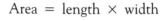

Because all sides of the square are equal, the length and width are often both referred to as the length of a side, s. So the area of a square can be written as:

$$\text{Area} = s^2$$

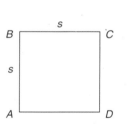

Perimeters of Rectangles and Squares

The perimeter of a simple closed figure is the length all the way around the figure. Because the opposite sides of rectangles are equal, the formula for the perimeter of a rectangle is:

$$\text{Perimeter of rectangle} = 2(\text{length} + \text{width}) = 2(l + w)$$

The same is true for any parallelogram. For a square, it's even easier. Because all four sides of a square are equal, the perimeter of a square is:

$$\text{Perimeter of a square} = 4(\text{length of any side}) = 4s$$

Area of Triangles

The area of a triangle is:

$$A = \left(\frac{1}{2}\right)bh$$

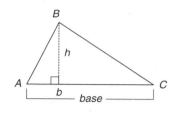

- b is the base;
- h is the height, a perpendicular line drawn from a vertex of the triangle to the base.

HINT

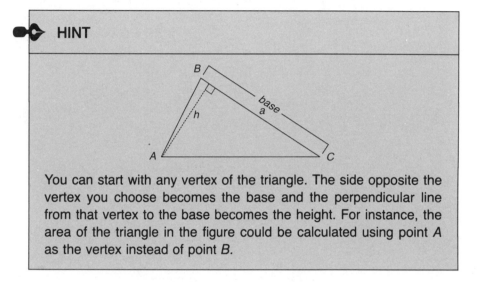

You can start with any vertex of the triangle. The side opposite the vertex you choose becomes the base and the perpendicular line from that vertex to the base becomes the height. For instance, the area of the triangle in the figure could be calculated using point *A* as the vertex instead of point *B*.

Area of Parallelograms

To find the area of a parallelogram, you "square up" the slanted side of the parallelogram by dropping a perpendicular—line *BE* in the figure shown below. This makes a right triangle *ABE*.

If you take this triangle away from the parallelogram and add it to the other side (triangle *DCF*) you have a rectangle with the same area as the original parallelogram.

The area of the rectangle is *length* × *width*.

The width of this rectangle is the same as the height of the parallelogram. So the formula for the area of a parallelogram is:

$$\text{Area} = \text{length} \times \text{height}$$

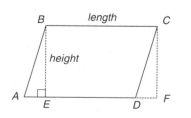

Other Polygons

Occasionally, a math question will ask you to work with polygons other than triangles and quadrilaterals. Here are a few things to remember about other polygons.

Angles in a Polygon

You can figure out the total number of degrees in the interior angles of most polygons by dividing the polygon into triangles:

- From any vertex, divide the polygon into as many nonoverlapping triangles as possible. Use only straight lines. Make sure that all the space inside the polygon is divided into triangles.
- Count the triangles. In this figure, there are four triangles.
- There is a total of 180° in the angles of each triangle, so multiply the number of triangles by 180. The product will be the sum of the angles in the polygon (720° in the hexagon shown below).

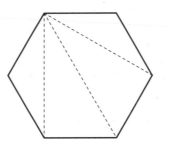

Sample Problem

In the figure shown below, lengths *AB*, *BD*, and *DC* are all $3\sqrt{2}$ units long. Angles *BAD* and *BCD* are both 45°. What is the perimeter of *ABCD*? What is the area of *ABCD*?

You are asked for the perimeter and the area of the figure. For the perimeter you will need to know the lengths of the sides. For the area you will need to know the length and height.

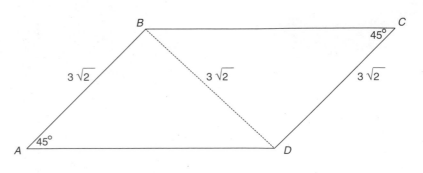

Perimeter

- You are given the lengths of 3 lines, all of which are the same: $3\sqrt{2}$.
- You are given two angles, both of which are the same: 45°.
- $\sqrt{2}$ and 45° are both characteristics of a special right triangle: 45°–45°–90°.
- ABD is a triangle with two equal sides.
- BCD is a triangle with two equal sides.
- So, they are both isosceles triangles.
- Angle BCD is 45°, so angle CBD has to equal 45°.
- The same is true for angles ADB and DAB, which both equal 45°.
- Both triangles are 45°–45°–90° triangles.
- You can figure out the lengths of AD and BC by the Pythagorean theorem:
$$AD^2 = (3\sqrt{2})^2 + (3\sqrt{2})^2 = 36, \text{ so } AD = 6$$
- Do the same for the length of BC to find that BC = 6.
- You now can add up the lengths of the sides to get the perimeter:
$$2 (6 + 3\sqrt{2}) = 12 + 6\sqrt{2}.$$

Area

- ABCD is a parallelogram. You know this because both sets of opposite sides are equal: AB = CD and AD = BC.
- That means that you can use the formula for the area of a parallelogram: area = length × height.
- To find the height, drop a perpendicular from B.
- That creates another 45°–45°–90° triangle whose hypotenuse is AB.
- The ratio of the sides of a 45°–45°–90° triangle is 1:1:$\sqrt{2}$.
- From that ratio, you know the height of the figure is 3.
- With the height, you can then calculate the area.

If you label everything you figure out as you go along, you will end up with a figure that looks like the one below.

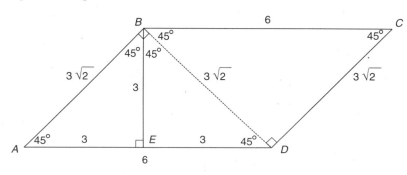

Circles   Diameter

The diameter of a circle is a line segment that passes through the center and has its end points on the circle. All diameters of the same circle have equal lengths.

Radius

The radius of a circle is a line segment extending from the center of the circle to a point on the circle. In the figure shown below, *OB* and *OA* are radii.

All radii of the same circle have equal lengths, and the radius is half the diameter. In the figure, the length of *OB* equals the length of *OA*.

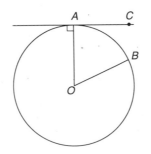

Arc

An arc is a part of a circle. In the figure above, *AB* is an arc. An arc can be measured in degrees or in units of length.

If you form an angle by drawing radii from the ends of the arc to the center of the circle, the number of degrees in the arc (arc *AB* in the figure) equals the number of degrees in the angle formed by the two radii at the center of the circle (∠*AOB*).

Tangent to a Circle

A tangent to a circle is a line that touches the circle at only one point. In the figure, line *AC* is a tangent.

Circumference

The circumference of a circle is equal to π times the diameter *d* (or π times twice the radius *r*).

$$\text{Circumference} = \pi d$$
$$\text{Circumference} = 2\pi r$$

If the diameter is 16, the circumference is 16π. If the radius is 3, the circumference is 2(3)π or 6π.

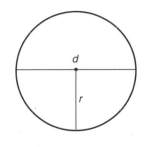

Area

The area of a circle is equal to π times the square of the radius.

$$\text{Area} = \pi r^2$$

Sample Question

In the figure shown below, A is the center of a circle whose area is 25π. B and C are points on the circle. Angle ABC is 45°. What is the length of line segment BC?

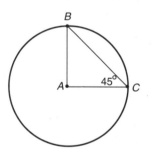

- Point A is the center of the circle.
- That makes both line segments AB and AC radii, which means that they are of equal length.
- Because AB and AC are equal, $\triangle ABC$ is an isosceles triangle.
- The area of the circle is 25π.
- The formula for the area of a circle is πr^2. You can use that formula to figure out the length of the radius, r. That length, r, is also the length of the legs of the triangle whose hypotenuse (BC) is the length you are trying to figure out.

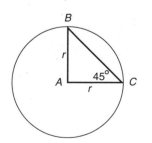

What is the value of r?

$$\text{Area} = \pi r^2$$
$$\text{Area} = 25\pi$$
$$r^2 = 25$$
$$r = 5$$

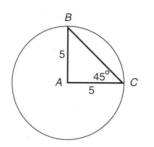

Now turn to the triangle:

- ABC is an isosceles triangle, so one angle opposite one of the equal sides is 45°.
- That means the angle opposite the other equal side is also 45°.
- The remaining angle is 90°.

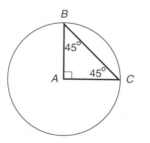

Figuring out the final answer to the problem is a simple matter of working through the Pythagorean theorem or remembering that the ratio of the sides of 45°–45°–90° triangles is $1:1:\sqrt{2}$. The answer is $5\sqrt{2}$.

Miscellaneous Math Questions

Most math questions fall into the three broad areas of arithmetic, algebra, and geometry. Some questions, however, do not fall neatly into one of these areas. Miscellaneous questions on the math test cover areas such as:

- Data interpretation;
- Counting and ordering problems;
- Special symbols;
- Logical analysis;
- Probability.

Data Interpretation

Your primary task in these questions is to interpret information in graphs, tables, or charts, and then compare quantities, recognize trends and changes in the data, or perform calculations based on the information you have found.

A question on a graph like the one shown below might require you to identify specific pieces of information (data), compare data from different parts of the graph, and manipulate the data.

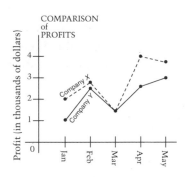

When working with data interpretation questions, you have to:

- Look at the graph, table, or chart to make sure you understand it. Make sure you know what type of information is being displayed.
- Read the question carefully.

HINT

With data interpretation questions—graphs, charts, and tables— always make sure you understand the information being presented:

- Read the labels.
- Make sure you know the units.
- Make sure you understand what is happening to the data as you move through the table, graph, or chart.

The graph below shows profits over time. The higher the point on the vertical axis, the greater the profits. (Each tic mark on the vertical axis is another $1,000.) As you move to the right along the horizontal axis, months are passing.

Sample Questions

1. In what month or months did each company make the greatest profit?

Follow the line labeled Company X to its highest point. Then check the month at the bottom of the graph. Follow the same procedure for Company Y.

For Company X, the greatest profit was made in April.
For Company Y, the greatest profit was made in May.

2. Between which two consecutive months did each company show the greatest increase in profit?

The increase (or decrease) in profit is shown by the steepness or "slope" of the graph.

For Company X, it's easy to see that the biggest jump occurred between March and April.

For Company Y, you have to be a little more careful. The biggest increase in profits occurred between January and February. You know this because the slope of the line connecting January and February is the steepest.

The increase between January and February is about $1,500, which is greater than the increase for any other pair of consecutive months.

3. In what month did the profits of the two companies show the greatest difference?

To figure this out, you have to compare one company to the other, month by month. The month in which the dots are farthest apart is the one in which there is the greatest difference between the two companies. The distance between the two graph lines is greatest in April.

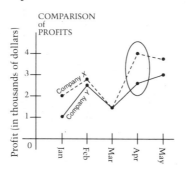

4. If the rate of increase or decrease for each company continues for the next six months at the same rate shown between April and May, which company would have higher profits at the end of that time?

This question is asking you to look at the graph and project changes in the future. To project changes, extend the lines between April and May for each company. The lines cross pretty quickly—well before six more months have passed. So the answer is that Company Y would be doing better in six months if the rates of change from month to month stay the same as they were between April and May.

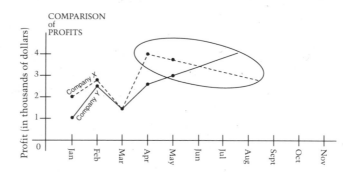

From Graph to Table

The same information presented in the profit chart could be presented in a profit table, which might look something like this:

	Profits (in dollars)				
	Jan.	Feb.	Mar.	Apr.	May
Company X	2,000	2,750	1,500	4,000	3,750
Company Y	1,000	2,500	1,500	2,500	3,000

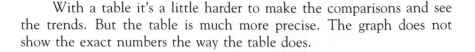

With a table it's a little harder to make the comparisons and see the trends. But the table is much more precise. The graph does not show the exact numbers the way the table does.

Counting and Ordering Problems

Counting and ordering problems involve figuring out how many ways you can select or arrange members of groups, such as letters of the alphabet, numbers, or menu selections.

Fundamental Counting Principle

The fundamental counting principle is the principle by which you figure out how many possibilities there are for selecting members of a group:

If one event can happen in *n* ways, and a second event can happen in *m* ways, the total ways in which the two events can happen is *n* times *m*.

For example:

On a restaurant menu, there are three appetizers and four main courses. How many different dinners can be ordered if each dinner consists of one appetizer and one main course?

The first event is the choice of appetizer, and there are three choices available. The second event is the choice of main course, and there are four main courses. The total number of different dinners is, therefore, $3 \times 4 = 12$.

This idea can be extended to more than two events:

If you had two choices for beverage added to your choices for appetizer and main course, you would multiply the total by 2:
$2(3 \times 4) = 24$.

If you also had three choices for dessert, you would multiply by 3:
$3(3 \times 4 \times 2) = 72$.

For example:

A security system uses a four-letter password, but no letter can be used more than once. How many possible passwords are there?

- For the first letter, there are 26 possible choices—one for each letter in the alphabet.
- Because you cannot reuse any letters, there are only 25 choices for the second letter (26 minus the letter used in the first letter of the password).
- There are only 24 choices for the third letter, and only 23 choices for the fourth.

The total number of passwords will be $26 \times 25 \times 24 \times 23$.

Special Symbols

To test your ability to learn and apply mathematical concepts, a special symbol is sometimes introduced and defined.

These symbols generally have unusual looking signs ($\star$, $*$, §) so you won't confuse them with real mathematical symbols.

The key to these questions is to make sure that you read the definition carefully.

A typical special symbol question might look something like this:

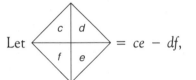

where c, d, e, and f are integers.

What is the value of

To answer this question, substitute the numbers according to the definition:

- Substitute 2 for c, 3 for d, 4 for f, and 1 for e.

- 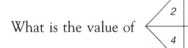 $= (2)(1) - (3)(4) = -10$

Some questions will ask you to apply the definition of the symbol to more complicated situations. For instance:

- You may be asked to compare two values, each of which requires the use of the symbol.

- You may be asked to evaluate an expression that involves multiplying, dividing, adding, squaring, or subtracting terms that involve the symbol.
- You could be asked to solve an equation that involves the use of the symbol.
- You may find a special symbol as part of a Quantitative Comparison question.

Logical Analysis

Some math questions emphasize logical thinking. You have to figure out how to draw conclusions from a set of facts.

Here's an example:

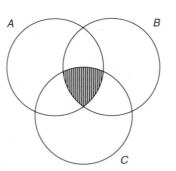

In the figure above, circular region A represents the set of all numbers of the form $2m$, circular region B represents the set of all numbers of the form n^2, circular region C represents the set of all numbers of the form 10^k, where m, n, and k are positive integers. Which of the following numbers belongs in the set represented by the shaded region?

(A) 2
(B) 4
(C) 10
(D) 25
(E) 100

Answering this question correctly depends on understanding the logic of the figure:

- The question is asking about the shaded region.
- The shaded region is part of *all* of the circles.
- Therefore, any numbers in the shaded region have to obey the rules for *all* the circles:

    The rule for A: The numbers must be of the form $2m$, which means that they must all be even numbers.

And the rule for B: the numbers must be of the form n^2, which means that they must all be perfect squares.

And the rule for C: the numbers must also be of the form 10^k, which means they have to be some whole-number power of 10 (10, 100, 1000, 10000, etc.)

- When you realize that the numbers in the shaded area must obey *all* the individual rules, you have figured out the logic of the question, and the answer is easy. The only choice that obeys *all* the rules is (E).

CHAPTER 10

Sample Mathematics Questions and Answers

Introduction

On the math test, the questions are grouped by question type: five-choice Multiple-Choice questions, Quantitative Comparison questions, and Grid-in questions (called "Student-Produced Response" on the SAT). But the content areas tested will change from question to question. You may have a geometry question, followed by an arithmetic question, followed by an algebra question.

This makes the mathematics section of the test different from most of your classroom math tests. To do well on the math portion, you must be flexible. You have to be able to shift quickly from one type of math content to another. To help you get used to these shifts, the sample math questions are presented the way they appear on the test, in mixed order in terms of the kinds of skills and concepts required to answer them.

Question Difficulty

The difficulty of every question is determined before that question is used in a test. The sample questions are labeled easy, medium, or hard.

Grid-in Questions

It's very important for you to get used to the Grid-in questions. The special rules for expressing and entering the answers to the Grid-in questions on the answer sheet were presented in Chapter 9. For many of the Grid-in questions, the answers that are acceptable and the different ways the answers can be entered are shown in this chapter.

Alternate Methods

As you work with the math questions, you'll find that many of them can be solved in more than one way. There is often a direct method that depends on your remembering and applying some specific pieces of information. Other methods may take longer, relying on your ability to reason out the problem step-by-step from the facts given. Still others will depend on some special insight.

The questions in this chapter are meant to give you practice with the different types of problems you'll meet on the SAT and to help you identify both your strengths and the areas where you need to do more work. In addition to the correct answers, solutions to the problems are also given. If you're able to answer a question correctly but used a different solution from the one given, don't worry. There are often several ways to solve a problem. However, if you *don't* know how to solve a problem, study the solution in the answer section. It could help you answer a similar question on the SAT.

> ### HINT
>
> The best method for approaching the math questions is the method that you can work with most comfortably, confidently, efficiently, and accurately. However, if you aren't familiar with one of the methods shown, it might be a good idea to study it carefully so you can increase your efficiency if you meet a similar type of problem later. You might also want to refresh your math skills by studying the concepts discussed in Chapter 9, Mathematics Review.

Five-Choice Multiple-Choice Questions

Practice Questions Chapter 9, Mathematics Review, discusses the five-choice format of multiple-choice math questions and suggests some approaches to solving the kinds of problems you'll find in that section of the SAT. Remember that while the questions are presented in the familiar five-choice (A) to (E) format, the content areas tested will vary from question to question.

If you find you're having trouble figuring out the solutions to the following 14 problems, turn to the Answers and Explanations, which start on page 172.

In this section solve each problem, using any available space on the page for scratchwork. Then decide which is the best of the choices given and fill in the corresponding oval on the answer sheet.

Notes:

(1) The use of a calculator is permitted. All numbers used are real numbers.

(2) Figures that accompany problems in this test are intended to provide information useful in solving the problems. They are drawn as accurately as possible EXCEPT when it is stated in a specific problem that the figure is not drawn to scale. All figures lie in a plane unless otherwise indicated.

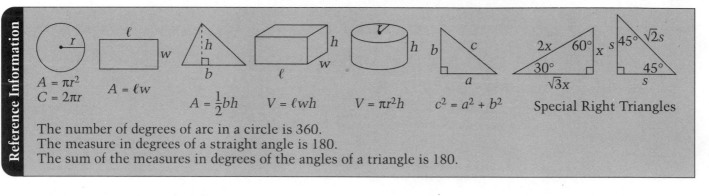

$A = \pi r^2$
$C = 2\pi r$

$A = \ell w$

$A = \frac{1}{2}bh$

$V = \ell w h$

$V = \pi r^2 h$

$c^2 = a^2 + b^2$

Special Right Triangles

The number of degrees of arc in a circle is 360.
The measure in degrees of a straight angle is 180.
The sum of the measures in degrees of the angles of a triangle is 180.

---

1 $\frac{1}{2} \cdot \frac{2}{3} \cdot \frac{3}{4} \cdot \frac{4}{5} \cdot \frac{5}{6} \cdot \frac{6}{7} =$

(A) $\frac{1}{7}$

(B) $\frac{3}{7}$

(C) $\frac{21}{27}$

(D) $\frac{6}{7}$

(E) $\frac{7}{8}$

2 If $\frac{x}{3} = x^2$, the value of x can be which of the following?

I. $-\frac{1}{3}$

II. 0

III. $\frac{1}{3}$

(A) I only
(B) II only
(C) III only
(D) II and III only
(E) I, II, and III

3 All numbers divisible by both 4 and 15 are also divisible by which of the following?

(A) 6
(B) 8
(C) 18
(D) 24
(E) 45

5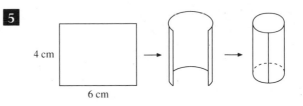

The figure above shows how a rectangular piece of paper is rolled to form a cylindrical tube. If it is assumed that the 4-centimeter sides of the rectangle meet with no overlap, what is the area, in square centimeters, of the base of the cylindrical tube?

(A) 16π
(B) 9π
(C) 4π
(D) $\dfrac{9}{\pi}$
(E) $\dfrac{4}{\pi}$

4 If United States imports increased 20 percent and exports decreased 10 percent during a certain year, the ratio of imports to exports at the end of the year was how many times the ratio at the beginning of the year?

(A) $\dfrac{12}{11}$

(B) $\dfrac{4}{3}$

(C) $\dfrac{11}{8}$

(D) $\dfrac{3}{2}$

(E) 2

6 The odometer of a new automobile functions improperly and registers only 2 miles for every 3 miles driven. If the odometer indicates 48 miles, how many miles has the automobile actually been driven?

(A) 144
(B) 72
(C) 64
(D) 32
(E) 24

169

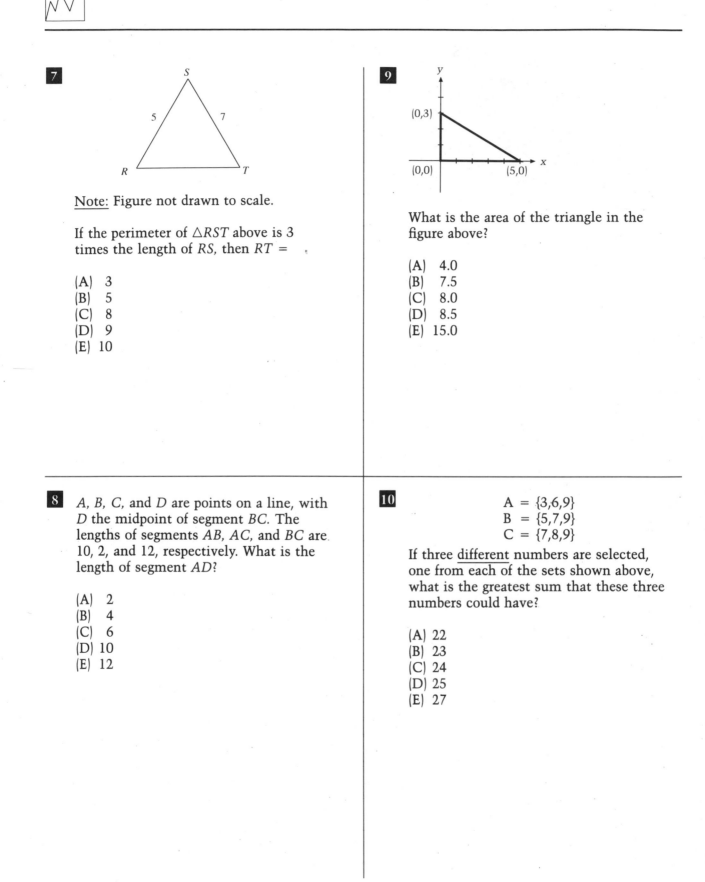

7

Note: Figure not drawn to scale.

If the perimeter of △RST above is 3 times the length of RS, then RT =

(A)   3
(B)   5
(C)   8
(D)   9
(E)   10

9

What is the area of the triangle in the figure above?

(A)   4.0
(B)   7.5
(C)   8.0
(D)   8.5
(E)   15.0

8   A, B, C, and D are points on a line, with D the midpoint of segment BC. The lengths of segments AB, AC, and BC are 10, 2, and 12, respectively. What is the length of segment AD?

(A)   2
(B)   4
(C)   6
(D)   10
(E)   12

10

A = {3,6,9}
B = {5,7,9}
C = {7,8,9}

If three different numbers are selected, one from each of the sets shown above, what is the greatest sum that these three numbers could have?

(A) 22
(B) 23
(C) 24
(D) 25
(E) 27

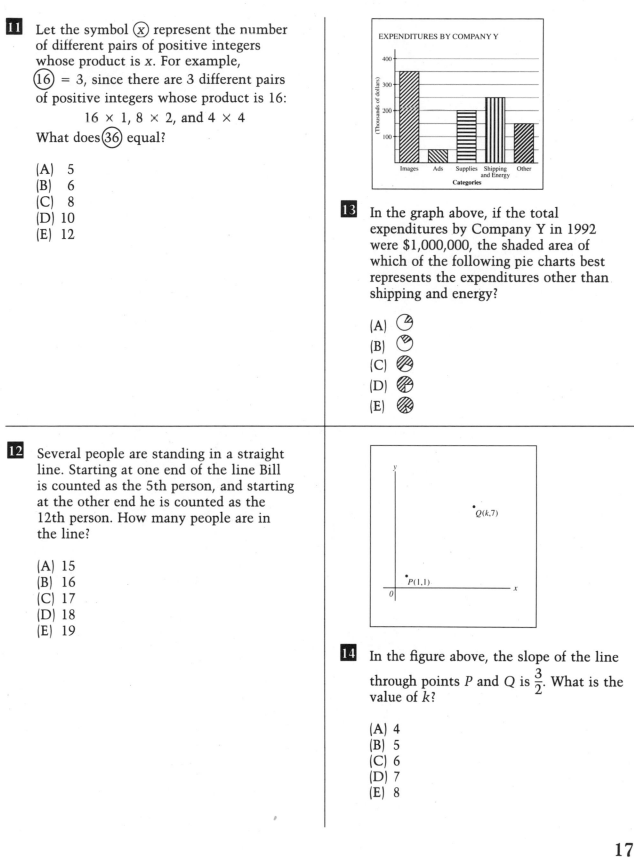

11 Let the symbol ⊗ represent the number of different pairs of positive integers whose product is x. For example, ⑯ = 3, since there are 3 different pairs of positive integers whose product is 16:

16 × 1, 8 × 2, and 4 × 4

What does ㊱ equal?

(A) 5
(B) 6
(C) 8
(D) 10
(E) 12

13 In the graph above, if the total expenditures by Company Y in 1992 were $1,000,000, the shaded area of which of the following pie charts best represents the expenditures other than shipping and energy?

(A)
(B)
(C)
(D)
(E)

12 Several people are standing in a straight line. Starting at one end of the line Bill is counted as the 5th person, and starting at the other end he is counted as the 12th person. How many people are in the line?

(A) 15
(B) 16
(C) 17
(D) 18
(E) 19

14 In the figure above, the slope of the line through points P and Q is $\frac{3}{2}$. What is the value of k?

(A) 4
(B) 5
(C) 6
(D) 7
(E) 8

Answers and Explanations

> **HINT**
>
> If it seems like you have a lot of calculating to do, look for a shortcut.

QUESTION 1
Arithmetic shortcuts

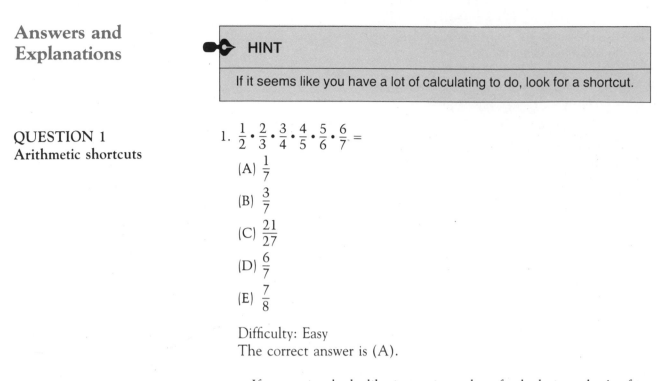

1. $\dfrac{1}{2} \cdot \dfrac{2}{3} \cdot \dfrac{3}{4} \cdot \dfrac{4}{5} \cdot \dfrac{5}{6} \cdot \dfrac{6}{7} =$

(A) $\dfrac{1}{7}$

(B) $\dfrac{3}{7}$

(C) $\dfrac{21}{27}$

(D) $\dfrac{6}{7}$

(E) $\dfrac{7}{8}$

Difficulty: Easy
The correct answer is (A).

If a question looks like it requires a lot of calculating, that's often a tip-off that something else is going on. There's usually a quick way to find the answer. In this question, all the fractions are being multiplied, so canceling is a possibility. The denominators cancel diagonally with the numerators that follow.

- The 2 from $\dfrac{1}{2}$ cancels with the 2 from $\dfrac{2}{3}$.

- The 3 from $\dfrac{2}{3}$ cancels with the 3 from $\dfrac{3}{4}$.

- And so on, right down to the equal sign.

$$\dfrac{1}{\cancel{2}} \cdot \dfrac{\cancel{2}}{\cancel{3}} \cdot \dfrac{\cancel{3}}{\cancel{4}} \cdot \dfrac{\cancel{4}}{\cancel{5}} \cdot \dfrac{\cancel{5}}{\cancel{6}} \cdot \dfrac{\cancel{6}}{7}$$

After you have canceled everything that can be canceled, you are left with the fraction $\dfrac{1}{7}$.

QUESTION 2
Roman numeral answer format

2. If $\frac{x}{3} = x^2$, the value of x can be which of the following?

I. $-\frac{1}{3}$

II. 0

III. $\frac{1}{3}$

(A) I only
(B) II only
(C) III only
(D) II and III only
(E) I, II, and III

Difficulty: Hard
The correct answer is (D).

HINT

When checking the values of expressions, remember the rules for multiplying positive and negative numbers:

$$(+)(+) = (+)$$
$$(-)(+) = (-)$$
$$(-)(-) = (+)$$

This means that the square of any nonzero number will be positive.

Question 2 uses what is referred to as the Roman numeral answer format. This format is used in both math and Reading Passage questions. The way to approach these is to work on each Roman numeral as a separate true/false question. Once you have decided (and marked) each Roman numeral as true or false, it's easy to find the correct answer.

Roman Numeral I: Can the Value of x Be $-\frac{1}{3}$?
You could test this answer by substituting $-\frac{1}{3}$ for x in the equation and seeing whether the result is true. But you can also reason this question out without substituting numbers:

- x^2 has to be a positive number, because any nonzero number squared is positive.

- If x were negative, $\frac{x}{3}$ would be negative.

- So $\dfrac{x}{3}$ is negative and x^2 is positive.
- Therefore, x cannot be $-\dfrac{1}{3}$.

    Mark Roman numeral I with an "F" for false.

Roman Numeral II: Can the Value of x Be 0?

This is a very easy substitution to make:

$$\dfrac{x}{3} = x^2$$
$$\dfrac{0}{3} = 0^2 = 0$$

Roman numeral II is true, so mark it with a "T" for true.

Roman Numeral III: Can the Value of x Be $\dfrac{1}{3}$?

Substitute $\dfrac{1}{3}$ for x:

If $x = \dfrac{1}{3}$, $\dfrac{x}{3} = \dfrac{1}{9}$.

Also, $x^2 = (\dfrac{1}{3})^2 = \dfrac{1}{9}$.

Roman numeral III is true, so mark it with a "T" for true.

Check the Answers:

You now know whether each of the Roman numeral statements is true or false:

    I is false.
    II is true.
    III is true.
    Find the answer that says only II and III are true, choice (D).

HINT

Remember the approach to Roman numeral format answers:

- Take each Roman numeral statement as a separate true/false question.
- Mark each Roman numeral with a "T" for True or an "F" for False as you evaluate it.
- Look for the answer that matches your "T"s and "F"s.

QUESTION 3
"Divisible by"

3. All numbers divisible by both 4 and 15 are also divisible by which of the following?

(A) 6
(B) 8
(C) 18
(D) 24
(E) 45

Difficulty: Medium
The correct answer is (A).

HINT

"Divisible by" means that the remainder is zero after the division.

8 is divisible by 4, but it is not divisible by 3.

First find a number that is divisible by both 4 and 15. One such number is 60. Now check each choice to see if 60 is divisible by that choice. 60 is divisible by choice (A) but is not divisible by any of the other choices. The answer must be (A).

HINT

When the arithmetic is simple and you understand what the question is asking, it's ok to find the answer by:

• checking each choice
• eliminating choices

In more complicated problems, this can take more time than finding a solution through mathematical reasoning.

175

QUESTION 4
Percent increase and decrease

4. If United States imports increased 20 percent and exports decreased 10 percent during a certain year, the ratio of imports to exports at the end of the year was how many times the ratio at the beginning of the year?

(A) $\frac{12}{11}$

(B) $\frac{4}{3}$

(C) $\frac{11}{8}$

(D) $\frac{3}{2}$

(E) 2

Difficulty: Hard
The correct answer is (B).

Express What You Know in Mathematical Terms

- State the ratio of imports to exports as $\frac{I}{E}$.

- At the end of the year, imports were up by 20%. So the change in imports can be expressed as 100% of beginning year imports *plus* 20%:

$$100\% + 20\% = 120\%$$

- At the end of the year, exports were down by 10%. So the change in exports can be expressed as 100% of beginning year exports *minus* 10%:

$$100\% - 10\% = 90\%$$

- Express the ratio of imports to exports at the end of the year:

$$\frac{I}{E} = \frac{120\%}{90\%}$$

Cancel the %s and reduce the fraction.

$$\frac{120\%}{90\%}$$
$$= \frac{12}{9}$$
$$= \frac{4}{3}$$

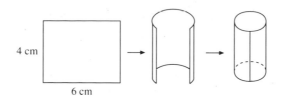

QUESTION 5
Two- and three-dimensional figures

5. The figure above shows how a rectangular piece of paper is rolled to form a cylindrical tube. If it is assumed that the 4-centimeter sides of the rectangle meet with no overlap, what is the area, in square centimeters, of the base of the cylindrical tube?

(A) 16π
(B) 9π
(C) 4π
(D) $\dfrac{9}{\pi}$
(E) $\dfrac{4}{\pi}$

Difficulty: Hard
The correct answer is (D).

HINT

Label diagrams and figures with the information you have. This often reveals key information that you need to answer the question.

What Do You Know?

- You know the *circumference* of the circle.
- Label the middle and right-hand figures in the diagram.

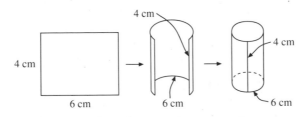

Notice that the 4-centimeter sides meet to form the seam in the cylinder and the 6 centimeter sides curl around to become the top and bottom of the cylinder.

- So the circumference of the circle is 6 centimeters.

177

Are There Any Formulas That Will Solve the Problem?

The question has now become a rather simple one. You know the circumference of the circle, and you have to figure out the area.

- There is no single formula to calculate the area, but you can get there in two steps:
  Relate the radius to the circumference by the formula:

$$\text{Circumference} = 2\pi r$$

  Relate the area to the radius by the formula:

$$\text{Area} = \pi r^2$$

- You know the circumference, so start there and work toward the area. The radius (r) is the common term in the two formulas so start by solving for r.

Apply the Formula to Get the Answer

$$\text{Circumference} = 2\pi r$$
$$6 = 2\pi r$$
$$\pi r = 3$$
$$r = \frac{3}{\pi}$$

- Now use the value for r in the formula for the area.

$$A = \pi r^2$$
$$r = \frac{3}{\pi}$$
$$A = \pi\left(\frac{3}{\pi}\right)^2$$
$$A = \pi\left(\frac{9}{\pi^2}\right)$$
$$A = \frac{9}{\pi}$$

QUESTION 6
Proportions

6. The odometer of a new automobile functions improperly and registers only 2 miles for every 3 miles driven. If the odometer indicates 48 miles, how many miles has the automobile actually been driven?

(A) 144
(B) 72
(C) 64
(D) 32
(E) 24

Difficulty: Medium
The correct answer is (B).

In this problem you are told that the odometer registers only 2 miles for every 3 miles driven. So the ratio of miles registered to miles driven is 2 to 3 or $\frac{2}{3}$. This can be expressed as

$$\frac{\text{odometer reading}}{\text{actual miles}} = \frac{2}{3}$$

If the odometer indicates 48 miles, the actual miles can be found using the above relationship as follows:

$$\frac{48}{x} = \frac{2}{3}$$
$$2x = 144$$
$$x = 72$$

So if the odometer indicates 48 miles, the actual number of miles driven is 72.

How to Avoid Errors When Working with Ratios

The most important thing with ratios is to be consistent in the way you set them up. If you mix up the terms, you won't get the correct answer. For instance, if you put the registered mileage in the numerator of one ratio but the actual mileage in the numerator of the other ratio, you will come up with a wrong answer:

$$\frac{3}{2} = \frac{48}{x}$$
$$3x = 96$$
$$x = \frac{96}{3} = 32 \text{ miles Wrong!}$$

Make a "Does-It-Make-Sense?" Check

When you arrive at an answer to a word problem, check to see whether it makes sense. The question states that the actual mileage is greater than the registered mileage. So the actual mileage has to be a number *larger* than 48.

Your check should warn you not to choose the incorrect answer (D) 32 that was obtained by setting up the wrong ratio.

HINT

A quick "make-sense" check before you start working on a question can help you eliminate some of the answers right away. If you realize that the actual mileage has to be greater than the registered mileage, you can eliminate answers D and E immediately.

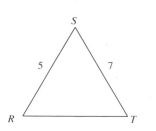

QUESTION 7
Figures not drawn to scale

7. If the perimeter of △*RST* above is 3 times the length of *RS*, then *RT* =

(A) 3
(B) 5
(C) 8
(D) 9
(E) 10

Difficulty: Easy
The correct answer is (A).

"<u>Note:</u> Figure not drawn to scale" means that the points and angles are in their relative positions, but the lengths of the sides and the sizes of the angles may not be as pictured.

What Do You Know?

- The perimeter of the triangle is the sum of the lengths of the three sides.
- The question states that the perimeter is 3 times the length of *RS*.
- *RS* is 5 units long.
- *ST* is 7 units long.

Express the Problem Using an Equation

- The perimeter is equal to three times the length of *RS*.
- That means that the perimeter is 3 times 5 or 15.
- So $5 + 7 + RT = 15$
$$RT = 3$$

HINT

It's always a good idea to draw the lines and figures that are described in a question if a figure is not given.

Make sure that what you draw fits the information in the question.

Don't worry about how pretty the figure is. It only has to be neat enough for you to work with it.

QUESTION 8
Draw your own figures . . . carefully

8. *A*, *B*, *C*, and *D* are points on a line, with *D* the midpoint of segment *BC*. The lengths of segments *AB*, *AC*, and *BC* are 10, 2, and 12, respectively. What is the length of segment *AD*?

(A) 2
(B) 4
(C) 6
(D) 10
(E) 12

Difficulty: Medium
The correct answer is (B).

The key to this question lies in *not* jumping to incorrect conclusions. The question names the points on a line. It gives you a variety of information about the points. The one thing it *does not* do is tell you the order in which the points fall.

Many students assume that the order of the points is A, then B, then C, then D. As you will see, if you try to locate the points in this order, you will be unable to answer the question.

What Is the Question Asking?

The question asks for the length of line segment *AD*. In order to find this length, you have to establish the relative positions of the four points on the line.

What Do You Know?

Try to draw the figure. You might be tempted to locate point A first. Unfortunately, you don't have enough information about A, yet, to place it.

- You can place B, C, and D because D is the midpoint of BC.

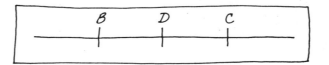

- You know the lengths of three of the line segments:

$$AB = 10$$
$$AC = 2$$
$$BC = 12$$

- Because you know where BC is, you can label the length of BC.

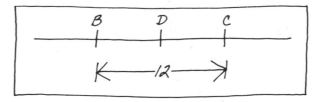

Build the Figure, Adding What You Know and What You Can Figure Out

Because D is the midpoint of BC, you know that BD and DC are each 6 units long.

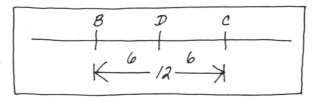

Where can you place point A?

It has to be 2 units from C, because AC = 2.

It also has to be 10 units from B, because AB = 10.

So the only location for A is between B and C, but closer to C.

- Place point A and mark the distances.

    It is now an easy matter to figure out the answer to the question:

- DC is 6 units.
- A is 2 units closer to D than C, so AD is 4 units.

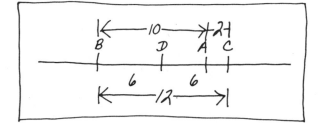

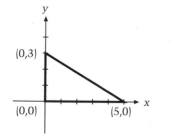

QUESTION 9
Figures on a coordinate plane

9. What is the area of the triangle in the figure above?

(A) 4.0
(B) 7.5
(C) 8.0
(D) 8.5
(E) 15.0

Difficulty: Medium
The correct answer is (B).

> **HINT**
>
> The coordinate system provides essential information for solving this problem.
>
> Your knowledge of the coordinate system can give you information about lengths and angles, such as:
>
> - Whether lines are parallel, perpendicular, or neither;
> - Whether figures are squares, special triangles, etc.;
> - How long line segments are;
> - Whether angles are right angles or other special angles.

The figure provides all the information you need to answer the question.

What Is the Question Asking?

You are asked to figure out the area of a triangle that is defined by three points on a coordinate plane.

What Do You Know?

- The triangle in the figure is a right triangle with the right angle at the lower left.
- Because it is a right triangle, its base and height are the two sides that form the right angle.
- The area of a triangle is $\frac{1}{2}bh$
- The base of the triangle extends from point (0,0) to point (5,0). So it is 5 units long.
- The height of the triangle extends from point (0,0) to point (0,3). So it is 3 units long.

$$\begin{aligned} \text{Area} &= \frac{1}{2}bh \\ &= \frac{1}{2}(3)(5) \\ &= \frac{1}{2}(15) \\ &= 7.5 \end{aligned}$$

HINT

If you are presented with a math question that shows the grid lines of a graph, you may rely on the accuracy of those lines.

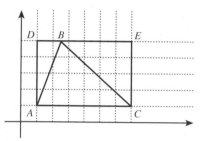

You can use the grid on the graph above to determine the following information:

- AC is 6 units long.
- ADEC is a rectangle.
- Side AD is 4 units long.
- The height of the triangle ABC is the same as the width of the rectangle (ADEC). So the height of the triangle is 4 units.
- The area of the triangle is $\frac{1}{2}$ the area of the rectangle.
- The area of a rectangle = width × length = AD × AC = 4 × 6 = 24 units.
- The area of the triangle = $\frac{1}{2}$(base × height) = $\frac{1}{2}$(AC × AD) = $\frac{1}{2}$(6 × 4) = 12 units.

QUESTION 10
Logical analysis

10.　　　　　　　A = {3,6,9}
　　　　　　　　B = {5,7,9}
　　　　　　　　C = {7,8,9}

If three <u>different</u> numbers are selected, one from each of the sets shown above, what is the greatest sum that these three numbers could have?

(A) 22
(B) 23
(C) 24
(D) 25
(E) 27

Difficulty: Medium
The correct answer is (C).

This question challenges your ability to reason with numbers. In other words, it is more a question of logic than of arithmetic.

What Is the Question Asking?

The question asks what is the largest sum you can get if you choose one number from each set and add those numbers together. There's a catch, however. Each number you select must be <u>different</u>. So you *cannot* take the largest number, 9, from each set, add the nines together, and come up with choice (E) 27.

What Do You Know?

- 9 is the largest number in each set.
- You can only take one number 9. This means that you will have to take the second largest number from two of the sets.

Make Your Selections

- The second largest number in set A is 6, which is smaller than the second largest number in sets B and C. So select 9 from set A.
- The other two choices are now easy. Take the largest numbers available from sets B and C.
- The greatest sum is 9 + 7 + 8 = 24.

QUESTION 11
Working with special symbols

11. Let the symbol $\widehat{x}$ represent the number of different pairs of positive integers whose product is x. For example, $\widehat{16} = 3$, since there are 3 different pairs of positive integers whose product is 16:

$$16 \times 1, 8 \times 2, \text{ and } 4 \times 4$$

What does $\widehat{36}$ equal?

(A) 5
(B) 6
(C) 8
(D) 10
(E) 12

Difficulty: Easy
The correct answer is (A).

Most SAT math tests have at least one question involving a newly defined symbol. Sometimes there will be an easy question, like this one, followed by a more difficult one in which you might have to use the new symbol in an equation.

To answer these questions, you have to read the definition of the special symbol carefully and follow the instructions. *It is not expected that you have ever seen the new symbol before.*

The question asks you to figure out how many pairs of positive integers can be multiplied together to give you the number in the question.

Put the Special Symbol to Work

- To figure out (36), list the pairs of positive integers whose product is 36:

1×36
2×18
3×12
4×9
6×6

- Count up the pairs. The answer is 5.

HINT

When you're faced with a special symbol, don't panic.

Read the definition carefully and use it as your instruction for working out the answer.

QUESTION 12
More logical analysis

12. Several people are standing in a straight line. Starting at one end of the line Bill is counted as the 5th person, and starting at the other end he is counted as the 12th person. How many people are in the line?

(A) 15
(B) 16
(C) 17
(D) 18
(E) 19

Difficulty: Easy
The correct answer is (B).

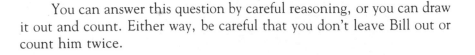

You can answer this question by careful reasoning, or you can draw it out and count. Either way, be careful that you don't leave Bill out or count him twice.

What Do You Know?

- Bill is the 5th person from one end of the line.
- Bill is the 12th person from the other end.

Using Logic to Solve the Problem

- If Bill is the 5th person from one end of the line, there are 4 people (not counting Bill) between him and that end of the line.
- If Bill is the 12th person from the other end of the line, there are 11 people (not counting Bill) between him and that end of the line.
- 4 people between Bill and one end, plus 11 people between Bill and the other end, add up to 15 people. Then you have to add Bill. So there are 16 people in the line.

HINT

Problems like this one focus on your ability to reason logically.

There's nothing wrong with drawing a figure using dots to represent the people in line. Just make sure that you follow the instructions carefully when you draw your figure.

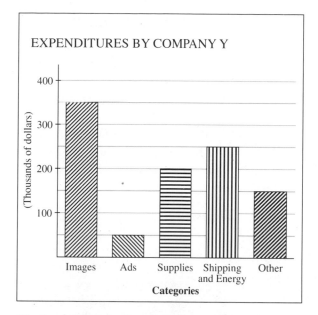

QUESTION 13
Working with data from a graph

13. In the graph above, if the total expenditures for Company Y in 1992 were $1,000,000, the shaded area of which of the following pie charts best represents the expenditures other than shipping and energy?

(A)

(B)

(C)

(D)

(E)

Difficulty: Medium
The correct answer is (D).

In this question you have to interpret information from one type of graph (bar graph) and translate that information into another type of graph (pie chart).

Questions that involve interpreting data presented on graphs or in tables will be common on the New SAT.

What Does the Question Ask?

The question asks you to identify the pie chart that shows all of Company Y's expenses *other than* shipping and energy. That *other than* is important. They're easy to overlook.

What Do You Know?

All you need to know to answer the question is the amount of money spent on Shipping and Energy and the total expenses for the company.

- You are given the total expenses: $1,000,000. (You also could have figured that total out from the graph by adding all the expenses from the individual categories.)
- The graph will show you that the expenditures for Shipping and Energy amount to $250,000.

Translating the Information

- The question really asks you to identify approximately what fraction of the total costs *did not* go for Shipping and Energy. Although the question does not ask this specifically, the pie charts in the answer choices show fractions of the whole. So that's the way you will have to express the information you have.
- Shipping and Energy expenses amount to $250,000 of the $1,000,000 of total expenses.
- Shipping and Energy cost $\frac{\$250,000}{\$1,000,000}$ or $\frac{1}{4}$ of the total.
- That means that the answer is (A) because the pie chart in (A) shows about $\frac{1}{4}$ of the total, right?... WRONG!!!!
- Remember, the question asks which pie chart "best represents expenditures *other than* shipping and energy?"
- If $\frac{1}{4}$ goes for shipping and energy, that leaves $\frac{3}{4}$ for other things.

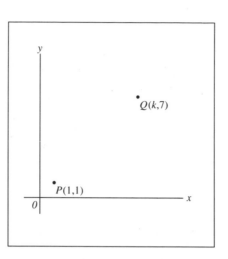

QUESTION 14
Slope of a line in a graph

14. In the figure above, the slope of the line through points P and Q is $\frac{3}{2}$. What is the value of k?

(A) 4
(B) 5
(C) 6
(D) 7
(E) 8

Difficulty: This question was written for this book. We do not know the difficulty.
The correct answer is (B).

Your ability to answer this question depends on your knowing and being able to apply the definition of "slope."
The **slope** of a line in a coordinate plane is:

$$\frac{\text{the change in } y \text{ between any two points on the line}}{\text{the change in } x \text{ between the same points on the line}}$$

The question asks for the value of k, which is the x coordinate of point Q.

What Do You Know?

- The slope of the line that goes between P and Q is $\frac{3}{2}$.

- That means for every 3 units that y changes, x will change 2.
- The coordinates of P are (1,1).
- The coordinates of Q are $(k, 7)$.
- The change in the value of y between P and Q is 6 units ($7 - 1 = 6$).

191

Apply What You Know

- y changes 6 units between the two points.
- That means that x will change 4 units, since for every 3 units that y changes, x changes 2 units.
- The x coordinate of point P is 1.
- The x coordinate of point Q will be 1 + 4 = 5.

RECAP: HINTS FOR FIVE-CHOICE MULTIPLE-CHOICE QUESTIONS

Remember the approach to Roman numeral format questions: Consider each Roman numeral statement as a separate true-false question.

A quick "make-sense" check before you start working on multiple-choice questions can help to eliminate some of the choices.

Quantitative Comparison Questions

Practice Questions

The next six questions are Quantitative Comparison problems. They do not require that you figure out a specific value or answer. Rather, you must determine which of two quantities has the greater value.

Here's how they work:

- Each Quantitative Comparison question shows two quantities to be compared—one in the left column (Column A) and one in the right column (Column B). Some may also have additional information that you'll find centered between the two columns.
- Your job is to determine which quantity, if either, has the greater value.

You choose the letter that indicates the correct relationship between the two quantities being compared.

If you find you're having trouble figuring out the solutions to these questions, turn to the Answers and Explanations that follow the questions.

Directions for Quantitative Comparison Questions

The questions each consist of two quantities in boxes, one in Column A and one in Column B. You are to compare the two quantities and on the answer sheet fill in oval

A if the quantity in Column A is greater;
B if the quantity in Column B is greater;
C if the two quantities are equal;
D if the relationship cannot be determined from the information given.

AN E RESPONSE WILL NOT BE SCORED.

Notes:

1. In some questions, information is given about one or both of the quantities to be compared. In such cases, the given information is centered above the two columns and is not boxed.
2. In a given question, a symbol that appears in both columns represents the same thing in Column A as it does in Column B.
3. Letters such as x, n, and k stand for real numbers.

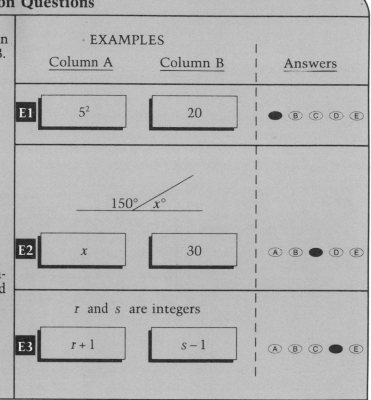

Special note: On the actual test, directions to Quantitative Comparison questions are summarized at the top of every page containing Quantitative Comparisons.

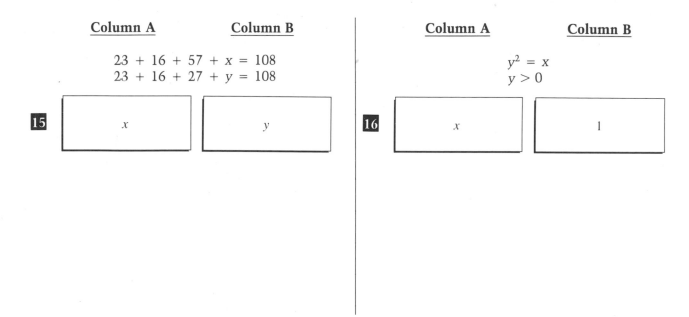

Column A	Column B
$23 + 16 + 57 + x = 108$	
$23 + 16 + 27 + y = 108$	

15 x y

Column A	Column B
$y^2 = x$	
$y > 0$	

16 x 1

SUMMARY DIRECTIONS FOR COMPARISON QUESTIONS

Answer: A if the quantity in Column A is greater;
B if the quantity in Column B is greater;
C if the two quantities are equal;
D if the relationship cannot be determined from the information given.

AN E RESPONSE WILL NOT BE SCORED.

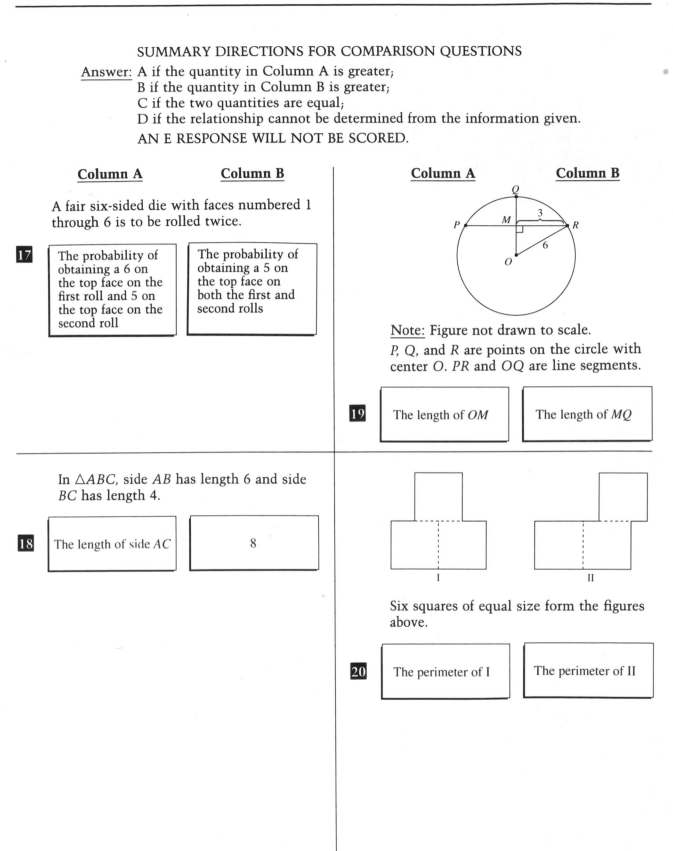

Column A	Column B

A fair six-sided die with faces numbered 1 through 6 is to be rolled twice.

17

| The probability of obtaining a 6 on the top face on the first roll and 5 on the top face on the second roll | The probability of obtaining a 5 on the top face on both the first and second rolls |

In $\triangle ABC$, side AB has length 6 and side BC has length 4.

18

| The length of side AC | 8 |

Column A	Column B

Note: Figure not drawn to scale.

P, Q, and R are points on the circle with center O. PR and OQ are line segments.

19

| The length of OM | The length of MQ |

Six squares of equal size form the figures above.

20

| The perimeter of I | The perimeter of II |

194

Answers and Explanations

$$23 + 16 + 57 + x = 108$$
$$23 + 16 + 27 + y = 108$$

QUESTION 15
Don't waste time doing calculations.

Column A	**Column B**
15. x	y

Difficulty: Easy
The correct answer is (B).

What Do You Know?

- The two equations contain some common terms. The only differences are in the two terms just before the equal sign.
- In both equations, the expressions on the left side of the equal sign add up to the same number.
- The numbers that are common to the two expressions will have no effect on which variable has the greater value, so you can eliminate them.

$$\cancel{23 + 16} + 57 + x = 108$$
$$\cancel{23 + 16} + 27 + y = 108$$

- Which has to be greater, x or y, in order for the sum to equal 108?
- Because y is added to a smaller number, y has to be greater.

> **HINT**
>
> By estimating and comparing, you can frequently establish which quantity is greater without figuring out the value of either quantity.

QUESTION 16
Substituting values

$$y^2 = x$$
$$y > 0$$

Column A	**Column B**
16. x	1

Difficulty: Medium
The correct answer is (D).

To answer this question, you can sample a few values for y, but you must make sure that you sample a variety of values.

> **HINT**
>
> When you are substituting values to answer a Quantitative Comparison question, make sure you check the special cases:
>
> - 0
> - 1
> - at least one number between 0 and 1
> - a number or numbers greater than 1
> - negative numbers

Substituting Values

Because y is greater than 0, you don't have to worry about 0 or negative values. But when you raise numbers to powers, fractions and the number 1 act differently than numbers greater than 1.

> **HINT**
>
> If any two of the answers (A), (B), or (C) can be true for particular values in a Quantitative Comparison question, then the answer to that question is (D).

So you need to sample:

The number 1;
A number between 0 and 1;
A number greater than 1.

Try $y = 1$.

$$y^2 = x$$
$$1^2 = x$$
$$1 = x$$

Try a value of y between 0 and 1, such as $\frac{1}{2}$.

$$y^2 = x$$
$$\left(\frac{1}{2}\right)^2 = x$$
$$\frac{1}{4} = x$$

We've found two possible values of x (1 and $\frac{1}{4}$). In the first case, the quantity in column A ($x = 1$) is equal to the quantity in Column B. In the second case, the quantity in column A ($x = \frac{1}{4}$) is less than the quantity in column B. So the answer is (D). You cannot tell.

QUESTION 17
Probability

A fair six-sided die with faces numbered 1 through 6 is to be rolled twice.

<u>**Column A**</u>

<u>**Column B**</u>

17. | The probability of obtaining a 6 on the top face on the first roll and 5 on the top face on the second roll

| The probability of obtaining a 5 on the top face on both the first and second rolls

Answer: C
Difficulty: Medium

You are given that a fair die is to be rolled twice. This means that on each roll each of the six numbered faces is equally likely to be the top face. For example, the face numbered 3 is just as likely to be the top face as the face numbered 4. The probability that any specific number will appear on the top face is $\frac{1}{6}$.

- In Column A, the probability of obtaining a 6 on the first roll and a 5 on the second roll is $\frac{1}{6} \times \frac{1}{6} = \frac{1}{36}$.

- In Column B, the probability of obtaining a 5 on the first roll and another 5 on the second roll is also $\frac{1}{6} \times \frac{1}{6} = \frac{1}{36}$.

Therefore, the two quantities are equal.

Caution: In this question, you are given the order in which the numbered faces appear. If in Column A you had been asked for "The probability of obtaining a 6 on the top face of one roll and a 5 on the top face of the other roll," the answer would be different. Why? Because there are *two* equally likely ways to succeed: a 6 on the first roll and a 5 on the second, or a 5 on the first roll and a 6 on the second. Each of these two outcomes has a probability of $\frac{1}{36}$. Therefore, in this case, the quantity in Column A would equal $\frac{2}{36}$.

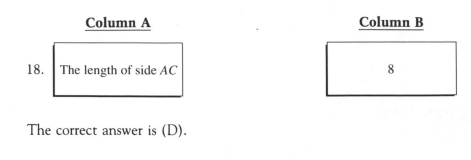

QUESTION 18
Draw your own figure

In △*ABC*, side *AB* has length 6 and side BC has length 4.

	Column A		**Column B**
18.	The length of side *AC*		8

The correct answer is (D).

> **HINT**
>
> The sum of the lengths of any two sides of a triangle is always greater than the length of the third side.

There are two related properties of triangles that you should remember. The length of any one side must be less than the sum of the lengths of the other two sides. And the length of any one side must be greater than the difference between the lengths of the other two sides.

If you remember these properties, the answer to this question is easy:

- The sum of lengths *AB* and *BC* is 6 + 4 or 10. So side *AC* has to be less than 10.
- The difference between lengths *AB* and *BC* is 6 − 4 or 2. So *AC* must be greater than 2.
- The length of *AC* can be greater than 8, equal to 8, or less than 8. In other words, you cannot tell which quantity (Column A or Column B) is greater.

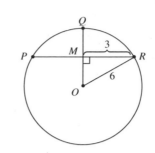

QUESTION 19
Use all the information

P, Q, and *R* are points on the circle with center *O*. *PR* and *OQ* are line segments.

	Column A		**Column B**
19.	The length of *OM*		The length of *MQ*

Difficulty: Hard
The correct answer is (A).

What Do You Know?

- *O* is the center of the circle. Therefore, *OR* is a radius of the circle with a length of 6.
- *OQ* is a line segment that starts from the center and extends to the edge of the circle. So it is also a radius with a length of 6.
- Angle *OMR* is a right angle. Therefore, triangle *OMR* is a right triangle.

What Lengths Do You Need to Find?

- *OQ* has a length of 6.
- *OM* is a side of right triangle (*OMR*). And you know the length of the other side and of the hypotenuse.
- Therefore, you can find the length of OM by using the Pythagorean theorem.

Apply the Theorem

The Pythagorean theorem:

$$a^2 + b^2 = c^2$$

Where:

> a and b are the lengths of the two perpendicular sides (the legs) of a right triangle.
> c is the length of the hypotenuse.

In the triangle in Question 19

> The two legs are OM and MR
> MR = 3
> The hypotenuse OR is 6.

Substitute these numbers into the Pythagorean theorem:

$$a^2 + b^2 = c^2$$
$$3^2 + (OM)^2 = 6^2$$
$$9 + (OM)^2 = 36$$
$$(OM)^2 = 27$$
$$OM = \sqrt{27}$$

Compare the Lengths

- OM = $\sqrt{27}$, which is a little more than 5.
- MQ = 6 − OM
- MQ = 6 − $\sqrt{27}$
- You don't have to figure out the exact lengths. If OM is more than 5, MQ has to be less than 1. So OM is longer than MQ.

HINT

The Reference section of the math test book gives the properties of some special triangles. Because the hypotenuse (6) is twice the shorter leg (3) you know the ratio of the sides of the right triangle in this question is 1: $\sqrt{3}$: 2. Then you can figure out that $OM = 3\sqrt{3}$, so $OM > MQ$.

You will probably find that if you are not familiar with most of the information in the Reference section before you take the test, you will have a hard time using it efficiently during the test.

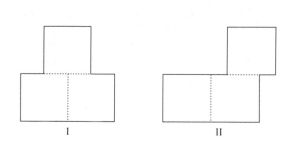

I   II

QUESTION 20
Visualizing

Six squares of equal size form the figures above.

Column A	**Column B**
20. The perimeter of I	The perimeter of II

Difficulty: Medium
The correct answer is (B).

Explanation:
   If you know the definition of perimeter, you should be able to figure out the answer to this question just by looking at the figures.

What Do You Know?

- Three squares make up each figure, and all the squares are of equal size.
- The perimeter of a figure is equal to the sum of the lengths of its sides, not the sides of the individual squares that make up the figure. The perimeters *do not* include any of the dotted lines.
- The lengths of the bottoms of both figures are equal. So your focus should be on what's happening where the top square and the top of the bottom squares meet.
- Look at the top square of I. Its entire bottom side overlaps with the upper sides of the lower squares, so its bottom side *does not* add to the perimeter.
- Now look at the top square of II. Some of its bottom side—the part that sticks out—does add to the perimeter.
- Therefore, the perimeter of II is greater.

RECAP: HINTS ON QUANTITATIVE COMPARISON QUESTIONS

With Quantitative Comparison questions, frequently you don't have to finish your calculations or determine an exact answer. You just have to know enough about the quantities to determine which one is greater.

Memorize the four answer choices for Quantitative Comparison questions.

If any two of the answers (A), (B), or (C) can be true for a particular Quantitative Comparison question, then the answer to that question is (D).

Think of the columns as a balanced scale. You are trying to figure out which side of the scale is heavier, so eliminate any quantities that are the same on both sides of the scale.

Try evaluating the quantities by substituting values for variables. Just remember:
- Make sure you check above the columns for any information about what the values can be.

When substituting values to answer a Quantitative Comparison question, make sure you check the special cases: 0, 1, at least one number between 0 and 1, a number or numbers greater than 1, and negative numbers.

Grid-in Questions

Practice Questions   The math skills and reasoning abilities required for Grid-in questions are much the same as those required for the other two types of math questions. In fact, many Grid-in questions are similar to regular Multiple-Choice questions except that no answers are provided.

There are, of course, some differences:

- Because no answers are given, you'll always have to work out the solutions yourself.

- If you have no idea of the correct answer, random guessing on Grid-in questions isn't very useful. Even though no points are deducted for wrong answers, your chances of guessing correctly are usually not good. But if you have worked out an answer and you think it might be correct, go ahead and grid it in. You won't lose any points for trying.

- You can enter your answers on the grid in several forms. When appropriate, you may use fractions or decimals. Fractions do not have to be reduced to lowest terms—e.g., $\frac{3}{12}$ is acceptable.

- The details of the gridding procedure are discussed in Chapter 8. There are strict rules for rounding and for expressing repeating decimals. Make sure you understand the grid-in procedure very well.

Use the sample grids on page 206 to practice gridding techniques. If you find you're having trouble figuring out the solutions to these eight problems, turn to the Answers and Explanations that follow the questions.

21 In a restaurant where the sales tax on a $4.00 lunch is $0.24, what will be the sales tax due, in dollars, on a $15.00 dinner?
(Disregard the $ sign when gridding your answer.)

23 If n is a two-digit number that can be expressed as the product of two consecutive <u>even</u> integers, what is one possible value of n?

22 A team has won 60 percent of the 20 games it has played so far this season. If the team plays a total of 50 games all season and wins 80 percent of the remaining games, what will be the percent of games it won for the entire season? (Disregard the % sign when gridding your answer.)

24 If the ratio of a to b is $\frac{7}{3}$, what is the value of the ratio of $2a$ to b?

25 If the population of a town doubles every 10 years, the population in the year $X + 100$ will be how many times the population in the year X?

27 If $\frac{X}{2} = y$ and $2y = y$, what is the value of x?

26

Number of Donuts	Total Price
1	$ 0.40
Box of 6	$ 1.89
Box of 12	$ 3.59

According to the information in the table above, what would be the <u>least</u> amount of money needed, in dollars, to purchase exactly 21 donuts? (Disregard the $ sign when gridding your answer.)

28

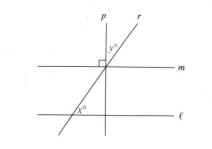

Note: Figure not drawn to scale.

In the figure above, line m is parallel to line ℓ and is perpendicular to line p. If $x = y$, what is the value of x?

21. 22. 23.

24. 25. 26.

27. 28.

**Answers and
Explanations**

QUESTION 21
Gridding dollar amounts

21. In a restaurant where the sales tax on a $4.00 lunch is $0.24, what will be the sales tax due, in dollars, on a $15.00 dinner? (Disregard the $ sign when gridding your answer.)

Difficulty: Easy
The correct answer is .90 or .9.

One way to solve this problem is to determine the tax on each $1.00 and then multiply this amount by 15 to get the tax on $15.00. The tax on a $4.00 lunch is $0.24. Then the tax on $1.00 would be one-fourth this amount, which is $0.06. So the tax on $15.00 would be $15 \times .06 = .90$ dollars.

 HINT

Zeros before the decimal point need not be gridded. (There isn't even a zero available in the far-left column of the grid.) So, don't try to grid 0.90; just grid .90 or .9.

The question asks for the number of dollars, so 90 for 90 cents would be wrong.

 HINT

Some seemingly difficult questions are really just a series of easy questions.

- Take the question one step at a time.
- Think about what you need to know in order to answer the question.
- Use what you know to figure out what you need to know.
- Make sure your *final* answer answers the question.

QUESTION 22
Work through a problem one step at a time

22. A team has won 60 percent of the 20 games it has played so far this season. If the team plays a total of 50 games all season and wins 80 percent of the remaining games, what will be the percent of games it won for the entire season? (Disregard the % sign when gridding your answer.)

Difficulty: Medium
The correct answer is 72 percent.

Express the Information in Mathematical Terms:

How many games has the team won so far?

$$60\% \text{ of } 20 \text{ games } =$$

$$\frac{60}{100} \times 20 = .6 \times 20 = 12 \text{ games}$$

How many games will the team win the rest of the season? The total number of games left is $50 - 20 = 30$.

The team will win 80% of 30 games during the rest of the season.

$$\frac{80}{100} \times 30 = .8 \times 30 = 24 \text{ games}$$

What percent of games will the team win for the entire season?

- The total number of games is 50.
- The total number of wins is: $12 + 24 = 36$.
- 36 is what percent of 50?

$$\frac{36}{50} = \frac{x}{100}$$

$$x = 72$$

Grid in 72. Disregard the % sign. Grid 72 not .72.

QUESTION 23
Properties of numbers: a question with multiple answers

23. If n is a two-digit number that can be expressed as the product of two consecutive <u>even</u> integers, what is one possible value of n?

Difficulty: Medium
There are three acceptable correct answers: 24, 48, and 80. You only have to find one.

Explanation:

Although there are several values for *n* that will work, you only have to find one.

Follow the Instructions

- *n* is the product of two consecutive even integers. In other words, the question tells you to multiply consecutive even integers.
- *n* is also a two-digit number.

Try Some Values

Start with two small consecutive even integers, 2 and 4.

- $2 \times 4 = 8$
- 8 is not a two-digit number, so *n* cannot be 8.

  Try the next two consecutive even integers, 4 and 6.

- $4 \times 6 = 24$
- 24 is a two-digit number.
- 24 is the product of two consecutive even integers.

  24 is an acceptable value for *n*. Grid in 24.

Other Correct Answers

The other possible values are 48 (6×8) and 80 (8×10). You can grid in *any one* of these three values and get credit for answering the question correctly.

HINT

Some questions have more than one correct answer.

You can grid any *one* of the correct answers and you will get full credit.

QUESTION 24
Ratios; gridding improper fractions

24. If the ratio of a to b is $\frac{7}{3}$, what is the value of the ratio of $2a$ to b?

Difficulty: Easy

The correct answer is $\frac{14}{3}$.

This question is easy as long as you know the definition of ratio. It is included in the sample section to show you how to grid the answer.

Express the Ratio

The ratio of a to b can be written as $\frac{a}{b}$.

The ratio of a to b is $\frac{7}{3}$, which can be expressed as $\frac{a}{b} = \frac{7}{3}$.

If $\frac{a}{b} = \frac{7}{3}$

then $\frac{2a}{b} = 2\left(\frac{7}{3}\right) = \frac{14}{3}$.

Grid in the answer 14/3.

HINT ON GRIDDING

$\frac{14}{3}$ cannot be gridded as $4\frac{2}{3}$. The grid-reading system cannot tell the difference between $4\frac{2}{3}$ and $\frac{42}{3}$. Also, if you change $\frac{14}{3}$ to a decimal, either 4.66 or 4.67 is an acceptable answer.

QUESTION 25
Working with powers

25. If the population of a town doubles every 10 years, the population in the year $X + 100$ will be how many times the population in the year X?

Difficulty: Hard
The correct answer is 1024.

Express the Population Growth in Mathematical Terms

Each time the population doubles, multiply it by 2. Let p represent the population in year X.

- In 10 years the population increases from p to $2p$.
- In 10 more years it increases to $2(2p)$
- In 10 more years it increases to $2[2(2p)]$ and so on for 100 years.

This repeated doubling can be expressed by using powers of 2:

- Another way to express $2(2)$ is 2^2.
- So a population of $2(2p) = (2^2)p$.
- In 10 more years the population is $2(2^2)$ or $(2^3)p$.
- In 10 more years the population is $2(2^3)p$ or $(2^4)p$, etc.

How Many Growth Cycles Are There?

- The population doubles (is raised to another power of 2) every 10 years.
- This goes on for 100 years.
- So there are $100/10 = 10$ cycles.
- The population increases 2^{10} times what it was in year X.

Figure Out the Answer

You can multiply ten 2s, but this invites error. You may want to use your calculator to find 2^{10}. Some calculators have an exponent key that allows you to find y^x directly. If your calculator does not have this feature, you can still quickly get the value of 2^{10} on your calculator as follows.

$$2^5 = 2 \times 2 \times 2 \times 2 \times 2 = 32$$
$$2^{10} = 2^5 \times 2^5 = 32 \times 32 = 1024.$$

Grid in the answer, 1024.

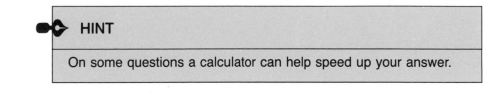

HINT

On some questions a calculator can help speed up your answer.

QUESTION 26
Using logic

26.

Number of Donuts	Total Price
1	$ 0.40
Box of 6	$ 1.89
Box of 12	$ 3.59

According to the information in the table above, what would be the least amount of money needed, in dollars, to purchase exactly 21 donuts? (Disregard the $ sign when gridding your answer.)

Difficulty: Medium
The correct answer is $6.68.

What Do You Know?

- You can save money by purchasing donuts by the box. A box of 6 donuts costs $1.89, but 6 individual donuts cost $2.40.
- You can save more money by purchasing the larger box. A box of 12 donuts costs $3.59, but 2 boxes of 6 donuts cost 2($1.89) = $3.78.
- The question says you have to buy exactly 21 donuts.

Use Your Head

You want to buy as few individual donuts as you can.

You want to buy as many donuts in large boxes as you can. You cannot buy 2 boxes of 12, because that would put you over the 21-donut limit. So start with 1 box of 12 donuts.

- Mark down 12 donuts, so you can keep track as you add more donuts.
- Mark down $3.59, so you can keep track as you spend more money.

You have 12 donuts, so there are 9 left to buy. You can save money by buying a box of 6 donuts.

- Add 6 to your donut total.
- Add $1.89 to your money total.

You now have 18 donuts, which means you will have to buy 3 individual donuts.

- Add 3 to your donut total. You now have exactly 21 donuts.
- Add 3 × $.40 = $1.20 to your money total.
- Add up the dollar figures: $3.59 + $1.89 + $1.20 = $6.68

Grid in 6.68. Remember to disregard the $ sign.

Note: Do not grid 668 without the decimal mark—it will be interpreted as $668!

◐← HINT

When you're working out an answer, jot down your calculations in the space provided in your test book.

QUESTION 27
Watch out for zero

27. If $\frac{x}{2} = y$ and $2y = y$, what is the value of x?

Difficulty: Medium
The correct answer is 0.

This is another question that takes some reasoning rather than simple mathematical manipulation.

Look at the Equations

The second equation may look a little unusual to you:

$$2y = y$$

If $2y = y$ then $y = 0$. Therefore:

$$\frac{x}{2} = 0$$
$$x = 0$$

Grid in the answer, 0.

◐← HINT ON GRIDDING

To grid zero, just enter 0 in a single column (*any* column where 0 appears). Leave the other three columns blank.

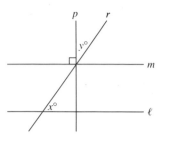

QUESTION 28
Lines and angles

28. In the figure above, line m is parallel to line ℓ and is perpendicular to line p. If $x = y$, what is the value of x?

Difficulty: Medium
The correct answer is 45.

⟜ HINT

Look for special properties that may help you answer the question. If it is about angles, look for special properties of angles. If it is about areas, look for special properties of areas.

Special properties that help you translate between different kinds of measurements can be especially useful.

For instance:
- If you know two sides of a triangle are of equal length, then you know that the measures of the angles opposite those two sides are equal.
- If you know two segments are radii of the same circle, you know that they are of equal length.

This question requires that you use your knowledge of lines, angles, and triangles to calculate values for parts of the figure that are not labeled. As you work on the question, remember:

- It's helpful to label parts of the figure as you work.
- Use your knowledge of special properties such as parallel lines, vertical angles, and special types of triangles.

What Do You Know?

- Lines l and m are parallel.
- Line p is perpendicular to line m.
- $x = y$.

> **HINT**
>
> Write relevant facts (angles, lengths of sides) on the figure as you pick up more information.

What Can You Figure Out From the Figure?

You can use the parallel lines in the figure to label other angles that are equal to $x°$.

Since line p is perpendicular to line m, $x° + y° = 90°$. You are told that $x = y$. Therefore,

$$x° + x° = 90°$$
$$2x = 90$$
$$x = 45$$

Grid the answer, 45. Disregard the degree sign (°).

RECAP: HINTS ON GRID-IN QUESTIONS

The slash mark (/) is used to indicate a fraction bar.

You don't have to reduce fractions to their lowest terms unless your answer will not fit in the grid.

You may express an answer as a fraction or a decimal: You can grid $\frac{1}{2}$ as 1/2 or .5.

Mixed numbers **must** be expressed as improper fractions: You must express $1\frac{3}{5}$ as 8/5. The grid-reading system cannot distinguish between 1 3/5 and 13/5.

Grid as much of a repeating decimal as will fit in the grid. You may need to round a repeating decimal, but round only the last digit: grid $\frac{2}{3}$ as 2/3 or .666 or .667. Do not grid the value $\frac{2}{3}$ as .67 or .66.

Since you don't have choices provided to help avoid careless errors on Grid-in questions:
- Carefully check your calculations.
- Always double-check your answers. Make sure the answer you enter makes sense.

Make sure you have gridded your answer accurately and according to all the Grid-in rules.

Practice a few Grid-in questions with a variety of answer types—whole numbers, fractions, and decimals. Get familiar with the mechanics of gridding.

Some Grid-in questions have more than one correct answer. You can grid any one of the correct answers and get full credit for the question.

To grid zero, just enter 0 in a single column (any column where 0 appears).

RECAP: GENERAL HINTS ON MATHEMATICAL REASONING QUESTIONS

Be thoroughly familiar with the Reference materials provided in the test booklet, so you can refer to them quickly if you need to.

Refresh your math knowledge by studying the skills and concepts discussed in Chapter 9, Mathematics Review.

Make notes in your test book:
- Draw figures to help you think through problems that relate to geometric shapes, distances, proportions, sizes, and the like.
- Write out calculations so that you can check them later.
- When a question contains a figure, note any measurements or values you calculate right on the figure in the test book.

If you have time to check your work, try to redo your calculations in a different way from the way you did them the first time.

Use the choices to your advantage:
- If you can't figure out how to approach a problem, the form of the choices may give you a hint.
- You may find that you can eliminate some choices so you can make an educated guess, even if you aren't sure of the correct answer.

If you decide to try all the choices, start with choice (C). This is *not* because (C) is more likely to be the correct answer, but because the choices are usually listed in ascending order, from smallest to greatest value or greatest to smallest.

With data interpretation questions—graphs, charts, and tables—always make sure you understand the information being presented.

If it seems like you have a lot of calculating to do, there may be a shortcut.

With relatively simple questions, it's ok to substitute and/or eliminate choices. With more complicated problems, this approach may take more time than using mathematical reasoning.

If you're told that a figure is not drawn to scale, lengths and angles may not be shown accurately.

Number lines and graphs are generally accurately drawn.

When you are faced with special symbols, don't panic. Read the definition carefully and use it as your instruction for working out the answer.

Some seemingly difficult questions are really just a series of easy questions. Take the solution one step at a time.

PART FIVE

Complete Practice Test and Answer Key

Time-30 Minutes — For each question in this section, select the best answer from among the choices given and
30 Questions   fill in the corresponding oval on the answer sheet.

Each sentence below has one or two blanks, each blank indicating that something has been omitted. Beneath the sentence are five lettered words or sets of words labeled A through E. Choose the word or set of words that, when inserted in the sentence, best fits the meaning of the sentence as a whole.

Example:

Medieval kingdoms did not become constitutional republics overnight; on the contrary, the change was ----.

(A) unpopular
(B) unexpected
(C) advantageous
(D) sufficient
(E) gradual

Ⓐ Ⓑ Ⓒ Ⓓ ●

1 When Harvard astronomer Cecilia Payne was ---- professor in 1956, it marked an important step in the reduction of ---- practices within the scientific establishment.

(A) accepted for..disciplinary
(B) promoted to..discriminatory
(C) honored as..unbiased
(D) denounced as..critical
(E) considered for..hierarchical

2 Like a parasitic organism, the most detested character in the play depended on others for ---- and ---- nothing.

(A) ideas..required
(B) diversion..spared
(C) assistance..destroyed
(D) survival..consumed
(E) sustenance..returned

3 Although refuse and ashes may seem ---- to some individuals, archaeologists can use such materials to draw conclusions about the daily lives of ancient people.

(A) undetectable
(B) fabricated
(C) insignificant
(D) historical
(E) abundant

4 Ryan was neither brusque nor cunning but was as ---- and as ---- a man as I have ever met.

(A) cordial..arrogant
(B) gentle..candid
(C) suave..wily
(D) insolent..tolerant
(E) treacherous..straightforward

5 The reporters' behavior was certainly ----, but they believed that such infringement on personal privacy was necessary to their work.

(A) dependable
(B) inconsequential
(C) predestined
(D) scintillating
(E) invasive

6 During the Middle Ages, plague and other ---- decimated the populations of entire towns.

(A) pestilences
(B) immunizations
(C) proclivities
(D) indispositions
(E) demises

7 Unlike most of their solitary relatives, arctic hares are ----, clumping into herds that can include as many as several thousand individuals.

(A) reserved
(B) cantankerous
(C) exclusive
(D) meritorious
(E) gregarious

8 Carolyn Bennett, a maker of kaleidoscopes, attributes the current ---- of intact nineteenth-century kaleidoscopes to the normal human desire to ---- a mysterious object in order to discover how it works.

(A) complexity..study
(B) uniqueness..acquire
(C) exorbitance..distribute
(D) paucity..disassemble
(E) fragility..discontinue

9 By nature he was ----, usually confining his remarks to ---- expression.

(A) acerbic..friendly
(B) laconic..concise
(C) garrulous..voluminous
(D) shrill..complimentary
(E) vague..emphatic

GO ON TO THE NEXT PAGE

220

Each question below consists of a related pair of words or phrases, followed by five pairs of words or phrases labeled A through E. Select the pair that best expresses a relationship similar to that expressed in the original pair.

Example:

CRUMB:BREAD::
(A) ounce:unit
(B) splinter:wood
(C) water:bucket
(D) twine:rope
(E) cream:butter

10 LUMBERYARD:LUMBER::

(A) supermarket:food
(B) jungle:vines
(C) drugstore:druggist
(D) wood:plank
(E) bakery:ovens

11 UNBUCKLE:BELT::

(A) unravel:yarn
(B) unlock:key
(C) unfold:napkin
(D) undress:coat
(E) untie:shoelace

12 PSEUDONYM:WRITER::

(A) alias:criminal
(B) alibi:defendant
(C) rank:officer
(D) disclaimer:producer
(E) dissertation:scholar

13 OFFICIATE:GAME::

(A) review:movie
(B) compete:contest
(C) preside:convention
(D) adjourn:meeting
(E) participate:rally

14 RIFT:ROCK::

(A) gale:wind
(B) constellation:star
(C) fracture:bone
(D) rust:iron
(E) tremor:earthquake

15 EXPOSITION:CLARIFY::

(A) rebuttal:humiliate
(B) refutation:disprove
(C) illumination:darken
(D) allegation:verify
(E) summary:end

GO ON TO THE NEXT PAGE

Each passage below is followed by questions based on its content. Answer the questions following each passage on the basis of what is <u>stated</u> or <u>implied</u> in that passage and in any introductory material that may be provided.

Questions 16-21 are based on the following passage.

The following passage is an adaptation of an excerpt from a memoir written by Elizabeth Bishop about the poet Marianne Moore. Bishop herself became a well-known poet.

I became a devoted reader of Marianne Moore's poetry while attending college in the early 1930's. A school friend and her mother, both better read and more sophisticated in their literary tastes than I was, were the
(5) first to mention her poetry, and soon I had read every poem of Moore's I could find.

I had not known poetry could be like that: her treatment of topics as diverse as glaciers and marriage struck me, as it still does, as a miracle of language and
(10) construction. Why had no one ever written about these things in this clear and dazzling way before?

As luck had it, when I first began searching for a copy of her volume entitled *Observations*, I found that the college library didn't own one. Eventually, though, I did
(15) borrow a copy, but from one of the librarians, Fanny Borden, not from the library. And I received an invitation to meet Marianne Moore in the process.

In retrospect, Fanny Borden seems like a most appropriate person to have suggested I might meet
(20) Marianne Moore. Borden was extremely shy and reserved and spoke in such a soft voice it was hard to hear her at all. The campus rumor was that her personality had been permanently subdued by her family history: the notorious Lizzie Borden* of Fall River was
(25) her aunt.

Contact with Fanny Borden was rare. Occasionally, in search of a book, students would be sent to her office, shadowy and cavelike, with books piled everywhere. She weighed down the papers on her desk with smooth,
(30) round stones, quite big stones, brought from the seashore. My roommate once commented on one in particular, and Borden responded in her almost inaudible voice, "Do you like it? You may <u>have</u> it," and handed it over.

*Lizzie Borden, the defendant in a highly publicized trial, was accused of murdering her parents.

(35) One day I was sent to her office about a book. During our talk, I finally got up my courage to ask her why there was not a copy of *Observations* by that wonderful poet Marianne Moore in the library. She looked ever so gently taken aback and inquired, "Do you <u>like</u>
(40) Marianne Moore's poems?" I said I certainly did, the few I had been able to find. She then said calmly, "I've known her since she was a girl," and followed that with the question that was possibly to influence the whole course of my life: "Would you like to meet her?"

(45) I was painfully—no, excruciatingly—shy and I had run away many times rather than face being introduced to adults of much less distinction than Marianne Moore. Yet I immediately said, "Yes."

16 To the author, Marianne Moore's poetry was

(A) reminiscent of poems by other great poets
(B) subtly satirical
(C) too scholarly for most readers
(D) inspiring and well crafted
(E) difficult but rewarding

17 The major purpose of the passage is to

(A) describe the events that led to a milestone in the author's life
(B) reveal the character of a college librarian
(C) relate the significant events of the author's college years
(D) analyze the impact of Marianne Moore's poetry on the author
(E) show the unexpected surprises that can happen in an ordinary life

GO ON TO THE NEXT PAGE

18 The reference to Lizzie Borden in line 24 provides all of the following EXCEPT

(A) one possible reason for the librarian's unusually quiet manner
(B) a piece of information about the librarian's family history
(C) a suggestion that the librarian might be deliberately hiding her true nature
(D) an indication that the students were curious about the shy librarian
(E) a fact that might be interesting to some readers

19 By mentioning the extent of her shyness (lines 45-48), the author primarily emphasizes

(A) her reasons for not asking Borden to introduce her to Marianne Moore
(B) her awareness of her own weakness
(C) how important meeting Marianne Moore was to her
(D) how hard it was for her to talk to people, even Borden
(E) how different her encounter with Borden was from her roommate's

20 The author most likely remembers Fanny Borden primarily with feelings of

(A) regret
(B) curiosity
(C) amusement
(D) gratitude
(E) loyalty

21 The passage suggests that the author's interest in meeting Marianne Moore was

(A) ultimately secondary to her interest in locating a copy of *Observations*
(B) prompted by a desire to have the poet explain a difficult poem
(C) motivated by the idea of writing a biography of the poet
(D) a secret dream she had cherished for many years
(E) sufficiently strong to make her behave uncharacteristically

Questions 22-30 are based on the following passage.

There has been a great deal of scientific debate about the nature of the object that exploded above Tunguska in 1908. The following passage presents one theory of what happened.

The thought came and went in a flash: there was not a chance in a billion years that an extraterrestrial object as large as Halley's comet would hit the Earth. But that
Line was 15 years ago, when I had little appreciation of
(5) geological time. I did not consider then the adage that anything that can happen does happen—given the time. My intuition was right—there is not a chance in a billion years for a big hit—but there have been more than 4 billion years of Earth history. Smaller collisions
(10) have happened frequently, as evidenced by many ancient impact craters. Even during the brief period of human history, there was a very real event at Tunguska.

Tunguska was a quiet hamlet in central Siberia. At
(15) 7:00 a.m. on June 30, 1908, a fireball appeared above the horizon to the southeast. More luminous than the rising Sun, the bright light streaked across the cloudless sky and exploded somewhere to the northwest. The scale of the explosion was unprecedented in recorded
(20) history. When seismographers consulted their instruments and calculated the energy that had been released, they were stunned. In today's terms the explosion had the force of a 10-megaton nuclear detonation.
(25) The brilliant object had been seen for hundreds of kilometers around, and the explosion was heard as far away as 1,000 kilometers.* The shock wave of wind circled the globe twice, and the ejecta from the explosion glowed over Northern Europe through the
(30) next two nights. Vast amounts of fire debris arrived at California two weeks later, noticeably depressing the transparency of the atmosphere over the state.

Fortunately, the object had exploded at a height of 8.5 kilometers above the ground, and the fall region was
(35) very sparsely populated. Hunters who were first to enter the disaster area reported that the whole forest had been flattened and gave accounts of wild forest fires. Systematic investigations did not begin until two decades later. The first team of experts visited the target
(40) area in 1927. They endured hardship to penetrate the devastated forest with horse-drawn wagons to investigate the aftereffect of the blast. Their mapping showed that trees within a radius of 30 to 40 kilometers had been uprooted and blown radially outward from the center of
(45) the blast. Within the blast zone, an area of 2,000 square kilometers had been ravaged by fire.

One kilometer is equal to 0.62 miles. One thousand kilometers equals 620 miles.

Study of the Tunguska site resumed after the Second World War and is still continuing. Although no meteorites have ever been found, soil samples from
(50) Tunguska contain small spherical objects similar to tektites, black glassy objects commonly believed to result from the impact of a meteorite. The material of which tektites are usually composed is only slightly contaminated by extraterrestrial substances from the meteorite
(55) itself. The spherical objects found at Tunguska have been compared to small tektites, or microtektites, which are commonly a fraction of a millimeter in diameter, but the chemical composition of the Tunguska objects resembles cosmic dust. Apparently they were not ejecta thrown
(60) out of an impact crater, but were derived directly from the explosion above the Earth, and descended as extraterrestrial fallout.

What was it that exploded on that sunny morning over Siberia? Astronomers have conjured everything from
(65) black holes to balls of antimatter, but dramatic as the Tunguska event was, it does not seem to require an exotic explanation. The more likely interpretation is conventional: the object was a large meteor.

22 In line 1, the statement "The thought came and went in a flash" refers to the idea that

(A) intuition is important in scientific research
(B) the Earth is immensely old
(C) the speed of Halley's comet is difficult to calculate
(D) the Tunguska event had an extraterrestrial origin
(E) the Earth could experience a collision with a large comet

23 In line 4, the word "appreciation" most nearly means

(A) increase in value
(B) artistic interest
(C) understanding
(D) curiosity
(E) gratitude

GO ON TO THE NEXT PAGE

24 In the third paragraph, the author mentions Northern Europe and California in order to emphasize which point about the Tunguska event?

(A) Although the explosion was locally destructive, the remainder of the world escaped harm.
(B) The magnitude of the explosion was so great that its effects were observable over much of the Northern Hemisphere.
(C) Although the explosion occurred in a remote area, more densely populated areas were also devastated.
(D) No part of the Earth can consider itself secure from the possibility of such an explosion.
(E) The explosion took place in the atmosphere rather than on the ground.

25 The word "depressing" in line 31 most nearly means

(A) reducing
(B) saddening
(C) indenting
(D) constraining
(E) probing

26 Which is most similar to the design of the fallen trees indicated in the 1927 "mapping" mentioned in line 42 ?

(A) The gridlike pattern of a checkerboard
(B) The spokes of a wheel
(C) The parallel lanes of a highway
(D) The spiral of a whirlpool
(E) The steps in a staircase

27 The author uses the evidence of tektite-like objects in the soil (lines 48-62) to establish that

(A) the Tunguska tektites were uncontaminated by extraterrestrial substances
(B) Tunguska had been the site of an earlier meteorite collision
(C) it was an extraterrestrial object that exploded above Tunguska
(D) normal tektites became deformed as a result of the impact of the Tunguska meteorite
(E) the effects of the Tunguska event were widespread

28 The author's conclusion at the end of the passage would be most directly supported by additional information concerning

(A) what quantity of cosmic dust routinely enters the Earth's atmosphere
(B) how an exploding meteor could generate conventional tektites
(C) why experts did not visit the forest until nineteen years after the explosion
(D) where and when the effect of the blast first registered on a seismograph
(E) why a large meteor would explode in the Earth's atmosphere rather than strike the Earth's surface

29 The author uses the example of the Tunguska event primarily to illustrate the

(A) origin and significance of tektites
(B) devastation caused when a meteorite strikes the surface of the Earth
(C) difference between collisions involving comets and those involving meteorites
(D) potential of the Earth's being struck by large extraterrestrial objects
(E) range of scientific theories advanced to explain an uncommon event

30 In maintaining that the Tunguska event was caused by a meteor, the author has assumed all of the following EXCEPT:

(A) The explosion was so destructive that only tiny fragments of the meteor survived.
(B) The altitude of the explosion accounts for the absence of a crater on the ground.
(C) The tektites found in the soil at Tunguska were formed by the 1908 event and not by an earlier event.
(D) The meteor that exploded near Tunguska is the largest one to have come close to the Earth.
(E) The Earth can be involved in collisions with a variety of cosmic objects.

IF YOU FINISH BEFORE TIME IS CALLED, YOU MAY CHECK YOUR WORK ON THIS SECTION ONLY. DO NOT TURN TO ANY OTHER SECTION IN THE TEST.

STOP

Time—30 Minutes
25 Questions

In this section solve each problem, using any available space on the page for scratchwork. Then decide which is the best of the choices given and fill in the corresponding oval on the answer sheet.

Notes:

(1) The use of a calculator is permitted. All numbers used are real numbers.

(2) Figures that accompany problems in this test are intended to provide information useful in solving the problems. They are drawn as accurately as possible EXCEPT when it is stated in a specific problem that the figure is not drawn to scale. All figures lie in a plane unless otherwise indicated.

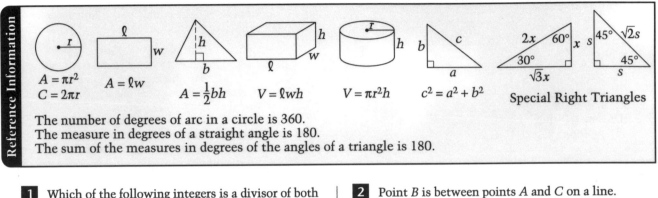

Reference Information

$A = \pi r^2$
$C = 2\pi r$
$A = \ell w$
$A = \frac{1}{2}bh$
$V = \ell wh$
$V = \pi r^2 h$
$c^2 = a^2 + b^2$
Special Right Triangles

The number of degrees of arc in a circle is 360.
The measure in degrees of a straight angle is 180.
The sum of the measures in degrees of the angles of a triangle is 180.

1 Which of the following integers is a divisor of both 36 and 90?

(A) 12
(B) 10
(C) 8
(D) 6
(E) 4

2 Point B is between points A and C on a line. If $AB = 2$ and $BC = 7$, then $AC =$

(A) 2
(B) 3
(C) 5
(D) 7
(E) 9

GO ON TO THE NEXT PAGE

When 3 times a number n is added to 7, the result is 22.

3 Which of the following equations represents the statement above?

(A) $3 + n + 7 = 22$
(B) $n + (3 \times 7) = 22$
(C) $3(n + 7) = 22$
(D) $3 + 7n = 22$
(E) $3n + 7 = 22$

5 The sales tax on a $6.00 meal is $0.36. At this rate what would be the tax on a $14.00 meal?

(A) $0.48
(B) $0.72
(C) $0.84
(D) $0.90
(E) $0.96

4 If $(y + 2)^2 = (y - 2)^2$, what is the value of y?

(A) 0
(B) 1
(C) 2
(D) 4
(E) 6

6 Apples are distributed, one at a time, into six baskets. The 1st apple goes into basket one, the 2nd into basket two, the 3rd into basket three, and so on until each basket has one apple. If this pattern is repeated, beginning each time with basket one, into which basket will the 74th apple be placed?

(A) Basket two
(B) Basket three
(C) Basket four
(D) Basket five
(E) Basket six

GO ON TO THE NEXT PAGE

7 If $4(x - 1) - 3x = 12$, then $x =$

(A) 4
(B) 8
(C) 11
(D) 13
(E) 16

9 25 percent of 16 is equivalent to $\frac{1}{2}$ of what number?

(A) 2
(B) 4
(C) 8
(D) 16
(E) 32

$$3, 6, 9, 12, \ldots$$

8 In the sequence above, each term after the first is 3 greater than the preceding term. Which of the following could NOT be a term in the sequence?

(A) 333
(B) 270
(C) 262
(D) 240
(E) 225

10 A car averages 20 miles per gallon of gas in city driving and 30 miles per gallon in highway driving. At these rates, how many gallons of gas will the car use on a 300-mile trip if $\frac{4}{5}$ of the trip is highway driving and the rest is city driving?

(A) 5
(B) 11
(C) 14
(D) 20
(E) 25

GO ON TO THE NEXT PAGE

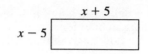

11 For which of the following values of x does the rectangle above have an area of 75?

(A) 5
(B) 10
(C) 15
(D) 20
(E) 25

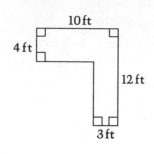

13 What is the perimeter, in feet, of the figure above?

(A) 38
(B) 41
(C) 44
(D) 46
(E) 48

12 To deliver a package, a delivery service charges $0.75 for the first pound, $0.50 per pound or part thereof for the next 5 pounds, and $0.25 per pound or part thereof for each additional pound. If the charge for delivering a package is $4.50, which of the following could be the weight, in pounds, of the package?

(A) 9

(B) 10

(C) $10\frac{1}{2}$

(D) 13

(E) $17\frac{1}{2}$

14 If the product of three consecutive integers written in increasing order equals the middle integer, what is the least of the three integers?

(A)   2
(B)   1
(C)   0
(D) −1
(E) −2

229

15 For all integers x, let

$\;\;\;\;\;\;\fbox{$x$} = x^2$ when x is an even integer, and

$\;\;\;\;\;\;\fbox{$x$} = x^2 - 1$ when x is an odd integer.

What is the value of $\fbox{$5$} - \fbox{$4$}$?

(A) 10
(B) 9
(C) 8
(D) 1
(E) 0

16 Which of the following is equal to $\dfrac{100 + n}{25}$?

(A) $\dfrac{4 + n}{5}$

(B) $\dfrac{20 + n}{5}$

(C) $4n$

(D) $4 + n$

(E) $4 + \dfrac{n}{25}$

17 Luis earns w dollars an hour for $3x$ hours and then earns y dollars an hour for x more hours. In terms of w, x, and y, how many dollars did he earn altogether?

(A) $\;\;x(3w + y)$
(B) $\;\;x(w + 3y)$
(C) $\;4x(3w + y)$
(D) $\;4x(w + y)$
(E) $\;4x(w + 3y)$

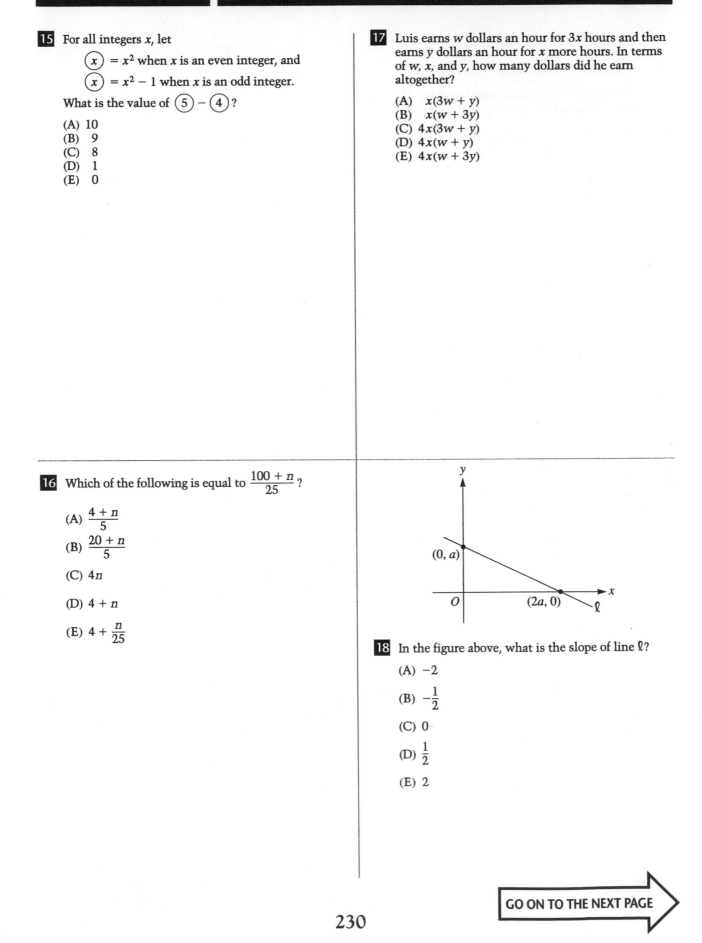

18 In the figure above, what is the slope of line ℓ?

(A) -2

(B) $-\dfrac{1}{2}$

(C) 0

(D) $\dfrac{1}{2}$

(E) 2

GO ON TO THE NEXT PAGE

19 A diagonal of a rectangle forms an angle of measure 60° with each of the two shorter sides of the rectangle. If the length of a shorter side of the rectangle is 2, what is the length of the diagonal?

(A) $2\sqrt{2}$
(B) $2\sqrt{3}$
(C) 3
(D) 4
(E) 5

21 There are 20 students in a class. For a given year, which of the following statements must be true?

I. At least two of these students have their birthdays on a Sunday.
II. At least two of these students have their birthdays on the same day of the week.
III. At least two of these students have their birthdays in the same month.

(A) I only
(B) III only
(C) I and II only
(D) II and III only
(E) I, II, and III

20 If $st^3u^4 > 0$, which of the following products must be positive?

(A) st
(B) su
(C) tu
(D) stu
(E) st^2

$$P = \left(1 - \tfrac{1}{2}\right)\left(1 - \tfrac{1}{3}\right)\left(1 - \tfrac{1}{4}\right)\cdots\left(1 - \tfrac{1}{16}\right)$$

22 The three dots in the product above represent eleven missing factors of the form $\left(1 - \tfrac{1}{n}\right)$, where n represents all of the consecutive integers from 5 to 15, inclusive. Which of the following is equal to P?

(A) $\dfrac{1}{16}$

(B) $\dfrac{1}{2}$

(C) $\dfrac{3}{4}$

(D) $\dfrac{7}{8}$

(E) $\dfrac{15}{16}$

GO ON TO THE NEXT PAGE

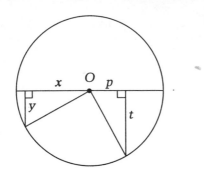

23 In the circle with center O above, the two triangles have legs of lengths x, y, p, and t, as shown. If $x^2 + y^2 + p^2 + t^2 = 72$, what is the circumference of the circle?

(A) 8π
(B) 9π
(C) 12π
(D) 24π
(E) 36π

24 A chemist has a solution consisting of 6 ounces of propanol and 18 ounces of water. She wants to change the solution to 40 percent propanol by adding x ounces of propanol. Which of the following equations could she solve in order to determine the value of x?

(A) $\dfrac{6}{18 + x} = \dfrac{40}{100}$

(B) $\dfrac{6 + x}{18} = \dfrac{40}{100}$

(C) $\dfrac{6 + x}{24} = \dfrac{40}{100}$

(D) $\dfrac{6 + x}{18 + x} = \dfrac{40}{100}$

(E) $\dfrac{6 + x}{24 + x} = \dfrac{40}{100}$

25 Which of the following could be the exact value of n^4, where n is an integer?

(A) 1.6×10^{20}
(B) 1.6×10^{21}
(C) 1.6×10^{22}
(D) 1.6×10^{23}
(E) 1.6×10^{24}

IF YOU FINISH BEFORE TIME IS CALLED, YOU MAY CHECK YOUR WORK ON THIS SECTION ONLY. DO NOT TURN TO ANY OTHER SECTION IN THE TEST.

STOP

232

NO TEST MATERIAL ON THIS PAGE

Time-30 Minutes — For each question in this section, select the best answer from among the choices given and 35 Questions fill in the corresponding oval on the answer sheet.

Each sentence below has one or two blanks, each blank indicating that something has been omitted. Beneath the sentence are five words or sets of words labeled A through E. Choose the word or set of words that, when inserted in the sentence, best fits the meaning of the sentence as a whole.

Example:

Medieval kingdoms did not become constitutional republics overnight; on the contrary, the change was ----.

(A) unpopular
(B) unexpected
(C) advantageous
(D) sufficient
(E) gradual

Ⓐ Ⓑ Ⓒ Ⓓ ●

1 Tarantulas apparently have little sense of ----, for a hungry one will ignore a loudly chirping cricket placed in its cage unless the cricket happens to get in its way.

(A) touch
(B) time
(C) hearing
(D) self-preservation
(E) temperature

2 Though she claimed to be portraying the human figure, her paintings were entirely ----, characterized by simple geometric shapes.

(A) lifelike
(B) emotional
(C) naturalistic
(D) formless
(E) abstract

3 Dr. Estella Jiménez believed that the experimental therapy would create new problems, some of them predictable but others totally ----.

(A) benign
(B) ineffective
(C) suggestive
(D) unexpected
(E) formal

4 Even more ---- in gesture than in words, the characters in the movie achieve their greatest ---- in pure silence.

(A) awkward..success
(B) expressive..eloquence
(C) trite..originality
(D) incompetent..performance
(E) skilled..repose

5 These studies will necessarily take several years because the ---- of the new drug involved in the project is not ----.

(A) availability..tested
(B) virulence..doubted
(C) effect..immediate
(D) background..practical
(E) value..expendable

6 Although he was ---- by nature, he had to be ---- at work because of the need to slash costs.

(A) prudent..profligate
(B) ferocious..indefensible
(C) industrious..productive
(D) extravagant..parsimonious
(E) pleasant..amiable

7 Like a martinet, Charles deals with all people in ---- manner that implies they must ---- him.

(A) a haughty..thwart
(B) an imperious..obey
(C) an egalitarian..salute
(D) a timorous..cheat
(E) a cowardly..understand

8 Because of their ---- to expand their share of the credit card market, banks may be ---- credit to customers who are poor risks.

(A) reluctance..increasing
(B) rush..decreasing
(C) inability..denying
(D) mandate..limiting
(E) eagerness..extending

9 The Roman soldiers who invaded Britain had little respect for the Britons, usually referring to them in ---- terms.

(A) pejorative
(B) hypocritical
(C) impressive
(D) irrational
(E) ambiguous

10 Many contemporary novelists have forsaken a traditional intricacy of plot and detailed depiction of character for a distinctly ---- presentation of both.

(A) convoluted
(B) derivative
(C) conventional
(D) conservative
(E) unadorned

GO ON TO THE NEXT PAGE

234

Each question below consists of a related pair of words or phrases, followed by five pairs of words or phrases labeled A through E. Select the pair that best expresses a relationship similar to that expressed in the original pair.

Example:

CRUMB:BREAD::
(A) ounce:unit
(B) splinter:wood
(C) water:bucket
(D) twine:rope
(E) cream:butter

(A) ● (C) (D) (E)

11 TIPTOE:STEP::

(A) pant:breathe
(B) smooth:wrinkle
(C) whisper:speak
(D) startle:frighten
(E) tickle:giggle

12 MARBLE:STONE::

(A) sand:cement
(B) gold:mine
(C) spoke:wheel
(D) copper:metal
(E) cloud:sky

13 FACTORY:MANUFACTURE::

(A) bookshop:read
(B) office:employ
(C) store:sell
(D) hospital:operate
(E) prison:escape

14 SHOULDER:ROAD::

(A) pane:window
(B) cup:bottle
(C) grain:leather
(D) driveway:garage
(E) margin:page

15 PACT:NATIONS::

(A) compromise:extremes
(B) certificate:qualifications
(C) treaty:hostilities
(D) border:municipalities
(E) contract:parties

16 SECEDE:ORGANIZATION::

(A) promote:job
(B) retreat:position
(C) retire:leisure
(D) bankrupt:wealth
(E) ally:country

17 ASYLUM:PERSECUTION::

(A) building:vandalism
(B) tomb:coffin
(C) refuge:safety
(D) infirmary:diagnosis
(E) shelter:storm

18 NOVICE:SEASONED::

(A) censor:offensive
(B) confidant:trustworthy
(C) ingrate:thankful
(D) tyrant:oppressed
(E) novelist:fictional

19 PARODY:IMITATION::

(A) farce:laughter
(B) caricature:likeness
(C) mask:disguise
(D) deviation:similarity
(E) gem:embellishment

20 MITIGATE:SEVERITY::

(A) weigh:measurement
(B) dissolve:solvent
(C) sterilize:heat
(D) stabilize:fluctuation
(E) examine:outcome

21 CONTROVERSY:DISPUTANT::

(A) stubbornness:pugilist
(B) antagonism:pacifist
(C) imperfection:purist
(D) meditation:hypnotist
(E) indoctrination:propagandist

22 CAREFUL:FASTIDIOUS::

(A) disobedient:mutinous
(B) patronizing:flattering
(C) religious:sacred
(D) mellow:harmonious
(E) fragrant:blooming

23 REPUGNANT:AVERSION::

(A) insatiable:satisfaction
(B) informed:knowledge
(C) bigoted:judgment
(D) shameless:regret
(E) admirable:esteem

GO ON TO THE NEXT PAGE

The passage below is followed by questions based on its content. Answer the questions on the basis of what is <u>stated</u> or <u>implied</u> in the passage and in any introductory material that may be provided.

Questions 24-35 are based on the following passage.

In this passage about language, the author, a Japanese American, recounts an experience he had just after the United States entered the Second World War. In the Midwest, where he lived and taught, hostility toward Japanese Americans at that time was not so severe as it was on the West Coast.

Although language is used to transmit information, the informative functions of language are fused with older and deeper functions so that only a small portion
(Line) of our everyday utterances can be described as purely
(5) informative. The ability to use language for strictly informative purposes was probably developed relatively late in the course of linguistic evolution. Long before that time, our ancestral species probably made the sorts of cries animals do to express feelings of hunger, fear,
(10) loneliness, and the like. Gradually these noises seem to have become more differentiated, transforming grunts and gibberings into language as we know it today.

Although we have developed language in which accurate reports may be given, we still use language as
(15) vocal equivalents of gestures such as crying in pain or baring the teeth in anger. When words are used as the vocal equivalent of expressive gestures, language is functioning in presymbolic ways. These presymbolic uses of language coexist with our symbolic system, so
(20) that the talking we do in everyday life is a thorough blending of symbolic and presymbolic language.

What we call social conversation is mainly presymbolic in character. When we are at a large social gathering, for example, we all have to talk. It is typical
(25) of these conversations that, except among very good friends, few of the remarks made have any informative value. We talk together about nothing at all and thereby establish rapport.

There is a principle at work in the selection of the
(30) subject matter we deem appropriate for social conversation. Since the purpose of this kind of talk is the establishment of communion, *we are careful to select subjects about which agreement is immediately possible.* Having agreed on the weather, we go on to further
(35) agreements—that the rate of inflation is scandalous, that New York City is an interesting place to visit but that it would be an awful place to live, and so on. With each new agreement, no matter how commonplace, the fear and suspicion of the stranger wears away, and the
(40) possibility of friendship emerges. When further conversation reveals that we have friends or political views or artistic values or hobbies in common, a friend is made, and genuine communication and cooperation can begin.

(45) An incident in my own experience illustrates these points. Early in 1942, a few weeks after war was declared between Japan and the United States and at a time when rumors of Japanese spies were still widely current, I had to wait two or three hours in a small
(50) railroad station in a city in the Midwest. I became aware as time went on that the other people waiting in the station were staring at me suspiciously and feeling uneasy about my presence. One couple with a small child was staring with special uneasiness and whispering to
(55) each other. I therefore took occasion to remark to the husband that it was too bad that the train should be late on so cold a night. He agreed. I went on to remark that it must be especially difficult to travel with a small child in winter when train schedules were so uncertain. Again
(60) the husband agreed. I then asked the child's age and remarked that the child looked very big and strong for his age. Again agreement—this time with a slight smile. The tension was relaxing.

After two or three more exchanges, the man asked, "I
(65) hope you don't mind my asking, but you're Japanese, aren't you? Do you think the Japanese have any chance of winning this war?"

"Well," I replied, "your guess is as good as mine. I don't know any more than I read in the papers. [This
(70) was true.] But I don't see how the Japanese with their lack of coal and steel and oil and their limited industrial capacity, can ever beat a powerful industrialized nation like the United States."

My remark was admittedly neither original nor well
(75) informed. Hundreds of radio commentators and editorial writers were saying exactly the same thing during those weeks. But because they were, the remark *sounded familiar* and was *on the right side,* so that it was easy to agree with. The man agreed at once, with what sounded
(80) like genuine relief. How much the wall of suspicion had broken down was indicated in his next question, "Say, I hope your folks aren't over there while the war is going on?"

"Yes, they are. My father and mother and two
(85) younger sisters are over there."

"Do you ever hear from them?"

"How can I?"

"Do you mean you won't be able to see them or hear from them until after the war is over?" Both he and his
(90) wife looked sympathetic.

There was more to the conversation, but the result was that within ten minutes after it had begun they had invited me to visit them in their city. The other people in the station ceased paying any attention to me and
(95) went back to staring at the ceiling.

GO ON TO THE NEXT PAGE

24 The phrase "older and deeper functions" (line 3) refers to the

(A) grammatical structure of language
(B) expression of emotions through sound
(C) transmission of information
(D) statement of cultural values
(E) original meanings of words

25 The word "differentiated" is used in line 11 to mean

(A) changeable
(B) fused
(C) defined
(D) functional
(E) communicative

26 The author uses the term "presymbolic language" to mean

(A) grunts and cries such as are made by animals
(B) language used between friends
(C) language that lacks an elaborate grammatical structure
(D) nonverbal expressions used in communicating
(E) language that does not convey specific information

27 The primary value of presymbolic language for humans is that it

(A) is easily understood
(B) is common to all languages rather than unique to any one language
(C) permits and aids the smooth functioning of interpersonal relationships
(D) helps us understand and express our emotions
(E) allows for a desirable amount of social mobility

28 Judging from the author's discussion in lines 29-44, the most important function of social conversation is to

(A) dispel suspicion among strangers
(B) discover topics that are interesting to debate
(C) impress others by expressing clever opinions
(D) perfect the use of effective gestures and facial expressions
(E) involve a large number of people in a conversation

29 Which of the following best captures the meaning of the word "communion" in line 32?

(A) Ritual
(B) Initiation
(C) Conversation
(D) Common ground
(E) Social group

30 The comment that New York City "would be an awful place to live" (line 37) is offered by the author as an example of the kind of statement that

(A) might lead to genuine communication
(B) will amuse the reader
(C) shows the author's distrust of New Yorkers
(D) is generally ignored
(E) expresses a basic emotion

31 The most crucial difference between presymbolic and symbolic language lies in the

(A) diversity of topics that can be discussed in each mode
(B) origin and developmental path of each mode in linguistic evolution
(C) degree to which each mode may be accompanied by expressive gestures
(D) purposes served by each mode
(E) clarity each mode makes possible

GO ON TO THE NEXT PAGE

32 The author's remark about Japan's industrial capacity (lines 71-72) helped to relieve the tension because

(A) it showed how much the author knew about Japan
(B) the information was already familiar to the couple
(C) it was not directly related to the war
(D) the author indicated that American newspapers were accurate
(E) the author did not offer the information until the couple asked for it

33 Which of the following best explains why the onlookers in the train station went back to "staring at the ceiling"?

(A) They sympathized with the writer because he was separated from his family.
(B) They did not want to get into conversation with the writer.
(C) They were embarrassed by the fact that the writer was from a country at war with the United States.
(D) The train was late and they had become bored.
(E) They had stopped viewing the author as a suspicious person.

34 The author uses the incident at the train station primarily to illustrate that

(A) distrust between strangers is natural
(B) people react positively to someone who is nice to children
(C) giving people the opportunity to agree with you will make it easier for them to trust you
(D) people of Japanese ancestry living in the United States during the Second World War faced prejudice
(E) it is easy to recognize hostility in strangers

35 Which piece of information about himself would have been most risky for the author to convey at the beginning of the conversation in the train station?

(A) He knows only what he reads in the newspapers.
(B) He believes that Japan lacks vital natural resources.
(C) He does not see how a powerful nation like the United States could be defeated by Japan.
(D) He has close relatives living in Japan.
(E) He does not expect to hear from his family in the near future.

IF YOU FINISH BEFORE TIME IS CALLED, YOU MAY CHECK YOUR WORK ON THIS SECTION ONLY. DO NOT TURN TO ANY OTHER SECTION IN THE TEST. STOP

238

NO TEST MATERIAL ON THIS PAGE

Time—30 Minutes
25 Questions

This section contains two types of questions. You have 30 minutes to complete both types. You may use any available space for scratchwork.

Notes:

(1) The use of a calculator is permitted. All numbers used are real numbers.

(2) Figures that accompany problems in this test are intended to provide information useful in solving the problems. They are drawn as accurately as possible EXCEPT when it is stated in a specific problem that the figure is not drawn to scale. All figures lie in a plane unless otherwise indicated.

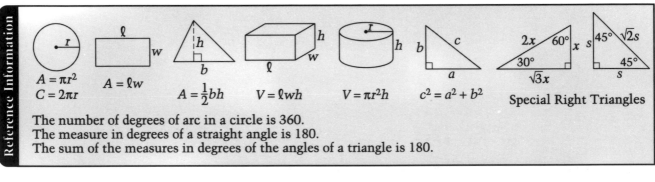

Reference Information

$A = \pi r^2$
$C = 2\pi r$

$A = \ell w$

$A = \frac{1}{2}bh$

$V = \ell wh$

$V = \pi r^2 h$

$c^2 = a^2 + b^2$

Special Right Triangles

The number of degrees of arc in a circle is 360.
The measure in degrees of a straight angle is 180.
The sum of the measures in degrees of the angles of a triangle is 180.

Directions for Quantitative Comparison Questions

Questions 1-15 each consist of two quantities in boxes, one in Column A and one in Column B. You are to compare the two quantities and on the answer sheet fill in oval

  A if the quantity in Column A is greater;
  B if the quantity in Column B is greater;
  C if the two quantities are equal;
  D if the relationship cannot be determined from the information given.

AN E RESPONSE WILL NOT BE SCORED.

Notes:

1. In some questions, information is given about one or both of the quantities to be compared. In such cases, the given information is centered above the two columns and is not boxed.
2. In a given question, a symbol that appears in both columns represents the same thing in Column A as it does in Column B.
3. Letters such as x, n, and k stand for real numbers.

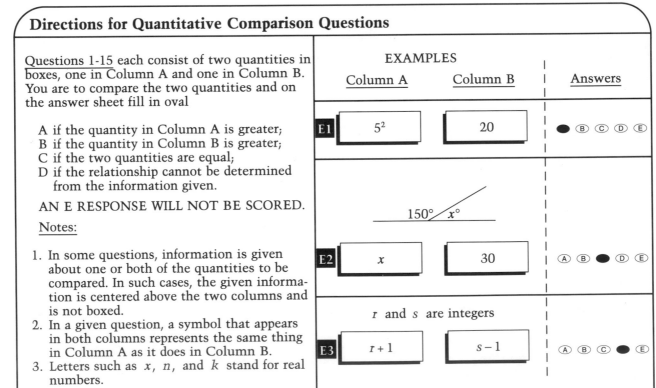

Column A   **Column B**

1 | The number of years from the year 1790 to the present | The number of years from the year 1780 to the present

$$x + 3 = 5$$
$$2y + 11 = 15$$

2 | x | y

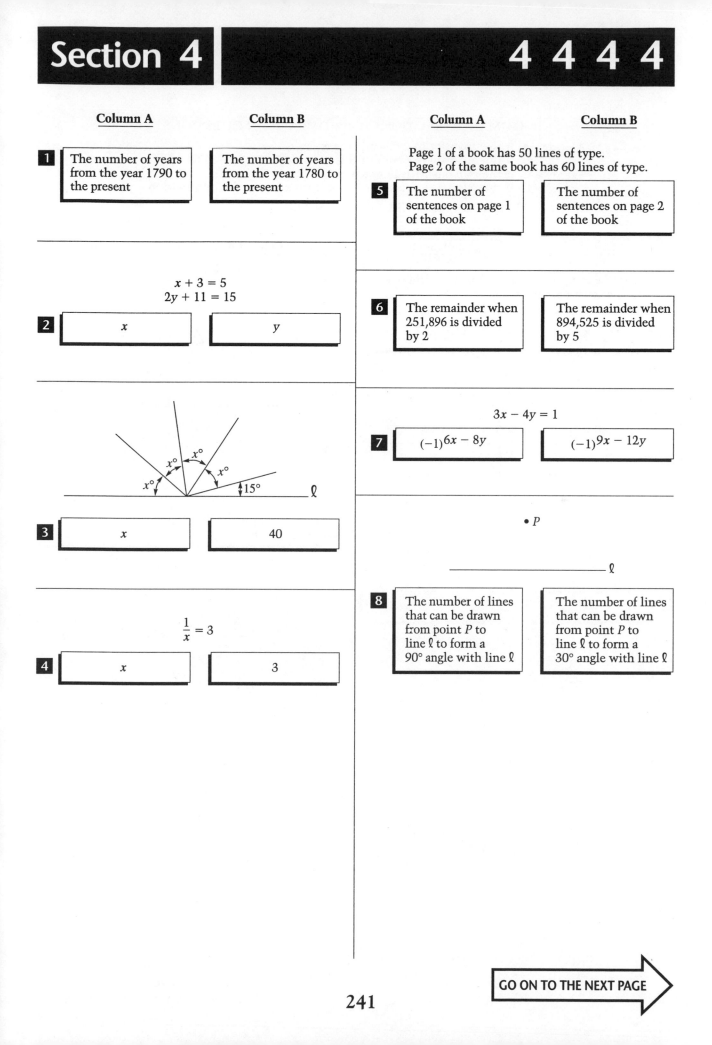

3 | x | 40

$$\frac{1}{x} = 3$$

4 | x | 3

Column A   **Column B**

Page 1 of a book has 50 lines of type.
Page 2 of the same book has 60 lines of type.

5 | The number of sentences on page 1 of the book | The number of sentences on page 2 of the book

6 | The remainder when 251,896 is divided by 2 | The remainder when 894,525 is divided by 5

$$3x - 4y = 1$$

7 | $(-1)^{6x - 8y}$ | $(-1)^{9x - 12y}$

$\bullet\, P$

─────────────── ℓ

8 | The number of lines that can be drawn from point P to line ℓ to form a 90° angle with line ℓ | The number of lines that can be drawn from point P to line ℓ to form a 30° angle with line ℓ

GO ON TO THE NEXT PAGE

241

SUMMARY DIRECTIONS FOR COMPARISON QUESTIONS

<u>Answer:</u> A if the quantity in Column A is greater;
B if the quantity in Column B is greater;
C if the two quantities are equal;
D if the relationship cannot be determined from the information given.

AN E RESPONSE WILL NOT BE SCORED.

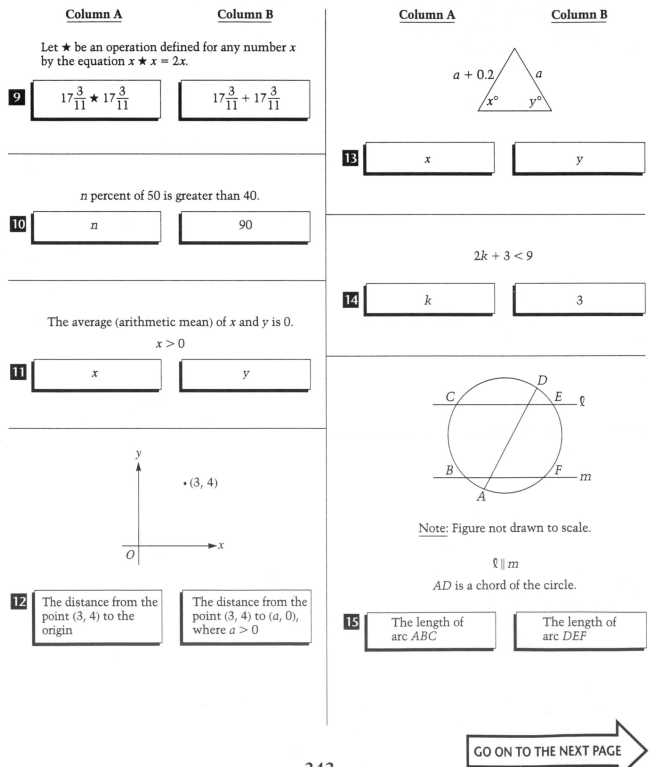

Column A	**Column B**

Let ★ be an operation defined for any number x by the equation $x \star x = 2x$.

9 | $17\frac{3}{11} \star 17\frac{3}{11}$ | $17\frac{3}{11} + 17\frac{3}{11}$ |

n percent of 50 is greater than 40.

10 | n | 90 |

The average (arithmetic mean) of x and y is 0.

$$x > 0$$

11 | x | y |

$\cdot (3, 4)$

12 | The distance from the point (3, 4) to the origin | The distance from the point (3, 4) to (a, 0), where $a > 0$ |

Column A	**Column B**

$a + 0.2$ ... a ... $x°$ ... $y°$

13 | x | y |

$$2k + 3 < 9$$

14 | k | 3 |

Note: Figure not drawn to scale.

$\ell \parallel m$

AD is a chord of the circle.

15 | The length of arc ABC | The length of arc DEF |

GO ON TO THE NEXT PAGE

242

Directions for Student-Produced Response Questions

Each of the remaining 10 questions (16-25) requires you to solve the problem and enter your answer by marking the ovals in the special grid, as shown in the examples below.

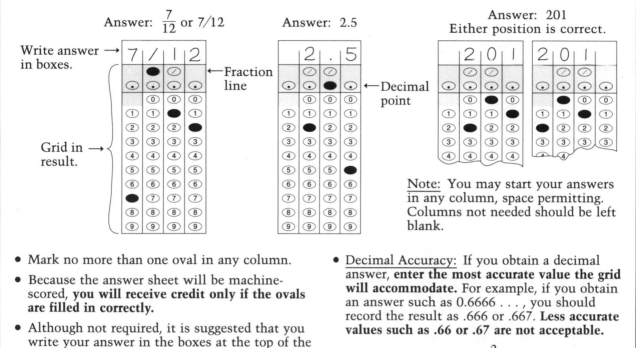

Answer: $\frac{7}{12}$ or 7/12

Answer: 2.5

Answer: 201
Either position is correct.

Write answer → in boxes.

← Fraction line

← Decimal point

Grid in → result.

<u>Note</u>: You may start your answers in any column, space permitting. Columns not needed should be left blank.

- Mark no more than one oval in any column.

- Because the answer sheet will be machine-scored, **you will receive credit only if the ovals are filled in correctly.**

- Although not required, it is suggested that you write your answer in the boxes at the top of the columns to help you fill in the ovals accurately.

- Some problems may have more than one correct answer. In such cases, grid only one answer.

- No question has a negative answer.

- **Mixed numbers** such as $2\frac{1}{2}$ must be gridded as 2.5 or 5/2. (If `2 1 / 2` is gridded, it will be interpreted as $\frac{21}{2}$, not $2\frac{1}{2}$.)

- Decimal Accuracy: If you obtain a decimal answer, **enter the most accurate value the grid will accommodate.** For example, if you obtain an answer such as 0.6666 . . . , you should record the result as .666 or .667. **Less accurate values such as .66 or .67 are not acceptable.**

Acceptable ways to grid $\frac{2}{3}$ = .6666 . . .

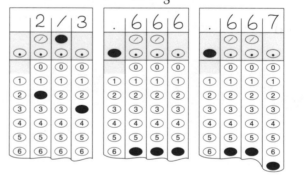

---

16 If $3x = y$ and $y = z + 1$, what is the value of x when $z = 29$?

17 An annual subscription to a certain monthly magazine is $9.60, including tax and postage. The cost of a single issue of the magazine at a newsstand is $1.25, including tax. How much money, in dollars, is saved in one year by subscribing to the magazine rather than by purchasing the magazine each month at a newsstand? (Disregard the $ sign when gridding your answer.)

GO ON TO THE NEXT PAGE

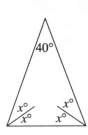

18 In the triangle above, what is the value of x?

19 If $2^n = 8$, what is the value of 3^{n+1}?

20 What is one possible value of x for which $\frac{1}{5} < x < \frac{1}{4}$?

FAMILIES IN CENTERVILLE—1990

Number of Children	Percent of Families
0	n%
1	18%
2	17%
3	11%
4 or more	10%

21 There were 5,000 families in Centerville in 1990. According to the chart above, how many of the families had no children?

GO ON TO THE NEXT PAGE

22 Two numbers form a "couple" if the sum of their reciprocals equals 2. For example, 8 and $\frac{8}{15}$ form a couple because $\frac{1}{8} + \frac{15}{8} = 2$. If x and y form a couple and $x = \frac{7}{3}$, what is the value of y?

Test Score	Number of Students
90	2
85	1
80	1
60	3

24 The test scores of 7 students are shown above. Let M and m be the median and mean scores, respectively. What is the value of $M - m$?

23 The entire surface of a solid cube with edge of length 6 inches is painted. The cube is then cut into cubes each with edge of length 1 inch. How many of the smaller cubes have paint on exactly 1 face?

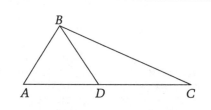

Note: Figure not drawn to scale.

25 In triangle ABC above, $AC = 12$. If the ratio of the area of triangle ABD to the area of triangle CBD is $3 : 5$, what is the length of segment AD?

IF YOU FINISH BEFORE TIME IS CALLED, YOU MAY CHECK YOUR WORK ON THIS SECTION ONLY. DO NOT TURN TO ANY OTHER SECTION IN THE TEST. **STOP**

245

Time-15 Minutes — For each question in this section, select the best answer from among the choices given and
13 Questions   fill in the corresponding oval on the answer sheet.

The two passages below are followed by questions based on their content and on the relationship between
the two passages. Answer the questions on the basis of what is <u>stated</u> or <u>implied</u> in the passages and in any
introductory material that may be provided.

Questions 1-13 are based on the following passages.

*The following passages, written in the twentieth century, present two views of the architectural design of cities.
Passage 1 discusses English "garden cities," planned medium-sized cities containing residential, commercial, and
open space. Passage 2 offers a critique of modern cities.*

Passage 1

Attempts have been made by architectural writers
to discredit the garden cities on the ground that they
lack "urbanity." Because the buildings in them are
Line generously spaced and interspersed with gardens, lawns,
(5) and trees, they rarely produce the particular effect of
absolute enclosure or packed picturesqueness not
undeservedly admired by visitors to many ancient cities.
This is true; garden cities exhibit another and a more
popular kind of beauty, as well as a healthier and more
(10) convenient form of layout.

But the garden city is, nonetheless, truly a "city."
The criticism exposes the confusion and aesthetic
narrow-mindedness of the critics. If the word
"urbanity" is used in the accepted sense of "educated
(15) tastefulness," the charge that the garden cities are
without it is an affront to the well-qualified architects
who have taken part in their design. If it is used in the
simple etymological sense of "city-ness," the users
unknowingly expose their crass ignorance of the infinite
(20) diversity that the world's cities display. And if it is used
(illegitimately) as a synonym for high urban density or
crowdedness, it stands for a quality most city dwellers
regard as something to escape from if they can. The
word "urbanity" has been so maltreated that it should
(25) now be eliminated from town planning discussions.

Tastes differ in architectural styles as they do in all the
arts, and the ability to judge is complicated by changes
in fashion, to which critics of the arts seem more
subject than people in general. Persons vary in stability
(30) of taste: for some a thing of beauty is a joy forever, for
others a joy till next month's issue of an architectural
periodical.

The garden cities have been obedient to the prevailing
architectural fashion. Luckily for the profession, average
(35) Britons, though not highly sensitive to architectural
design, do not mind it, so long as the things they really
care about in a house or a town are attended to. They
take great pleasure in grass, trees, and flowers, with
which the garden cities are well endowed. The outlook
(40) from their windows is more important to them than the
look of their dwellings from the street. And though they
would have preferred their dwellings to have some
element of individuality, they accept harmonious
design and grouping without resentment. Thus, given
(45) due respect for their major interest, a pleasing ensemble
is attainable.

Passage 2

To the visually trained person today, the architecture
of the modern city is a remorseless and unremitting
assault on the senses. This kind of urban anarchy is an
(50) outstanding fact of modern life, an expression of
brutalism as harsh and as significant as modern warfare.
Our cities are neither expressions of civilization nor
creators of civilized individuals.

We see this rampant ugliness not only in the
(55) crumbling hearts of older American cities, but in
America's most modern urban areas as well—the tangle
of superhighways that seem to strangle certain West
Coast cities or in suburbs that project the image of a
standardized, anonymous, dehumanized person. Nor
(60) have we escaped this gloomy catalog when we visit cities
that have erected "good taste" into an inoffensive—but
equally repugnant because false—urban "style." Urban
uglification is not limited to any single country: the
posters in the travel agent's office promise famous
(65) monuments and picturesque antiquities, but when you
look through your hotel room window you see smog,
unsanitary streets, and neighborhoods ruined by
rapacious speculation in land and buildings.

Those who do not reject modern cities are condi-
(70) tioned not to see, hear, feel, smell, or sense them as
they are. The greatest obstacle to seemly cities has
become our low expectations, a direct result of our
having become habituated to the present environment

GO ON TO THE NEXT PAGE

and our incapacity to conceive of any better alternative.
(75) Those of us who have made this adjustment are permanently disabled in the use of our senses, brutalized
victims of the modern city.

   We can get at what's wrong with a city like
Washington D.C. by considering the question once
(80) asked seriously by a European visitor, "Where can you
take a walk?" He didn't mean an arduous hike, but a
stroll along a city street where you can see the people,
admire the buildings, inspect the goods, and learn about
life in the process.

(85)   Perhaps we need a simple litmus-paper test of the
good city. Who lives there? Where is the center? What
do you do when you get there? A successful urban design
involves urbanity, the quality the garden city forgot. It is
found in plazas and squares, in boulevards and prom-
(90) enades. It can be found in Rome's railroad station.
When you find it, never let it go. It is the hardest thing
to create anew.

1 In line 4, the word "generously" most nearly
   means

   (A) charitably
   (B) helpfully
   (C) unselfishly
   (D) widely
   (E) benevolently

2 The author of Passage 1 objects to using the
   "simple etymological sense" (line 18) of the word
   "urbanity" for which reason?

   (A) Different individuals value different aspects of
       urban life.
   (B) The traditional idea of what is desirable in a
       city changes greatly over time.
   (C) Discovering the history of a word is often
       difficult.
   (D) Not all of the world's cities are alike.
   (E) It is dangerous to disregard the opinion of
       experts.

3 In Passage 1, the reference to "next month's
   issue of an architectural periodical" (lines 31-32)
   serves to

   (A) show that the plans for the garden cities are
       well thought of in professional journals
   (B) indicate that what seems like a random
       process is actually an ordered process
   (C) suggest that some people lack their own firm
       ideals of beauty
   (D) imply that only those who are knowledgeable
       about a subject should offer their opinions
   (E) emphasize the importance of what the experts
       say

4 In lines 34-41, by considering the relative
   importance to "average Britons" of the view
   from their homes, the author of Passage 1
   suggests that

   (A) natural light is an important element of urban
       design
   (B) Britons are not particularly concerned about
       the architectural design elements that catch
       the attention of critics
   (C) the appeal of grass, trees, and flowers has been
       overrated by many architectural theorists
   (D) the importance of designing buildings that
       have a pleasing exterior form needs to be
       remembered
   (E) Britons often object to being treated like
       members of a group rather than like
       individuals

5 In the last paragraph of Passage 1, the author
   acknowledges which flaw in the design of
   the garden city?

   (A) The uniformity of the dwellings
   (B) The view from many of the windows
   (C) The constraint imposed by the landscape
   (D) The emphasis placed on plantings
   (E) The outmodedness of the architecture

GO ON TO THE NEXT PAGE

6 The references in Passage 2 to "posters" (line 64) and the view from the "hotel room window" (line 66) serve to

(A) give an accurate sense of the two places
(B) highlight the distinction between the ideal and the reality
(C) show what could be, as opposed to what is
(D) criticize those who would say negative things about well-loved places
(E) invoke past splendor in order to point out present flaws

7 In line 68, the phrase "rapacious speculation" refers to

(A) rapid calculations
(B) endless deliberation
(C) immoral thoughts
(D) exploitative investments
(E) illegal gambling

8 If modern cities are so terrible, why, according to Passage 2, do people continue to live in them?

(A) Cities provide more varied employment opportunities than other places.
(B) People see cities for what they are and actually enjoy living in such places.
(C) The cultural opportunities available in cities are more varied than those in rural areas.
(D) Despite their drawbacks, cities have a quality of life that makes them desirable as places to live.
(E) As a consequence of living in cities, people have become unable to think objectively about their environment.

9 The distinction made in Passage 2 between a "walk" and a "hike" (lines 81-84) can best be summarized as which of the following?

(A) The first is primarily a social experience, the second primarily exercise.
(B) The first involves a greater degree of physical exercise than the second.
(C) The first is more likely to be regimented than the second.
(D) The first covers a greater distance than the second.
(E) The first is a popular activity, the second appeals only to a small group.

10 The questions in lines 86-87 chiefly serve to

(A) ask the reader to compare his or her experience with the author's
(B) show that it is easier to point out problems than to find solutions
(C) suggest what the author's definition of urbanity might involve
(D) answer the charges made by the author's critics
(E) outline an area in which further investigation is needed

11 In lines 87-88, the author of Passage 2 is critical of garden cities primarily because

(A) they are too crowded
(B) they lack that quality essential to a good city
(C) their design has not been carried out rationally
(D) people cannot readily accommodate themselves to living in them
(E) they are better places for plants than for people

12 The author of Passage 1 would most likely react to the characterization of garden cities presented in lines 87-88 by pointing out that

(A) recent research has shown the inadequacy of this characterization
(B) the facts of urban life support this characterization
(C) this characterization is dismissed by most authorities
(D) this characterization is neither accurate nor well defined
(E) this characterization expresses poor taste

13 How would the author of Passage 1 respond to the way the author of Passage 2 uses the word "urbanity" to describe the quality found in "Rome's railroad station" (line 90)?

(A) The quality is not to be found in so common a structure as a railroad station.
(B) The word "urbanity" is being used to denigrate an otherwise positive quality.
(C) The word "urbanity" has been so misused as to be no longer meaningful.
(D) "Urbanity" is, in fact, one of the leading characteristics of the garden city.
(E) It is a sign of arrogance to refuse to value this quality.

IF YOU FINISH BEFORE TIME IS CALLED, YOU MAY CHECK YOUR WORK ON THIS SECTION ONLY. DO NOT TURN TO ANY OTHER SECTION IN THE TEST.

STOP

NO TEST MATERIAL ON THIS PAGE

Time—15 Minutes 10 Questions	In this section solve each problem, using any available space on the page for scratchwork. Then decide which is the best of the choices given and fill in the corresponding oval on the answer sheet.

Notes:

(1) The use of a calculator is permitted. All numbers used are real numbers.

(2) Figures that accompany problems in this test are intended to provide information useful in solving the problems. They are drawn as accurately as possible EXCEPT when it is stated in a specific problem that the figure is not drawn to scale. All figures lie in a plane unless otherwise indicated.

Reference Information

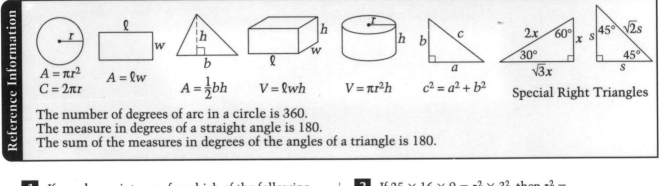

$A = \pi r^2$
$C = 2\pi r$

$A = \ell w$

$A = \frac{1}{2}bh$

$V = \ell wh$

$V = \pi r^2 h$

$c^2 = a^2 + b^2$

Special Right Triangles

The number of degrees of arc in a circle is 360.
The measure in degrees of a straight angle is 180.
The sum of the measures in degrees of the angles of a triangle is 180.

1 If x and y are integers, for which of the following ordered pairs (x, y) is $2x + y$ an odd number?

(A) (0,2)
(B) (1,2)
(C) (2,1)
(D) (2,4)
(E) (3,0)

2 If $25 \times 16 \times 9 = r^2 \times 3^2$, then $r^2 =$

(A) 4^2
(B) 5^2
(C) 10^2
(D) 15^2
(E) 20^2

GO ON TO THE NEXT PAGE

DISTRIBUTION OF $10,000 IN
SCHOLARSHIP MONEY

3 The circle graph above shows the distribution of $10,000 in scholarship money to five students. Which of the students received an amount closest to $2,500?

(A) Maria
(B) Bob
(C) Yuriko
(D) Diane
(E) Ed

5 In a sack there are exactly 48 marbles, each of which is either red, black, or yellow. The probability of randomly selecting a red marble from the sack is $\frac{5}{8}$, and the probability of randomly selecting a black marble from the sack is $\frac{1}{8}$. How many marbles in the sack are yellow?

(A) 6
(B) 12
(C) 16
(D) 18
(E) 24

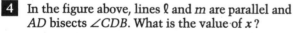

4 In the figure above, lines ℓ and m are parallel and AD bisects $\angle CDB$. What is the value of x?

(A) 55
(B) 60
(C) 65
(D) 70
(E) 75

6 If the area of rectangle $ABCD$ above is 70 square units, what is the value of p?

(A) 8
(B) 10
(C) 12
(D) 14
(E) 16

GO ON TO THE NEXT PAGE

7 In a certain basketball league, a player has an average (arithmetic mean) of 22 points per game for 8 games. What is the total number of points this player must score in the next 2 games in order to have an average of 20 points per game for 10 games?

(A) 18
(B) 20
(C) 22
(D) 24
(E) 34

9 Let x and y be positive integers and $n = x^y$.
If $n + \sqrt{n} + \sqrt[3]{n} = 76$, then x CANNOT equal

(A) 64
(B) 16
(C) 8
(D) 4
(E) 2

Note: Figure not drawn to scale.

8 In the figure above, $AB = 1$ and $BC = CD = 3$. What is the length of line segment AD?

(A) 5

(B) $2\sqrt{3} + \sqrt{2}$

(C) $3 + \sqrt{2}$

(D) $\sqrt{19}$

(E) 4

10 A faulty clock is set to the correct time at 12:00 noon. If the clock gains 5 minutes per hour, what is the correct time when the faulty clock indicates that 13 hours have passed?

(A) 11:55 p.m.
(B) 12:00 midnight
(C) 1:00 a.m.
(D) 1:05 a.m.
(E) 2:05 a.m.

IF YOU FINISH BEFORE TIME IS CALLED, YOU MAY CHECK YOUR WORK ON THIS SECTION ONLY. DO NOT TURN TO ANY OTHER SECTION IN THE TEST.

STOP

252

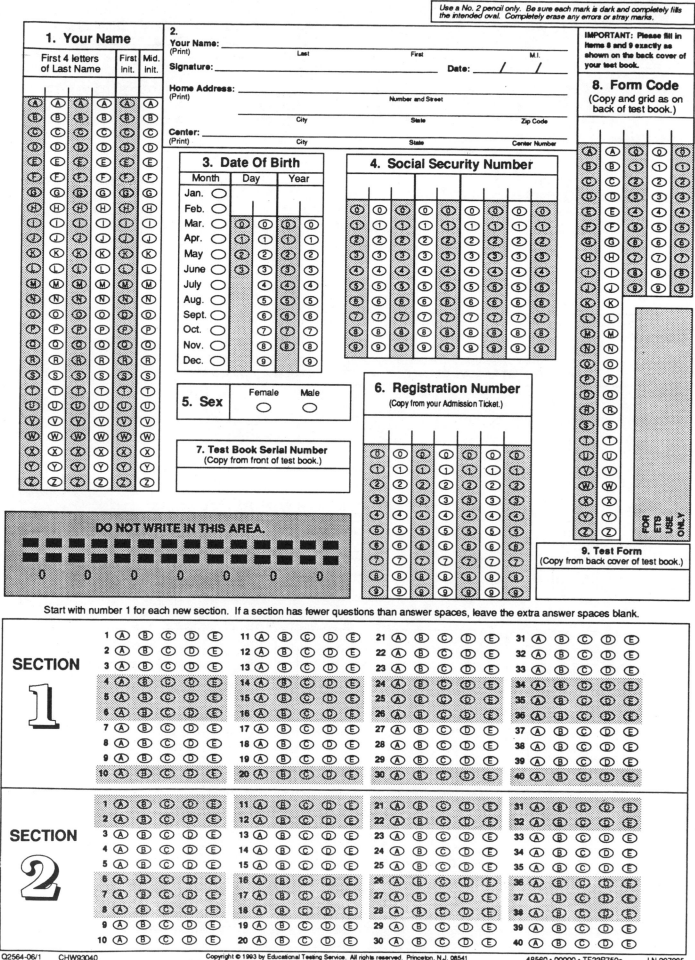

Start with number 1 for each new section. If a section has fewer questions than answer spaces, leave the extra answer spaces blank.

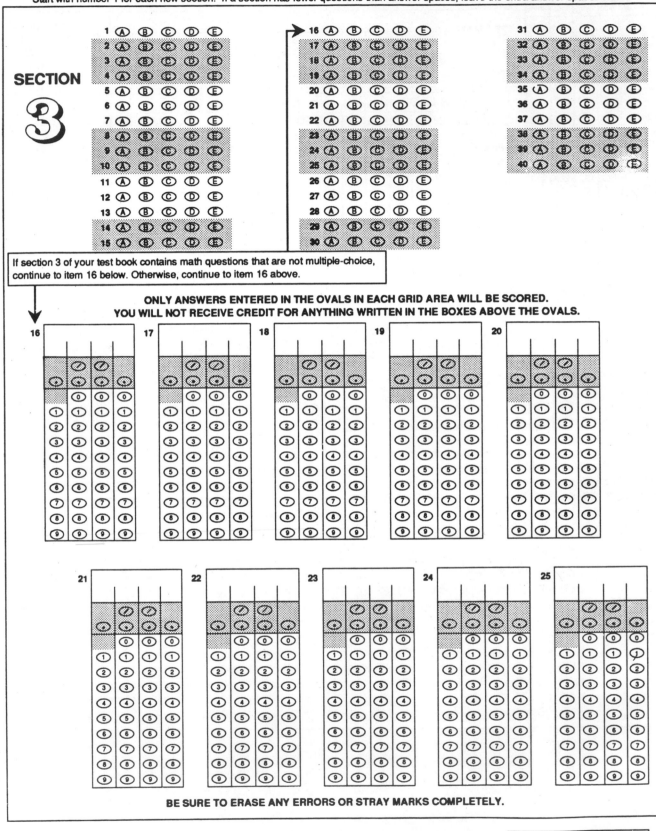

SECTION 3

If section 3 of your test book contains math questions that are not multiple-choice, continue to item 16 below. Otherwise, continue to item 16 above.

ONLY ANSWERS ENTERED IN THE OVALS IN EACH GRID AREA WILL BE SCORED.
YOU WILL NOT RECEIVE CREDIT FOR ANYTHING WRITTEN IN THE BOXES ABOVE THE OVALS.

BE SURE TO ERASE ANY ERRORS OR STRAY MARKS COMPLETELY.

PLEASE PRINT YOUR INITIALS

First   Middle   Last

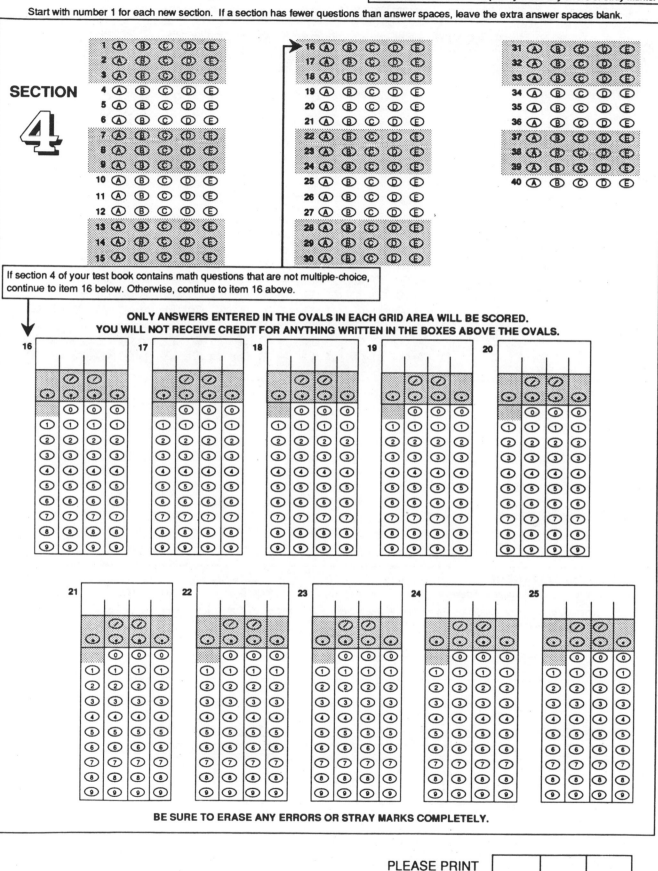

Use a No. 2 pencil only. Be sure each mark is dark and completely fills the intended oval. Completely erase any errors or stray marks.

Start with number 1 for each new section. If a section has fewer questions than answer spaces, leave the extra answer spaces blank.

SECTION

4

If section 4 of your test book contains math questions that are not multiple-choice, continue to item 16 below. Otherwise, continue to item 16 above.

ONLY ANSWERS ENTERED IN THE OVALS IN EACH GRID AREA WILL BE SCORED.
YOU WILL NOT RECEIVE CREDIT FOR ANYTHING WRITTEN IN THE BOXES ABOVE THE OVALS.

BE SURE TO ERASE ANY ERRORS OR STRAY MARKS COMPLETELY.

PLEASE PRINT
YOUR INITIALS

First Middle Last

255

Start with number 1 for each new section. If a section has fewer questions than answer spaces, leave the extra answer spaces blank.

SECTION 5

1 Ⓐ Ⓑ Ⓒ Ⓓ Ⓔ   11 Ⓐ Ⓑ Ⓒ Ⓓ Ⓔ   21 Ⓐ Ⓑ Ⓒ Ⓓ Ⓔ   31 Ⓐ Ⓑ Ⓒ Ⓓ Ⓔ
2 Ⓐ Ⓑ Ⓒ Ⓓ Ⓔ   12 Ⓐ Ⓑ Ⓒ Ⓓ Ⓔ   22 Ⓐ Ⓑ Ⓒ Ⓓ Ⓔ   32 Ⓐ Ⓑ Ⓒ Ⓓ Ⓔ
3 Ⓐ Ⓑ Ⓒ Ⓓ Ⓔ   13 Ⓐ Ⓑ Ⓒ Ⓓ Ⓔ   23 Ⓐ Ⓑ Ⓒ Ⓓ Ⓔ   33 Ⓐ Ⓑ Ⓒ Ⓓ Ⓔ
4 Ⓐ Ⓑ Ⓒ Ⓓ Ⓔ   14 Ⓐ Ⓑ Ⓒ Ⓓ Ⓔ   24 Ⓐ Ⓑ Ⓒ Ⓓ Ⓔ   34 Ⓐ Ⓑ Ⓒ Ⓓ Ⓔ
5 Ⓐ Ⓑ Ⓒ Ⓓ Ⓔ   15 Ⓐ Ⓑ Ⓒ Ⓓ Ⓔ   25 Ⓐ Ⓑ Ⓒ Ⓓ Ⓔ   35 Ⓐ Ⓑ Ⓒ Ⓓ Ⓔ
6 Ⓐ Ⓑ Ⓒ Ⓓ Ⓔ   16 Ⓐ Ⓑ Ⓒ Ⓓ Ⓔ   26 Ⓐ Ⓑ Ⓒ Ⓓ Ⓔ   36 Ⓐ Ⓑ Ⓒ Ⓓ Ⓔ
7 Ⓐ Ⓑ Ⓒ Ⓓ Ⓔ   17 Ⓐ Ⓑ Ⓒ Ⓓ Ⓔ   27 Ⓐ Ⓑ Ⓒ Ⓓ Ⓔ   37 Ⓐ Ⓑ Ⓒ Ⓓ Ⓔ
8 Ⓐ Ⓑ Ⓒ Ⓓ Ⓔ   18 Ⓐ Ⓑ Ⓒ Ⓓ Ⓔ   28 Ⓐ Ⓑ Ⓒ Ⓓ Ⓔ   38 Ⓐ Ⓑ Ⓒ Ⓓ Ⓔ
9 Ⓐ Ⓑ Ⓒ Ⓓ Ⓔ   19 Ⓐ Ⓑ Ⓒ Ⓓ Ⓔ   29 Ⓐ Ⓑ Ⓒ Ⓓ Ⓔ   39 Ⓐ Ⓑ Ⓒ Ⓓ Ⓔ
10 Ⓐ Ⓑ Ⓒ Ⓓ Ⓔ   20 Ⓐ Ⓑ Ⓒ Ⓓ Ⓔ   30 Ⓐ Ⓑ Ⓒ Ⓓ Ⓔ   40 Ⓐ Ⓑ Ⓒ Ⓓ Ⓔ

SECTION 6

1 Ⓐ Ⓑ Ⓒ Ⓓ Ⓔ   11 Ⓐ Ⓑ Ⓒ Ⓓ Ⓔ   21 Ⓐ Ⓑ Ⓒ Ⓓ Ⓔ   31 Ⓐ Ⓑ Ⓒ Ⓓ Ⓔ
2 Ⓐ Ⓑ Ⓒ Ⓓ Ⓔ   12 Ⓐ Ⓑ Ⓒ Ⓓ Ⓔ   22 Ⓐ Ⓑ Ⓒ Ⓓ Ⓔ   32 Ⓐ Ⓑ Ⓒ Ⓓ Ⓔ
3 Ⓐ Ⓑ Ⓒ Ⓓ Ⓔ   13 Ⓐ Ⓑ Ⓒ Ⓓ Ⓔ   23 Ⓐ Ⓑ Ⓒ Ⓓ Ⓔ   33 Ⓐ Ⓑ Ⓒ Ⓓ Ⓔ
4 Ⓐ Ⓑ Ⓒ Ⓓ Ⓔ   14 Ⓐ Ⓑ Ⓒ Ⓓ Ⓔ   24 Ⓐ Ⓑ Ⓒ Ⓓ Ⓔ   34 Ⓐ Ⓑ Ⓒ Ⓓ Ⓔ
5 Ⓐ Ⓑ Ⓒ Ⓓ Ⓔ   15 Ⓐ Ⓑ Ⓒ Ⓓ Ⓔ   25 Ⓐ Ⓑ Ⓒ Ⓓ Ⓔ   35 Ⓐ Ⓑ Ⓒ Ⓓ Ⓔ
6 Ⓐ Ⓑ Ⓒ Ⓓ Ⓔ   16 Ⓐ Ⓑ Ⓒ Ⓓ Ⓔ   26 Ⓐ Ⓑ Ⓒ Ⓓ Ⓔ   36 Ⓐ Ⓑ Ⓒ Ⓓ Ⓔ
7 Ⓐ Ⓑ Ⓒ Ⓓ Ⓔ   17 Ⓐ Ⓑ Ⓒ Ⓓ Ⓔ   27 Ⓐ Ⓑ Ⓒ Ⓓ Ⓔ   37 Ⓐ Ⓑ Ⓒ Ⓓ Ⓔ
8 Ⓐ Ⓑ Ⓒ Ⓓ Ⓔ   18 Ⓐ Ⓑ Ⓒ Ⓓ Ⓔ   28 Ⓐ Ⓑ Ⓒ Ⓓ Ⓔ   38 Ⓐ Ⓑ Ⓒ Ⓓ Ⓔ
9 Ⓐ Ⓑ Ⓒ Ⓓ Ⓔ   19 Ⓐ Ⓑ Ⓒ Ⓓ Ⓔ   29 Ⓐ Ⓑ Ⓒ Ⓓ Ⓔ   39 Ⓐ Ⓑ Ⓒ Ⓓ Ⓔ
10 Ⓐ Ⓑ Ⓒ Ⓓ Ⓔ   20 Ⓐ Ⓑ Ⓒ Ⓓ Ⓔ   30 Ⓐ Ⓑ Ⓒ Ⓓ Ⓔ   40 Ⓐ Ⓑ Ⓒ Ⓓ Ⓔ

CERTIFICATION STATEMENT

Copy in longhand the statement below and sign your name as you would an official document. **DO NOT PRINT.**

I hereby agree to the conditions set forth in the *Registration Bulletin* and certify that I am the person whose name and address appear on this answer sheet.

_____

_____

_____

SIGNATURE: _____   DATE: _____

FOR ETS USE ONLY	VTR	VTFS	CRR	CRFS	ANW	SCR	SCFS	5MTW	MTFS		5AAW	AAFS	5GRW	GFS
	VTW	VTCS	CRW	ANR	ANFS	SCW	MTR	4MTW	MTCS	AAR	4AAW	GRR	4GRW	
								0MTW			0AAW		0GRW	

DO NOT WRITE IN THIS AREA.

0   0   0   0   0   0   0

Answer Key

Section 1 VERBAL	Section 2 MATHEMATICAL	Section 3 VERBAL	Section 4 MATHEMATICAL	Section 5 VERBAL	Section 6 MATHEMATICAL
1. B	1. D	1. C	1. B	1. D	1. C
2. E	2. E	2. E	2. C	2. D	2. E
3. C	3. E	3. D	3. A	3. C	3. E
4. B	4. A	4. B	4. B	4. B	4. A
5. E	5. C	5. C	5. D	5. A	5. B
6. A	6. A	6. D	6. C	6. B	6. A
7. E	7. E	7. B	7. A	7. D	7. D
8. D	8. C	8. E	8. B	8. E	8. A
9. B	9. C	9. A	9. C	9. A	9. B
10. A	10. B	10. E	10. D	10. C	10. B
11. E	11. B	11. C	11. A	11. B	
12. A	12. C	12. D	12. D	12. D	
13. C	13. C	13. C	13. B	13. C	
14. C	14. D	14. E	14. B		
15. B	15. C	15. E	15. D		
16. D	16. E	16. B	16. 10		
17. A	17. A	17. E	17. 5.40		
18. C	18. B	18. C	18. 35		
19. C	19. D	19. B	19. 81		
20. D	20. A	20. D	20.*$1/5 < x < 1/4$ or $.200 < x < .250$		
21. E	21. D	21. E	21. 2200		
22. E	22. A	22. A	22. 7/11 or .636		
23. C	23. C	23. E	23. 96		
24. B	24. E	24. B	24. 5		
25. A	25. B	25. C	25. 9/2 or 4.5		
26. B		26. E			
27. C		27. C			
28. E		28. A			
29. D		29. D			
30. D		30. A			
		31. D			
		32. B			
		33. E			
		34. C			
		35. D			

* There is more than one correct answer to mathematics question 20. In this question, $1/5 < x < 1/4$ means that the answer, represented by x, can be any value between 1/5 and 1/4 that can be gridded

258

HOW TO SCORE THE SAT I: REASONING TEST

Verbal

Count the number of correct and incorrect answers in verbal sections 1, 3, and 5. Enter these numbers on the worksheet. Multiply the number of incorrect answers by 1/4. Subtract the result from the number of verbal questions answered correctly; record the result on the worksheet (A), keeping any fractions. Round A to the nearest whole number: 1/2 or more, round up; less than 1/2, round down. The number you get is your **total verbal raw score**. Enter this number on line B.

Mathematics

Count the number of correct and incorrect answers in math sections 2 and 6. Enter these numbers on the worksheet. Multiply the number of incorrect answers by 1/4. Subtract the result from the number of questions answered correctly; record the result on the worksheet (subtotal A), keeping any fractions.

Count the number of correct and incorrect answers in math section 4, questions 1-15. **Note: Do not count any E responses to questions 1 through 15 as correct or incorrect. Because these four-choice questions have no E answer choices, E responses to these questions are treated as omits.** Enter these numbers on the worksheet. Multiply the number of incorrect answers by 1/3. Subtract the result from the number of questions answered correctly; record the result on the worksheet (subtotal B), keeping any fractions.

Count the number of correct answers in math section 4, questions 16-25. Enter the number on the worksheet (subtotal C).

Add subtotals A, B, and C to get D, keeping any fractions. Round D to the nearest whole number: 1/2 or more, round up; less than 1/2, round down. The number you get is your **total mathematics raw score**. Enter this number on line E.

WORKSHEET FOR CALCULATING YOUR SCORES

Verbal

A Sections 1, 3, and 5   _____ − (1/4 x _____) = _____
                              no. correct   no. incorrect   A

B Total rounded verbal raw score   _____
                                                                            B

Mathematics

A Sections 2 and 6   _____ − (1/4 x _____) = _____
                          no. correct   no. incorrect   subtotal A

B Section 4   _____ − (1/3 x _____) = _____
   Questions 1-15   no. correct   no. incorrect   subtotal B

C Section 4   _____   = _____
   Questions 16-25   no. correct   subtotal C

D Total unrounded math raw score (A + B + C)   _____
                                                                     D

E Total rounded math raw score   _____
                                                                     E

Use the table on the next page to convert your raw scores to scaled scores. For example, a raw verbal score of 39 corresponds to a verbal scaled score of 450; a math raw score of 24 corresponds to a math scaled score of 430.

Scores on the new SAT I range from 200 to 800.

SCORE CONVERSION TABLE

Raw Score	Verbal Scaled Score	Math Scaled Score	Raw Score	Verbal Scaled Score	Math Scaled Score
78	800		36	430	540
77	750		35	430	530
76	740		34	420	520
75	730		33	420	510
74	710		32	410	500
73	700		31	400	490
72	690		30	400	480
71	680		29	390	470
70	680		28	380	460
69	670		27	380	450
68	660		26	370	450
67	650		25	370	440
66	640		24	360	430
65	630		23	350	420
64	620		22	350	410
63	610		21	340	400
62	600		20	330	390
61	590		19	330	390
60	590	800	18	320	380
59	580	770	17	310	370
58	570	760	16	300	360
57	570	750	15	300	350
56	560	740	14	290	340
55	550	730	13	280	340
54	550	720	12	270	330
53	540	710	11	270	320
52	530	700	10	260	310
51	530	690	9	250	300
50	520	670	8	250	300
49	510	660	7	240	290
48	510	650	6	230	280
47	500	640	5	220	270
46	490	630	4	210	270
45	490	620	3	210	260
44	480	610	2	200	250
43	480	600	1	200	250
42	470	590	0	200	240
41	470	580	−1	200	230
40	460	570	−2	200	230
39	450	560	−3	200	220
38	450	550	−4	200	210
37	440	550	−5 and below	200	200

This table is for use only with the test in this booklet.

MAKE YOUR MAJOR DECISION A WISE ONE

"This is an easy-to-use guide and contains very useful information." —*Voice of Youth Advocates*

"This unique book offers [students] information they need to make sound choices about bachelor's degree majors at 4-year colleges."
—*The International Educator*

"...presents a multitude of college majors."
—*Booklist*

The College Board Guide to 150 Popular College Majors is a unique guide that will help students and their parents make informed choices concerning college majors. It contains detailed, up-to-the-minute descriptions of the most widely offered undergraduate majors, each written by a leading professor in the field.

Majors are grouped into 17 fields ranging from the arts, business, and engineering to health services and the physical sciences.

Each entry in *The College Board Guide to 150 Popular College Majors*:

- describes the content of the major
- explains what a student will study
- lists related majors for a student to consider

In addition to an overview of the major, including new territory being explored, each description lists:

- interests and skills associated with success in the major
- recommended high school preparation
- typical courses in the major
- specializations within the major
- what the major is like
- careers the major may lead to
- where to get more information

The introduction provides authoritative advice on what a major is, how to choose a major, and the connection of majors to careers and further education. In an introductory chapter, college students tell how they chose their majors. 004000 ISBN: 0-87447-400-0, 1992, 328 pages, glossary, indexes, $16.00